Real Estate Millions in Any Market

TERRY EILERS

WILEY

John Wiley & Sons, Inc.

Published by John Wiley & Sons, Inc., Hoboken, New Jersey.
Published simultaneously in Canada.

For general information on our other products and services, or technical support, please contact our Customer Care Department within the United States at 800-762-2974, outside the United States at 317-572-3993 or fax 317-572-4002.

Wiley also publishes its books in a variety of electronic formats. Some content that appears in print may not be available in electronic books.

For more information about Wiley products, visit our web site at www.wiley.com.

Library of Congress Cataloging-in-Publication Data

Eilers, Terry (Terry Lynn), 1948–
    Real estate millions in any market / Terry Eilers.
        p. cm.
    Includes index.
        ISBN 0-471-66761-7 (pbk.)
    1. Real estate investment—United States.   2. Real property—Purchasing—
United States.   I. Title.
        HD255.E3713 2004
        332.63'24'0973—dc22

                                                                        2004005519

10 9 8 7 6 5 4 3 2 1

Contents

PART II
THE COMPONENTS NECESSARY FOR IMMEDIATE AND LONG-TERM REAL ESTATE WEALTH

PART III
CREATING YOUR OWN PLAN FOR SUCCESS

APPENDIX

Acknowledgments

Many years ago I read a quote by Margaret Mead that said, "Never doubt that a small group of thoughtful people can change the world. Indeed, it is the only thing that ever has." Each time that we complete a new project, I revisit those words and though I hardly believe that we are changing the world, we are, if only in a small way, making a contribution toward improving the lives of a few thousand people. We are pleased and proud if we accomplish that.

Hardly any venture, large or small, is conceived, created, and fulfilled through the efforts of only one person. It is certainly *always* a team effort for my projects and I am blessed with a magnificent team. My thanks go out to:

This great country, where we are given the opportunity to succeed at any level we choose. God Bless the USA.

Royce Dunn, the first person to put a pen in my hand and convince me that I should record "the thoughts that matter most."

"Wild" Bill Elliott, my first and best mentor—you are always there.

Scott Landrum, Debbie Baker, Nick Morrow, Mitchell Perigo, Richard Neufell—the crew who labor tirelessly to turn out so much great work. You are the best!

Virgil Baker and Mike Sullinger—my guidance, my partners, and my friends. I couldn't do it without you.

Those who contribute every day to our real estate success—Timmie Handy, Bev and Bill Gallaher, Dennis Wolfe, Jon Sarchett, John Belza, Gary Miller, and the Magnificent Mortgage Man, Roger Smith, my self-appointed conscience.

The support crew in the background, always cheering: Greg, Andy and Diana, Lewis and Kristin, Alex, Chris and Kim, Carol, Cody and Suzanne, Dean, Ray, A.J., Holly and Larry, Big John, Blain,

Ernie and Laurie, Sam and Sabrina, Jay and Tyler, Laura, Jean, Josh, Betty and the "Tucker Man."

All the kids, Tara, Risa, Kara, Tyler, Jaime, Jeni, and Sean, who have put up with the excuse, "I would love to go . . . but I have a project to finish that has to be done by . . . ," more times than anyone ever should.

My super agent and great friend, A. Richard Barber.

John Wiley and Sons, the undisputed, nonfiction king-of-the-hill, with special thanks to my talented, insightful, and patient editor, David Pugh.

Most importantly, my wife, partner, and soul mate—Neesie, your incredible patience, tireless work, remarkable talent, and miraculous love make every day a joy and our life truly a wonderful journey.

Introduction

Was It Better in the Good Old Days or Are These the Good Old Days?

Some Things Never Change

Three things *never* change in the real estate business.

1. Every buyer wants to purchase the best property available, at the absolute lowest price and with as little cash out of pocket as possible.
2. Every seller wants to sell his or her property at the highest feasible price and net the most money possible.
3. Everyone wants to get rich.

Having said that, I must add that there are very few buyers, sellers, and investors who actually accomplish those desires. Why is that? The answer is simple: Most buyers, sellers, and investors do not apply six very common principles to their efforts when buying and selling real property:

1. Don't believe everything that you read or that you are told, unless you check it out for yourself—*you must be self-sufficient*!
2. If you do not ask for a better deal, you probably won't get it—*so always ask*!
3. If you expect to have someone else do all of the work for you, do not expect that you will receive all of the rewards—*learn what to do* and *then get it done*!
4. If you don't have a map to get you where you want to go, you probably won't ever get there—*you must have a plan*!

5. Those that snooze will lose and you cannot wait. Once you know what to do—*you must go out and make it happen*!

6. And most important—*never forget!* It does not take money to make money, it takes a *deal* to make money.

If you take into account these concepts and principles that seem never to change, add in the fact that the real estate business is booming more and more every decade, why is it that so few people ever achieve what they say they would really like to achieve? Or worse yet, why do most people never even make an effort to achieve what they say they would like to accomplish? The answer in one word is *fear*.

It may be fear of risk, fear of asking, fear of hearing no, fear of ignorance, fear of criticism, fear of loss, or any number of other fears, including the big one—fear of failure. But the fact is—*we do not do most of the things in life that we say we would like to do because we are afraid of something*!

Why Are You Interested in Real Estate?

Let me ask you another question. Why are you reading this introduction or this book?

Is it because you are killing time in the business book aisle, waiting for your husband or wife to finish shopping at the mall? Is it because you are bored with the spy novels that seem to tell the same story again and again? Is it because you just have nothing better to do?

Or is it because you have stood on the sidelines of the real estate investment game and you have watched friends and relatives and acquaintances build fortunes and you have said to yourself, "I could do that." And, when those words fell out of your mouth, they were followed immediately by, "If I only knew how to do it."

So now, you stand here, thumbing through the myriad of real estate publications and you're saying, "There is so much to know." Worse yet, there is that little voice in your head that is saying, "I'm afraid, you better not do this, there is risk, people may laugh at you, you're not smart enough, you might fail, and worst of all *you don't have any money—how can you buy real estate?*"

Well, address that little voice with the words from Macauley Culkin, in the classic movie *Home Alone*, when he was so afraid to go down to the basement because the monstrous furnace made awful noises and he knew it was going to eat him, *"Shut Up!"*

If you have the desire and you are willing to make the effort, you can generate tremendous wealth in the real estate investment business and you can make it happen whether or not you have any money to invest. However, to do so, you must have a plan that will work. But, I must warn you, not every plan will work for every person who decides to build a fortune in real estate. You must be given lots of choices, lots of methods, and lots of alternatives, and you *must do what works for you*!

My System for Success

Many times, I have wished that I could wave a magic wand and teach my seminar students everything that I have learned in 30 years in this business, as well as everything that they needed to know to be able to go out and create phenomenal wealth in the real estate investment industry. Although that is not possible, what I have been able to do with this book and the many programs that we have created is to provide a step-by-step system that can be adapted and used by nearly anyone, in any market. Granted, it will take some time, it will take some effort, and it will take a *major* commitment on your part. But, it can work for you, quickly and dramatically, just as it has for hundreds and thousands of other people who once may have been in exactly the same position that you are at this moment.

In this book, you will see many specific and successful techniques, but the six most important general topics that you will learn are:

1. Many ways to buy and sell real estate, often with little or no money down
2. How to find hundreds, even thousands of the best properties that are great deals and possibly never leave your home
3. How to negotiate the best deals with every buyer and seller
4. When to buy and when to walk away
5. How to generate both quick and substantial cash, as well as long-term wealth
6. How to plan and execute your own personal wealth-building program

How to Use This Book

Using this book in the most effective manner is a three-step process:

1. *Read the entire book.* Acquaint yourself with the terminology. Try to get an overall picture as to how the whole game works. Begin to draw a mental picture of how you will structure your own real estate success plan.

Throughout the book you will find many actual examples of investment, buying, and selling techniques used by some of the most successful real estate investors in the country. Each of these individuals has achieved great success in the business, and they have graciously come forth to share their many secrets, tips, and tricks, in the hope that you will achieve that same success. Whether you are buying or selling your first or your tenth property, you will find many new suggestions that will help you to achieve better success.

2. *Get out into the market and begin using what you learn.* Remember, it is not a difficult process if you simply learn and follow the proper steps, and who better to learn from than those who have already done it and done it well.

If you reflect on your own job or your favorite hobby, and if you are good at that job or hobby, you realize that the activities involved have become second nature. You don't really have to think about it, you just do it and it comes naturally. In the beginning, you may have been a little clumsy. You didn't have the right moves, so to speak. However, as you learned the correct techniques, possibly from recognized authorities in the field, and you practiced those proper methods, you became very proficient and soon you began to feel that *you* were the expert. You will have that same experience in a short period of time with regard to real estate investing.

3. *Use this book as your reference guide for successful buying, selling, and managing techniques* This book will become your constant companion and all of the experts who have contributed to this publication will, in a sense, become your support staff, helping you to achieve the success that you desire.

Where Do You Start?

So the question is: Whether you have a lot of money and a lot of time, or have virtually no money and no time, or have any combination of those two scenarios, how do you get started, and more importantly, how do you succeed, *today*?

The answer is simple. You have already started! If you read this book, put a plan together as I suggest, become serious about the task ahead of you, spend a little time each day working to achieve the goals that you desire to accomplish, and most importantly, persevere and do not give up, you will succeed. It's that simple! There has never been a better time to begin to create your own path to *real estate millions in any market.*

Part I

An Overview of Your Wealth-Building Process

1

Identify Exactly What You Want to Achieve

Turning Dreams into Reality

Everyone has dreams. Unfortunately, most people never achieve much, if any, of what they dream. Why do you suppose that is?

As a seminar instructor, for many years I have traveled around the world and had the opportunity to spend time helping many people build fortunes in real estate. In most respects, these people are just like many of you reading this book. In their lives, they had done many of the things that you do every day. They went to work, they cooked, they went to work, they took the kids to school, they went to work, they went to soccer practice, they went to work, they went on diets, they went to work, they had their car serviced, they went to work, they went to the health club, they went to work, they shopped for groceries.... Sound familiar?

However, ultimately, there is a difference between the people who become very successful and most of the rest of the world: Successful people are successful because they do the things they like the most. The most! Let me explain. People go to work day after day and many of them don't really care for their jobs. The job is not what they most like to do. Frankly, almost all of them would rather be doing something different, be paid more, have more time off, have better benefits, have more freedom—and the list goes on and on. So why do they stay where they are? The answer can be explained in three words: security, procrastination, and fear!

- Security because they at least have a job and don't really have to make a change.
- *Procrastination* because they want to change, but never quite get around to it.
- *Fear* because they might be worse off if they do make a change.

Again I ask you, does that sound familiar?

But are they really secure? How many layoffs have occurred this year? How many companies have closed their doors? How many thousands of people have lost their retirements?

Remember this: *Your own personal security can only exist when you can independently generate whatever income you desire and your future is totally in your control.*

One of the most prominent personal development trainers over the past few years has been a man named Tony Robbins. Although similar training programs have been taught for decades, Tony has successfully combined much of the world's success training into a very compact package of daily do's and don'ts. Think about that for a moment—the daily do's and don'ts of success. How simple would life have been if we had been given that handbook when we walked into first grade?

Well, as you have been taught and as we all know, it is just not that easy! Or is it?

You Decide What You Will Achieve

A few years ago in Memphis, Tennessee, a young man named Mac approached me after a seminar and told me that he'd been quite ill for some time, but had finally started to recover physically. He had been in and out of hospitals for two years, had no insurance, had a low-paying but *secure* job, was deeply in debt, had no liquid assets, his one car was about to quit on him, he was about to lose his house in foreclosure, and he was considering bankruptcy. He had a wife and two children and said that he was, and I quote, "digging himself deeper and deeper into a hole every month." He asked a very simple question: "Can you help someone that is as far down as I am?"

As you might imagine, my heart went out to this man and I thought very carefully before I answered, because the last thing he needed was false hope. Our conversation went something like this.

"First, I want you to understand that I can only help you if you're willing to help yourself. Since you are here today, I assume that you have at least taken the first step to try to make a change that will improve your life. Is that correct?"

Mac's response was one that I have heard a thousand times. "Yes, I'm willing to try anything, but I don't know what to do. I just need a plan that will help me pay my bills and get me some money so I can go out and make a few deals."

I would venture a guess that nearly every person reading this book, at one or more times in their lives, has felt the fear and frustration and maybe even the desperation that Mac felt that day. And, worse yet, many of you are still struggling. Do those words, "I just need a plan that will help me to pay my bills and get me some money so I can go out and make a few deals," sound at all familiar? Maybe his grammar wasn't the best, but his message was strong and clear.

The two concepts that Mac didn't understand are the same two concepts that most people who are desperate have a hard time understanding: You cannot expect things to change, *if you don't make a change*. And, most importantly, many times, *the money comes from making or having the deal*, not necessarily, or exclusively, from closing the deal!

It was very evident that Mac's need for security, fear of change, and sheer procrastination were killing him. He needed to get out of the job that wasn't cutting it. And he needed to realize that it doesn't take money to generate money; it takes a deal to generate money! But, he probably said it best—he needed a plan!

My next statement to Mac was, "You said that you're in a hole that keeps getting deeper and deeper. Well, the first rule when you are in a hole is stop digging!"

It is always pleasing to me when someone uses our techniques and enjoys success from their actions. In Mac's case, it was especially gratifying. In the following 12 months after our conversation, Mac paid all of his hospital bills, purchased two nice rental properties, got current on his home mortgage obligation (he had been four months behind on his payments), purchased a nearly new pickup for himself and a car for his wife, and generated an income of just over $88,000. That was just over six years ago and since that time Mac and his wife have accumulated over 20 properties, their annual income is in six figures, and their net worth is over $2 million.

Sound like a dream? Well, you're right—it was Mac's dream and he made it a reality.

Now let's add one more piece to this puzzle. For those of you who are thinking that you must move to a large city to create high returns, think again. Mac lives in a fairly small college town with a population of approximately 50,000, about 60 miles from Memphis, and all of his investment, buying and selling, has taken place in that area. Understand that what he has accomplished can be done virtually anywhere in North America and in many other countries around the world.

This is only one of many hundreds of stories that can be told of people who have started with practically nothing and built a fortune from real estate and related industries. When you finish this book, you can have a plan that will work for you to accomplish as much or more than Mac has accomplished. Your success will be up to you.

Goals—The Most Valuable Building Blocks

"Goal setting," you groan, "not that again. Every time I read a book or watch a video or go to a seminar, they talk about how important it is to set goals."

Yes, and once again, I will tell you what you have already heard 10 or 100 or 1,000 times: *Setting concise but flexible goals, writing them down, continually reviewing those goals, and measuring your accomplishments is critical to your own success!* Period. Like it or not, it is an absolute necessity.

Right now is a good time to begin asking yourself: What exactly do I want to achieve out of this new real estate investment undertaking?

- Do you want to build an ongoing, income-generating business at which you can work full time?
- Do you want to keep your current job and begin buying and selling periodically for either additional income or a more fruitful retirement?
- Do you simply want to become a real estate mogul and buy and hold as many properties as possible to secure your future?
- Do you just want to buy your first house?

Identifying your goals is very important for many reasons. Most importantly, because you will learn many, many techniques from this book, it is important that you utilize the information that will best suit your needs and desires. It may take you years to utilize every method that will be shown to you. Concentrating on a specific plan and specific methods will provide the best results. As you become more and more knowledgeable and proficient with the techniques, the entire process will become less cumbersome and you will be able to branch out and use other methods.

However, remember that your goals also need to be *reasonable* and *flexible*. Reasonable, in that you must honestly evaluate the time and resources that you have to put into your own real estate investing venture. Flexible, because you may start out with a goal to only buy your first house and find that the process was so easy that you want to buy several more. Setting the goals, measuring your achievements, and moving the bar up to the next level is the progression of success in nearly every venture in life. The investment goal form shown in Figure 1.1 will help you break down each of the actions that you will need to take to accomplish your aspirations. Note that the form requires you to state a goal, show the action that will be required, and then break down the specific actions that will be necessary.

One example might be:

Investment Goal: To purchase two properties within 60 days

Actions: Search the classified ads for properties

                 Contact a real estate broker and have her or him
                 search

                 Search foreclosures and notices of default

                 Drive around the area and look for "For Sale by
                 Owner" signs

Specific Actions: Classifieds: contact a minimum of 20 sellers, do
                  follow-up letters to sellers, and view at least six
                  properties

                  Broker contact: identify 20 potential properties
                  and view a minimum of six properties

                  Foreclosures and notices of default: contact a minimum of six sellers, six lenders, and six trustees

                  Driving: identify a minimum of four sellers, view
                  a minimum of two properties, and negotiate
                  offers on two properties

By breaking down your goals in this manner, you will know the exact actions that you need to take every day to accomplish your goals.

It also is very important to segregate your goals into three categories:

1. Daily action goals
2. Short-term achievement goals
3. Long-term success goals

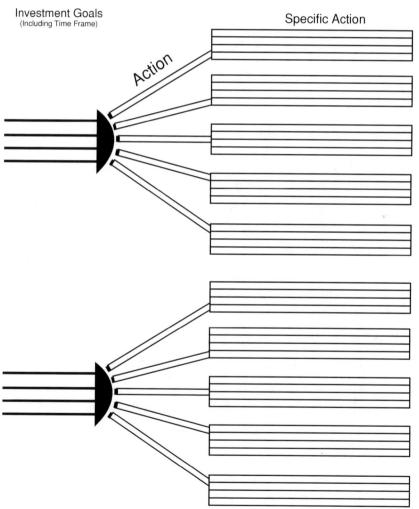

FIGURE 1.1   Sample investment goal form to help you set goals and the actions needed to reach them.

Daily Action Goals

These goals can best be defined as daily, weekly, and monthly activities such as personal contacts with potential sellers, viewing properties, creating and distributing flyers, and follow-ups on potential deals—everyday activities that will be necessary for you to find and close the transactions that will allow you to achieve your short-term achievement goals. Daily action goals will become almost second nature, but you must continue to track your results or you may become scattered and disorganized. Time is your most important asset and setting and prioritizing specific daily action goals will help you to utilize your time most efficiently.

Short-Term Achievement Goals

These are those goals that you want to achieve in one year or less. These include making a monthly or annual income, paying off bills, buying one or two or three properties, taking a certain vacation, buying a new car, creating more time to spend with your family, quitting your job and working full time in real estate, etc. Short-term achievement goals are the stepping stones that move you sequentially closer to achieving your long-term success goals.

Long-Term Success Goals

These goals should be broken into two parts: those goals that you want to achieve in five years or less and those that you want to achieve in 10 years. Some examples of five-year long-term success goals might be net worth of $1 million, ownership of 20 properties producing a net income of $75,000 a year, an annual income of $150,000, etc. Ten-year goals can be moved up substantially, but keep in mind, things change. Your five-year and 10-year long-term success goals need to be the most flexible.

As you gain more knowledge, experience, and confidence, you also will become more astute at setting goals and you'll find that you have a tendency to push yourself a little more than you did when you were first beginning your new venture. As I said before, as you work with the process, the easier it will become and the less complicated it will seem to you. It will be the same with your goal setting. It will become habitual and second nature.

In Part III of this book, after you have learned many specific buying and selling techniques, you will be asked to prepare your own personal action plan. You will have been given many choices and it will be critical for you to choose to do the things that you like the most. The most! The fact is, if you *like* doing it, you're much more likely to *keep* doing it! At that time you will begin setting your goals and writing your first personal plan for success.

Time—Your Most Valuable Asset

How many times have you heard someone say, "I would love to be able to have the time to do this or that or be able to go here or there, but I am so busy and have so little time that I just can't do it." Many of you have probably said or thought those same things at one time or another. But, the real truth is that there are only 24 hours in a day and we all make the time that we need or want to for the things that are the *real* priorities in our lives. If you want something different than what you have, you must first, and honestly, change your priorities.

Many people enjoy looking and acting and being *busy*. The problem is that most people are highly unproductive, whether they are busy or not. Like any other venture, if you are to be successful in the real estate business, you *must* prioritize and manage your time to allow you to complete the actions that will be necessary for you to achieve your goals. Remember, a commitment of four or five hours a week might be all that is necessary for you to become a successful real estate investor.

Managing Your Time

There have been many books written on time management, but I believe that most of them are entirely too complex. Why make it harder than it really is? Here is my simple, two-part formula for successful time management, broken into preparation and actions.

Preparation

1. Simplify your life. Stop doing the things that are not essential or that you really don't want or have to do—the things that are getting in the way of the success that you want to achieve.
2. Control what people and actions get your time. Do not let other people's priorities take control of your life.
3. Balance your actions, and balance your life. Figure 1.2 shows a pie chart representing a sample allocation of the 24 hours in your day. This shows that you should designate allotted time for the essential activities in your life and strive to maintain that balance.
4. Identify and control procrastination. Learn to prioritize and focus. Do no allow yourself to waste valuable time.

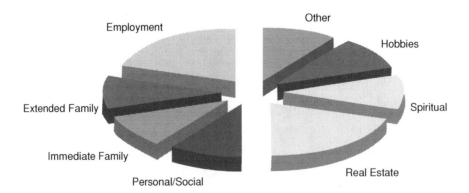

FIGURE 1.2   The pie chart shows that you must allow time for the essential activities of your life.

Actions

1. Establish daily priority and action lists. Write down every activity and action that you wish to accomplish. It seems easiest to use the ABC method to identify the different levels of importance that will be attached to each activity or action. The A activities or actions are the ones that are absolutely necessary to accomplish. The B activities or actions are the ones that are important, but that can wait until the A's have been completed. The C's are the activities or actions that have the least importance and can wait until the A's and B's are done or that can be worked intermittently into your schedule and not interfere with your priorities. Create your priority and action lists every evening while your current day is fresh in your mind.

2. Create weekly completion reports. Track what you accomplish. You must be consistent and if you begin to see a pattern of reduced productivity or accomplishment, go back to the basics and make sure you are doing the right things at the right times.

3. Follow the progress of your short-term achievement goals. At the end of every month revisit your personal plan for success, which is broken incrementally into 12 months. Check your progress and see that you are on track. If not, make the changes necessary to put you back on schedule.

Time management is not difficult if you keep it simple: Plan your work and work your plan. That is all there is to it.

2

Taking Inventory of Your Personal Resources

Where Is Your Starting Line?

In my seminars, I reach a point where I say to everyone, "Okay, now we're going to take inventory of each of your personal resources." Without fail, someone will utter, "What resources?" or "This won't take long," or the best one, "I have no resources, I spent my last $139 to come to the seminar!"

Everyone always laughs, but often the people who made the remarks stated exactly what they believed to be the truth—*they believed that they had no resources*. However, if you look around, you'll see that we live in a world abundant with resources for success:

- Do you have access to a computer or the Internet?
- Do you have access to a telephone?
- Do you have a recorder's office in your county?
- Do you have a library in your town?
- Do you have any real estate offices in your city?
- Do you have a local newspaper?

If you answered yes to any one of these questions, and you have this book to guide you, you have all the resources necessary to make you as rich as you wish to be. Most of you answered yes to all of the questions and if you are thinking, that increases your chances for even greater success, you are right. The question becomes: How do you use those resources that are available to you? The answer is very simple: *You must take the right actions, in the right order, at the right time.* So, what are the right actions, what is the right order, and when is the right time?

The Basic Action Plan

The order of action that you must adhere to is actually very straightforward. Everything that you will learn in this book is based on the following basic action plan. You must:

1. Identify potential properties and sellers
2. Choose the best prospects from your list of potentials
3. Always be making contacts with potential sellers
4. Negotiate a win-win transaction for you and the seller
5. Find the money to fund the deal
6. Use all resources to close the transaction
7. Never forget to follow up on all commitments and promises
8. Don't stop—use, move, or lose the cash

It is imperative that you follow each and every one of these actions. If you try to skip steps, attempting to move ahead or make things happen more quickly, you may find yourself wasting a lot of time, not closing any transactions, and never making any money.

How do you remember every step? Very simple. You memorize them and you use them every day If you look at the first letter of each action step, you will find that it spells out "I CAN FUND," which is exactly what you will do.

Remember when I was telling you about Mac in Chapter 1, his concern was to find a plan that would help him to pay his bills and get him some money so he could go out and make a few deals. However, if you look at the order of action that I have given you, you will see that finding the money to fund the deal is actually number 5 on the list. So, now you are probably thinking about how you make the deal *before* you have the money. That is a fair concern, so let me give you an actual example.

Believe You Can Before You Do It

A young lady who used our action plan in Albuquerque, New Mexico, sent a letter to me after she had completed her first no-cash-out-of-pocket transaction. I was especially impressed with Carol's story because she told me in the letter that she was only 22 years old, a single mother, living paycheck to paycheck, had no savings, had substantial credit card debt, and a car payment, had only a high school education, and was working nights as a receptionist at a hospital. She had *no* experience in real estate, and *no* higher education, but as she put it, "I realized that I had more guts than money or knowledge, and, I was desperate— I *had* to make a change."

Because she had no cash or other liquid resources, this young entrepreneur said that she thought she would start off learning the lower-end markets, mostly homes that were selling for $70,000 or less. However, while doing her research, and before she could find a property on which she could write an offer, she found a vacant property that was quite run down in a moderately expensive neighborhood. She said that she had been driving through the area, looking at homes and dreaming about where she wanted to live when she became very successful. She said that this particular property "stuck out like a sore thumb."

When Carol got out of her car to take a closer look at the home, the next-door neighbor had approached her and asked if she was looking for a rental. The neighbor said that the owner lived out of town and that she had a key if Carol was interested. Carol indicated that she would like to see the property. The entire time that Carol was going through the property, the neighbor was giving her a detailed history of everything that was wrong with the home. But, for the most part, the home and property needed a professional cleaning, a coat of paint, and some work on the yard. The only major item of repair was a toilet that was cracked, not operable, and needed replacement. According to the neighbor, that was the reason that the owner had not been trying to re-rent the home. She said, "He just doesn't have time to get up here from Phoenix."

Carol thanked the neighbor and within two hours of first seeing the property, she had contacted the county recorder's office, picked up a copy of the plat map, identified the lien that was against the property, found out that the taxes were delinquent by one installment, identified the owner, and obtained his address and telephone number in Phoenix, Arizona, used her computer to obtain the sales prices for homes listed in the area of the property, contacted a local realtor with whom her family had been friends for several years, and obtained the sale price of every home that had sold in that area for the past year.

That evening the young investor made her first contact with a potential seller, using a dialogue that you will learn later in this book. According to her letter, she found the process to be much easier than she expected. The seller indicated that he had purchased the property when he was stationed at the Air Force base in Albuquerque, 13 years prior, for $61,000. He had since retired and was teaching school in Phoenix. He said that the Albuquerque property had been rented to the same people for over six years for $400 per month, and he stated that he simply would not have time until the end of the school year (three months later) to go over and work on the property. He said that the home had been vacant for almost three months and mentioned that he did miss the money coming in each month. He further indicated that he had been contacted by a couple of the neighbors who were complaining about the maintenance of the property for the past year and that he might be interested in selling.

Carol offered the seller the exact solution he was seeking. She would purchase the property in its "as is" condition and see that everything was handled so that the seller would not have to make the 500-mile trip back to New Mexico. The seller agreed to the following terms:

1. Sale price: $212,000
2. Down payment: $12,000
3. Interest rate: 6 percent
4. Monthly payments: interest only—$1,000 per month
5. Owner to carry the loan that would be all due and payable in one year, with no prepayment penalty
6. 60-day escrow
7. Buyer to pay title insurance, escrow fees, and termite and roof inspection

Carol prepared a written offer, faxed it to the seller, and received his faxed approval back the next morning.

You Can Make Deals with What You Have—or Don't Have

Now, I'm sure you are thinking, how in the world is this young buyer, who is starting out in her investing career, going to come up with a $12,000 down payment and the $1,000 monthly payments? You may remember at the beginning of this chapter I said, "Often the money comes from making or having the deal, rather than from closing the deal." Let me see if I can put this in a different perspective that may be easier to understand.

What if I offered to sell you a diamond that was perfect in color and clarity and was just over three carats for, let's say, $2,000? Most of you are not diamond experts or have many contacts in the field of fine gems, but you would probably recognize that this is a deal you might not want to pass up. If you did your homework, determined that the diamond was real and that it had a wholesale market value of over $40,000, and identified that there were buyers who would purchase the stone for at least half of the value, my guess is that you would probably make a concerted effort to come up with the $2,000 and put the deal together. Am I right?

Even though you don't have a great deal of money or knowledge, you know that this is a deal that you just can't pass up. Now, let me ask you another question. If you went to your best friend, mother, father, sister, brother, neighbor, coworker, or anyone else and said, "I want to borrow $2,000 and I'll pay you back as soon as I can," do you believe that you might have some difficulty getting the money?

However, if you went to those same people with all of the information about the diamond transaction, put together in a concise and understandable form, including offers to purchase from gem buyers, and you offered to pay back $3,000 in 60 days or less, for the $2,000 loan, would you have more interest from the potential lenders? Of course you would!

With that scenario in mind, you will appreciate how Carol managed to close her first deal. She determined that comparable sales in the area, for homes in good condition, were in the neighborhood of $368,000. Listing prices ranged between $355,000 and $389,000 and the time on the market ranged between 30 days and four months. Carol decided that the easiest way to get the money was to go to someone who would understand the value of the property and the potential for profit that existed. She called the Realtor who had given her the comparable sales information, explained the deal, and offered her a 50/50 split on the profits and *the listing on the property when they were ready to sell*, if she would pay $30,000 up front. Carol explained that this money was to close the transaction, do the work on the property, and make the monthly payments until it sold. Naturally, the Realtor took the deal with no hesitation.

It Does Not Take Your Money to Make Money

Here's how the transaction played out over the next four months:

Sale price	$212,000
Down payment	$ 12,000
Closing costs	$ 400
Repairs, equipment, parts, etc.	$ 8,300
Water damage repair	$ 1,100
Miscellaneous expenses	$ 600
Payments made to seller	$ 2,500
Total expenses	$ 24,900

Out of the original $30,000, Carol put $ 5,100 in her pocket for the work she did. When the home resold, the results were:

Sale price	$371,000
Closing costs	$ 1,400
Commission to Realtor	$ 19,300
Loan payoff	$200,000
Gross to Carol (seller)	$150,300

Net to Carol: $75,150 + $ 5,100 = $ 80,250

Net to Carol's realtor partner: $75,150 − $30,000 upfront money + $9,650 commission = $54,800

This was a perfect example of a win-win situation for all parties. The seller was happy with the deal because he sold the home for over three times what he paid for it, after he had enjoyed the rental income and tax writeoffs for many years, and he did not have to come back to Albuquerque to refurbish and/or sell the home. The Realtor who put the closing and repair money up made a 150 percent return on her investment in less than four months, plus had a nice listing and a $9,600 commission. Carol made nearly four years of her current salary in four months. With that money she paid off her bills, bought a house, and still had $16,000 left to use for her next deal, on which she was already working when she wrote to us.

Once again, I repeat: It does not necessarily take money to make money—it takes a deal to make money!

There Are Professionals Available to Help You—Use Them!

Let's face it. You can't be an expert in every area relating to real estate or any other investment field. I have been involved in the business from just about every aspect imaginable for over 28 years and I still learn something nearly every day. As much as I try to be self-reliant and independent, I have learned that becoming successful in the real estate investment business must be a team effort. Fortunately, there are a lot of experts out there that will want to be part of your team.

Why is that, you ask? Because, while they are helping you to make a lot of money, you are going to be helping them to make a lot of money. When I first began doing seminars years ago, I did programs with a man named Zig Zigler and I cannot remember how many times that I heard him say, "To get everything you want out of life, you have to help a lot of other people to get everything that they want out of life!" How true that statement has proven to be over the years.

Putting Your Investment Team Together

While preparing a training program for sales people in the mid-1980s, I had the opportunity to interview dozens of agents, brokers, investors, and entrepreneurs who had started with virtually nothing and were all self-made multimillionaires. These success superstars all had many things in common, but the aspect that stood out more than any other was the fact that every one of them recognized that if you want to achieve greatness, happiness, and success, you must have a superstar team surrounding you every day of your life.

You cannot do it alone. And frankly, why would you want to? There are only so many hours in a day, there is only so much liability that you can carry on your own, there is only so much that you can know, there are only so many places that you can be in one day, and there are only so many phone calls that you personally can make. Let's face it. You need help! So, where do you get the help that you need? Like everything else in life, you ask for it!

Here is the process you need to follow to build your own investment team.

1. Start with the people who will help you to get the deals. The real estate brokers and agents, title and escrow people, the bird-dog referral people, recorder's office employees, bank Real Estate Owned (REO) and foreclosure people, and anyone else who can help you find a good property to purchase.
2. Create a banking relationship. Even if you have bad credit and you are very short of funds, find a banker who will believe in you and help you to start, or restart, a banking affiliation. Make them believe in you.
3. Develop a relationship with professionals who can guide you when you need assistance: a lawyer, an accountant, a tax expert, an appraiser, a property manager, a home inspector, an insurance

agent, city and county inspectors, pest control inspectors, and even surveyors.

4. Develop a list of every individual currently in your life or from your past experiences that can and will be able to help you with your investment business. Past employers, teachers, relatives, employees—everyone, and I do mean *everyone,* who can assist in your efforts and that you will be able to repay for their efforts. If you are going to belong to an investment club or organization, a few of the other members will go on your list as well.

5. Create a team of high-quality, honest maintenance, yard-care, and repair people who will work with you on an ongoing basis. Take care of these people—they are very important to your long-term success.

As you begin searching for properties and sellers, take the time to begin meeting the potential team players. Convince the experts that you are serious about your efforts, and you will be amazed how much help they will provide to get you going. When you produce—and reward them as you said you would—you will have a winning team that will stick by you through thick and thin. Below are some details on the specific professionals who may be especially critical to your success.

Real Estate Brokers and Agents

The licensed professionals can be your greatest asset if you can develop a good working relationship with a broker or an agent that understands exactly for what type of properties and for what type of sellers you are searching. Licensed real estate brokers or agents who are members of the local multiple listing service (MLS) have access to nearly every listing that comes up in their area. They are also generally familiar with the local financing market and usually know the service levels of the local title and escrow companies.

If I had to choose only one group of professionals with whom I had to work to develop my real estate investment business, without a doubt, it would be the brokers and agents. All of the other professionals with whom you will work can help to bring you business and build your portfolio, but the agents and brokers can bring you instant business once they have an understanding of exactly how you want to structure your transactions.

Find a broker or agent with whom you can work on an ongoing basis in every area where you will be working. Develop and maintain those relationships— they will prove to be your greatest assets.

Title Companies and Escrow Agents

Title companies and escrow agents are important to your success. The information that the employees of these companies can provide is without a doubt important to your success in the investment business. Foreclosure notices, notices of default, recorded owner information, escrow and notary information, and other recorded data can be gleaned from title companies and escrow agents. They are unquestionably the greatest information resource in our real estate investment world.

Build a strong relationship with one or more title companies and escrow agents and you will be able to create an enormous amount of success from the information and help that these people will provide for you.

Banking Relationships

In the next few chapters you will be shown many ways in which you will be able to buy real estate with little or no money down, good or bad credit, whether you have a large bank account or no money in the bank. However, if you have aspirations to build a fortune in real estate, it will be extremely important for you to establish good credit and strong banking relationships. It is one thing to be able to go out and put a few deals together. It is another thing to build a multimillion-dollar business and portfolio. Banking relationships give you the opportunity to grow in exponential leaps and bounds.

Throughout the years, many people who have attended my seminars started out with virtually no money and built fortunes in the real estate industry. Eventually, nearly every one of those individuals who achieved great success developed great banking relationships and utilized credit lines, bank loans, and equity lines of credit, as well as many other services offered by banks.

Attorneys

Attorneys are another professional entity that can be tremendous assets in your real estate investment business. Most people, when they think of attorneys, think only of litigation, defendants, plaintiffs, and remedies. However, attorneys can provide more services than just legal defense. In fact, attorneys should be viewed as the people who can keep you out of trouble rather than those who you run into when it is too late and you are already in hot water.

You may decide to have attorneys draw up contracts for you or advise you as to how you should structure your transactions. In some states, attorneys handle the closing procedures in transactions, and some actually issue title insurance or title guarantees.

When choosing legal representation, it is important to find an attorney who has a solid background in real estate. Just because an attorney has done a great job handling your last three divorces does not mean that same attorney is the right person to help you with your real estate contracts. Granted, nearly any attorney will know more about contract law than the average person, but if you are going to pay for representation, get the best representation that you can afford. Attorneys also can be a great source of business in that they may handle bankruptcies and other financial distress situations that might produce properties that you could be interested in purchasing.

I am fortunate that my own attorney is a man that I have known, worked with, and have been close friends with for over 30 years, and the mutual trust that we have developed and maintained has been a tremendous asset over the years. Providentially, Mike is what I call a "legal deal maker" and not a "legal deal breaker." When you look for the lawyer that you will want on your team, make sure that he or she is a deal maker.

As you begin working in your local area, ask the title and escrow people and the real estate agents and brokers whom they might recommend as a good real estate lawyer.

Insurance Agents

As you're probably aware, having insurance coverage for general liability and potential loss of your personal and real properties is critical in today's world. Having an insurance agent that will assist you in obtaining and changing coverages quickly and efficiently is extremely important to your success.

Not long ago, I was closing a transaction—and it turned out that at the last moment the lender wanted the insurance coverage increased on the property before they would allow the funding to take place. This was not something that had been previously mentioned, but came up just prior to recording. It was critical that this transaction close as there were two other transactions that were being funded out of the original closing escrow. Often, you will have this domino effect when you have several concurrent transactions closing.

Because I had a good working relationship with my insurance agent, I was able to increase the coverages on my policy, as requested by the lender, with just a phone call. If I had been a new client, the agent would have been required to inspect the property, prior to allowing the coverage increase, and that would have delayed the closing of all three transactions.

Insurance agents also can help to direct business to you because they may have clients who sometimes have financial difficulty and end up with properties that they must sell. Get to know your insurance agents, send them business on an ongoing basis, and stay in touch with them so they know who you are personally and do not have to pull your policy up on their computer to remember who you are.

Accountants

Nearly 30 years ago I met a man who was very good with numbers. He was not a CPA or an accountant. As matter of fact at that time he was a bookkeeper and a manager for several automobile service companies. However, the man was very good at what he did and eventually went back to school, became an accountant and tax expert, and ultimately became the CFO of the conglomeration of businesses that we have built, developed, operated, and in some cases sold over the past three decades. Virgil's help, guidance, and friendship over those many years have been immeasurable.

When it comes to managing your revenues, doing your taxes, and generally keeping your assets in order, an accountant is a very important part of your success team.

Professional Management Companies

If you develop a large real estate portfolio or your investments include large multi-unit projects, you probably will utilize the services of a property management company. Unfortunately, many investors wait too long before they begin using these types of services and they find themselves becoming rent collectors and maintenance workers, rather than deal makers. Make sure that you hire a management company *before* you reach the point that the time and effort necessary to manage your properties are overwhelming.

Once again, find out from the professionals in the area which management companies have a good reputation and spend some time talking with them before you need their services.

The Other Professionals

As you build your investment business, you will find the need to utilize the services of other professionals and it pays you to identify the people in your community who are the best at what they do. Pest control and other inspectors, appraisers, city and county inspectors, recording office employees, building inspectors, surveyors, and maintenance people are just a few of the individuals with whom you will have contact in your business. Meet them, make friends with them, and make sure that you are always honest and ethical in your dealings with them. The level of your success often depends on the relationships that you have with the professionals in your own working community.

3

The Basic Education —What You Really Need to Know

It All Seems So Complicated

Real estate transactions generally are not complicated. That is not to say that you never will have a difficult or complex transaction. However, learning to simplify every part of the transaction as much as possible is as important as any other facet of your education. As you know, there is almost always an easy way to get things done, or a hard way to get things done. You probably know people who, no matter what they're doing, *always* make things much more difficult than they need to be. Unfortunately, in the real estate business, many so-called professionals make the transactions appear much more difficult than they really are.

In Chapter 2, we discussed how you can build a team of professionals who can help you to create the success that you want to achieve. But, for the time being, I want you to make a commitment to be as self-sufficient as possible. To become a well-versed and successful investor, you must understand not only the basics of real estate, but also the basics of goal setting, the basics of finance, the basics of time management, and the basics of long- and short-term investment.

You will notice that I repeated three words again and again. Those words are "the basics of." Too many people spend too much time trying to learn everything there is to know before they ever go out and try to use what they've learned.

If you have a computer and can use it properly, you probably understand what I mean. Learning the computer has been an ongoing process, correct? You didn't learn it all at one or two or three sittings. It may have taken you years of use to learn everything that you know about the computer. And, you realize now that you will never know *everything* that there is to know about your computer.

However, most of you learned the basics of at least one technique, one software or one Internet function, the first time that you used the keyboard. But, you also realize that hardly a day goes by that you do not learn something new about your computer. You are learning as you go—exactly what you will do with your real estate investments.

Like the computer, real estate investing is nothing more than understanding the basics of how you can achieve the results that you want and being willing to learn more and more every day. When you run into a problem with your computer, you simply call someone who knows more than you know and is willing to help you. That is exactly what you will do when you begin putting real estate transactions together.

Real Estate—Quick and Easy

There are seven main areas in which you will become proficient in a fairly short period of time. Those areas are:

1. Terminology
2. Technology
3. Prospecting

4. Finance

5. Negotiation

6. Contracts

7. Property management

Do not worry if you have no experience in these areas. You will have a strong grasp of the basics when you finish this book and you will learn as you go along. Before you know it, you will have developed your skills and you will be quite amazed at you own capabilities.

Technology—The New World of Information Availability

Whether you love it or hate it, the Internet has dramatically changed the world in which we live. Only a few years ago it was virtually impossible, unless you were a licensed real estate agent or broker, to find properties in quantity that were listed by brokers. The boards of realtors and multiple listing services (MLSs) were organizations that only shared information with their members. Buyers and sellers could only obtain specific information on properties that were for sale by contacting a licensed agent or broker who was a member of the local board or MLS. Additionally, ownership information and other pertinent information about properties that were or were not listed were only available at the county recorder's office and often were very difficult to obtain.

With the advent and extensive application of the Internet, most of the listed properties and much of the information previously available only from the recorder's offices are now easily accessible to anyone who has access to the World Wide Web.

Not only is a tremendous amount of information available, but transactions are now occurring start to finish online. Foreclosure information, special sale opportunities, credit reports, loan information, and a great deal of legal guidance are all available, much of it *free*, if you know where and how to search the Internet. Several years ago one of the large national telephone companies had a media campaign that was based around the slogan, "Let your fingers do the walking." With the Internet, the slogan could be changed to, "Let your fingers do the walking, talking, seeing, buying, and selling."

However, there is one facet of deal making that never may be replaced by the Internet. That component is the very important personal relationship that can be developed, very quickly, between a potential buyer and the seller of a property. A successful investor will need to develop the ability to build trust from sellers in a very short period of time, usually one or two contacts. Although not impossible, that trust relationship can be very difficult to build when the only contact is online. Face to face, nose to nose, and eye to eye will get you more good deals than any other technique that you will ever use. That being said, utilizing the Internet and other available technology to search out properties, owners, and any other information that is available, *before* you begin making personal contacts, can save you weeks and months of time and effort. Most importantly, technology can allow you to move your wealth-building plan along much faster than any time in the past.

Outsmarting the So-Called Experts

As we just explained, learning successful real estate investing, buying, and selling is very much like learning to use your computer. You learn to use the keyboard, you learn to use the mouse, you learn how to utilize software programs, you learn to navigate through the Internet, and one day you wake up and realize that you have mastered the functions that you need to use on your computer. As with the computer, you learn bits and pieces of real estate investing and eventually you will have a very good grasp of the entire business. Prospecting, negotiating, writing offers, opening escrows, and handling the last-minute closing details all will become second nature in a very short period of time.

Keep in mind that you may make mistakes and that is perfectly all right if you learn from those mistakes. If you think back to the time as a child when you were learning to ride a two-wheeled bicycle, you probably fell off a time or two and scraped your elbows or knees. But that didn't stop you from getting back on and riding the bike until you became proficient, and hopefully you didn't continue to fall off. So it will be with your real estate investing—you will make mistakes, learn from them, and move on.

I am sure that many of you reading this book have thought to yourselves, "How will I be able to compete with the many real estate professionals out there in the market?" The fact is that most licensed real estate agents and brokers are not necessarily out in the market looking to buy and sell properties for themselves. They instead are looking for listings and buyers that they can represent. I have purchased many properties directly from sellers who had been contacted by numerous agents and brokers who were trying to obtain listings on the properties, but never offered to purchase the property.

Another very important aspect for you to understand is that licensed real estate agents and brokers have a much greater legal responsibility to sellers, to advise those sellers in every way possible about the valuation of their properties. As a nonlicensed buyer, you may offer as little or as much as you please for the properties and as long as you are not taking some unfair advantage of the seller, you are within the law. The concept of "willing buyer, willing seller" is the basis for making good deals. However, keep in mind, as I have said previously, the very best investors always attempt to make every deal a win-win situation for all parties involved.

When we talk about outsmarting the so-called experts, you must keep in mind that you will have a real advantage. Your goal will be to find only *specific, bargain properties* and locate *accommodating, flexible sellers,* which considerably narrows your focus and makes your job fairly simple. I equate that to the difference between shooting a rifle or a shotgun. With a rifle you aim the bullet at one circle on the target. Conversely, many real estate licensees are out in the market with very little focus, more like shotgunning, trying to list every property that they can get their hands on and sell every buyer who walks into their office, often bypassing a property that could be a good personal purchase opportunity.

The Most Important Component

When I ask a new investment class, "What is the single most important factor in finding great deals in the real estate investment market today?," their answer is almost always the same. Something along the lines of "You need to find the best properties, in the best locations."

We all have heard over and over again that the most important factor to consider when purchasing real estate is location, location, location. And, there is no doubt that location is a very important factor in the real estate investment puzzle. However, as you begin to make purchases of real property, you will realize very quickly that *finding the most accommodating, flexible sellers is by far the most important aspect of your real estate deal making.* But remember, there are usually two types of accommodating sellers:

1. The ones who have a problem of their own that can be solved by liquidating the property.
2. The ones who have a problem property and just want to dump the problem into someone else's lap.

Obviously, you are looking for the sellers in the first category.

Identifying and Qualifying Sellers

There are some important things to remember when you are looking for those accommodating, flexible sellers:

1. Accommodating, flexible sellers are everywhere and own every type of property. However, you'll probably find one particular niche where you will be able to minimize your efforts and maximize your results.
2. The quicker you can identify the seller's true motivation, the quicker you will be able to move to satisfy that seller's needs and put a deal together.
3. Many times, finding the accommodating, flexible seller is more important than finding the perfect property.
4. The very best deals will come from a small percentage of the sellers with whom you will come in contact.
5. It will be critical for you to learn to communicate properly with sellers to help them to realize that you are interested in creating win-win situations.
6. There are three types of accommodating, flexible sellers: those who are flexible on the price, those who are flexible on the terms, and those who are flexible on both price and terms.

Utilizing the dialogues that will be provided for you in this book, you will be able to make contact with sellers and very quickly determine how accommodating and flexible they will be with regard to the type of transaction that you want to put together. Once you have made a few contacts, the process will become streamlined and almost second nature.

As you probably have recognized from the information provided so far in this book, more times than not you'll be dealing with sellers who have some type of problem for which the solution will be to sell a property. As I said earlier, the quicker you can identify the seller's exact motivation, the quicker you will be able to structure a transaction that will satisfy both the needs of the seller and your desires as the investor.

There are primarily two categories of problems that exist for sellers who will have the greatest propensity to be accommodating and flexible, and with whom you will be structuring transactions:

1. *Personal problems*: These might include health issues, transfers, divorces, deaths, job loss, retirement, location of seller in relation to the property, no longer wanting to handle the real estate such as in the case of a rental property, or any other personal issue that would cause the seller to believe that selling the property will ease the problem.

2. *Economic problems*: These might include bankruptcy, foreclosure, income reduction for any number of reasons, local area economic difficulty, increased living expenses incurred from an event such as children going to college or an elderly party coming to live with the family, the real estate reaching a point of deterioration that requires immediate financial input, or any other issue that financially and dramatically effects the seller and his or her family.

Of course, many of these personal and economic problems will cross lines, one into the other. Health issues can very quickly create difficult economic problems, and bankruptcy or foreclosure can certainly create health issues. The important thing to understand is that when sellers are suffering with either personal or economic problems, they may become accommodating, flexible sellers if you can show them an acceptable solution to their problems.

When identifying and qualifying sellers, you will be looking for the most efficient and cost-effective ways to solve the seller's problem and allow you the opportunity to structure a transaction that can create a strong investment position for you. The first question that you must always ask yourself is: To what extent will the seller's problems affect me or my position as the new owner of the property? Let me give you an example.

A few months ago I found a vacant property in the outskirts of Reno, Nevada, that appeared to have great potential in that it needed some minor cosmetic work such as paint and windows repaired. When I contacted the seller, he stated that he was very interested in selling the property since he was living in Las Vegas and could not properly manage the rental. He indicated that he had some financial difficulties and that if he could get $5,000 to $7,000 out of the property fairly quickly, he would be willing to sell it at a price that he knew was below market value, but it would have to be strictly "as is." He said that he would not be able to pay for any work that was required to obtain a new loan on the property. The seller was very cooperative and provided all the information with regard to the current loans against the property.

When I received a title report on the property, it was evident why the seller was willing to be flexible. There were three loans against the property totaling $97,000. The first loan for $55,000 and had an interest rate of 7½ percent, with 30-year amortization and fairly low payments. The second loan, with a balance of $15,000, was an equity line of credit that was maxed out, with an interest rate of 12½ percent. This loan was two payments in arrears and was about to foreclose. The third loan was a private loan for $27,000 with interest-only payments and interest at 24 percent. The third loan was also two months in arrears.

When I ran the seller's name through the county records, I discovered that several lawsuits were pending against the man. Comparable sales in the area showed that the property would have been worth approximately $185,000 if the repairs and refurbishing were completed and the property brought back up to an acceptable standard. However, considering the potential loss from the pending lawsuits and the possibility that there might be problems with the title, I made the decision not to purchase the property.

Sometimes, no matter how good the deal sounds, it will take entirely too much time and effort to resolve the seller's problems and you are better off to walk away. There are too many other good, smooth transactions out there for you to waste your time on a problem that may be incurable.

Basic Real Estate Terminology

There are numerous real estate terms that you will work with on a continual basis. The following is a list of terminology that you need to become acquainted with before you move into actual investment training. Take the time, at least an hour, to review the following words and definitions so that you may begin to develop a basic understanding of the most used real estate terminology. Do not skip this terminology lesson. It is very important in your effort to become successful in real estate investing.

Absentee owner: A person or entity owning property and residing elsewhere, usually some distance from the property.

Accrued interest: All interest accumulated and unpaid to date.

Acknowledgment: A formal declaration made before an authorized officer, usually a notary public, by the person who has signed a document, that such execution is his or her own act or deed. In many cases, documents must be notarized before they can be **accepted for recording.**

Adjustable-rate mortgage (ARM): A real estate loan in which the interest rate varies over time according to a prescribed formula or set of conditions. Also known as a variable-rate mortgage.

Agreement of sale: An agreement entered into between two or more parties for the sale and purchase of property.

All-inclusive deed of trust: A security document for a new encumbrance that encompasses or "wraps around" a senior or prior deed of trust. In most cases, upon recordation the all-inclusive deed of trust is junior to the existing lien. These type of liens are also known as a wraparound deed of trust or wraparound mortgage.

Amortization: The gradual or incremental payoff of a debt through regular and scheduled payments of principal and interest over a stated period of time until the debt is fully paid or until a specified payoff date at which a balloon payment might become fully due and payable.

Appraiser: A person who is qualified to determine the value of property.

Appreciation: An increase in the value of property.

Assessed value: The value of property for taxation purposes, as determined by the tax assessor.

Assessments: Specific and special taxes, in addition to normal taxes, imposed on real property.

Assessor: The county official who determines the value of property for taxation purposes.

Assessor's parcel number (APN): Number assigned by the county assessor. In most areas this number must appear on any documents that are recorded.

Assets: Any property, real or personal, with value.

Assign: To transfer all, or part, of one's interest in property.

Assumption agreement: An agreement to assume or take responsibility for a debt or obligation that was originally contracted by another person.

Balance sheet: A statement of financial condition showing assets, liabilities, and net worth as of a specific date.

Balloon payment: Any payment that is greater than twice the amount of the normal or periodic payment. Generally used to refer to the final payment of a note with a predetermined due date.

Bankruptcy: A legal process in the U.S. District Court wherein assets of the debtor are liquidated to pay off the claims of his or her creditors.

Basis: The property owner's original cost, plus capital improvements, less depreciation. Basis is used for the computation of income tax liability if a property has been liquidated in a tax-liable sale. Also known as book value.

Beneficiary: One who is in receipt of benefit, profit or advantage. With regard to real estate lending, beneficiary is used to identify the party to whom trustor is obligated—usually the lender or person intended to benefit.

Blanket deed of trust or mortgage: A security document that finds more than one parcel of land as the security for a loan.

Bona fide: Made in good faith.

Broker: A person who brings parties together and assists in negotiating contracts between them for a commission or fee.

Building code: A set of regulations setting forth minimum building construction standards in a city, county, parish, or state.

Building restrictions: Zoning ordinances and regulatory laws that require the construction be protective of the population's health and safety.

Buyer's broker agreement: An agreement used between a buyer and a broker, establishing a fiduciary relationship between those parties and stating that the broker will work for the buyer and make every effort to locate a property and that the broker will be paid a commission if the property is found and purchased.

Call: With regard to real estate, to require payment of loan money. Often called a demand. The terminology usually is "to *call* a note."

Capital gain: Profit gained from the increase in value of a capital asset after sale.

Carryback: Usually referring to a seller carryback, whereby a seller acts as a lender of purchase money and holds or carries back a loan for the purchaser.

Chain of title: The chronological list of recorded documents affecting title to a specific parcel of real property.

Clear title: A title that is free from any encumbrance obstruction or limitation that would cloud the title.

Closing: Closing of escrow; the final act of a transaction wherein papers are signed, monies are exchanged, and the title is transferred.

Closing costs: The expenses incurred in a real estate transaction including costs or title examination, title insurance, attorney's fees, lender's service charges, documentary transfer tax, etc.

Cloud on a title: An outstanding claim of title that is yet to be proven invalid.

Collateral: The property secured as a security interest for a debt.

Condition: A qualification or restriction attached to the conveyance of property wherein it is predetermined upon the occurrence of a specified event, an estate shall commence, enlarge, or be defeated.

Constructive notice: Public notice given by public records.

Contingency: An item in a contract dependent on a specific condition for its fulfillment.

Contingent: That which is dependent upon a future event.

Contract: A promise, or a set of promises; an agreement to do or not to do certain things, as between two or more parties. A binding agreement between two or more parties.

Contract of sale or contract sale: Also known as conditional sales contract or a land contract of sales, whereby the title remains in the name of the seller until the buyer fulfills certain conditions of the contract.

Convey: To transfer title to property from one person to another.

Conveyance: A written document that transfers title to property from one person to another.

Credit report: A report on the credit history of a person or business.

Debit: A charge or debt.

Debtor: Someone who owes a debt or is liable for a claim.

Deed: A written document transfers an interest in property from one person or entity to another.

Deed in lieu of foreclosure: The conveyance of title to a mortgagor or beneficiary in order to circumvent foreclosure.

Deed of trust: A security document used to transfer beneficial interest in title from the trustor or the borrower to the trustee (usually a corporation—always a neutral party), to be held in trust for the benefit of the beneficiary until the trustor completes performance of an obligation.

Deed restrictions: Limitations on the use of real estate written into the deed.

Deferred payments: Payments that are extended over a period of time or put off until some date in the future.

Demand: A term used in escrow to identify the consideration pay-off required to execute a reconveyance, relinquishment, or an interest, or a right to property.

Deposit receipt: A written document used to secure a firm offer to purchase property and provide a receipt for the buyer's earnest money. Also known as a purchase agreement or purchase offer.

Depreciation: A decline in the value of a property. May be actual or for tax purposes only. Depreciation can be an exceptional tax write-off.

Documentary transfer tax: Tax levied by the county, city, etc., on the transfer of title of real property.

Down payment: The portion of the purchase price of a property that the buyer pays in cash or does not finance.

Due date: Fixed time for a payment.

Due on sale clause: A provision in a security document calling for the automatic payoff of a loan in the event of sale or transfer of title to the property.

Earnest money: Something of value given as part of the purchase price to show good faith and to secure an agreement.

Easement: An interest in land owned by another that entitles its holder to a specific limited use or enjoyment.

Equity buildup: The increase in the value of a property due to appreciation.

Encumber: To place a legal claim on a property.

Escrow: A transaction wherein an impartial third party, usually an escrow company or officer, acts as agent to both parties, buyer and seller, acting only under instructions in delivering papers drawing and/or recording documents and disbursing funds. Escrow agents may also handle the signing of loan documents for the lenders and buyers.

Exclusive agency agreement: A written listing agreement between an owner and agent that gives the agent the right to sell a property within a specified period of time, while allowing the owner the right to sell the property without paying the agent a commission.

Exclusive right to sell: A written agreement between an owner and a broker that gives the broker the exclusive right to sell the property. If the property is sold to anyone during specified listing period, the broker is entitled to receive the specified commission.

Extension agreement: A mutual agreement that grants additional time for the completion of performance; such an agreement should be in writing.

Fair Credit Reporting Act: A consumer protection law that sets a procedure for correcting mistakes on one's credit record.

Farming: A term for prospecting, used in the real estate industry.

Federal Housing Administration (FHA): A federal agency that sets guidelines and ensures loans for residential housing.

Fixed-rate mortgage: A mortgage in which the interest rate does not change during the term of loan.

For valuable consideration: A statement that reflects the money or something of value that is being given in exchange for the property.

Foreclosure: The involuntary procedure to sell real property according to the terms and conditions of the deed of trust that identified the subject property as security for a lien, when the loan (a note) is in default.

Foreclosure sale: The involuntary sale of property that was used as security for a lien.

Free and clear title: Title to real property that is free of liens.

Good faith: Clear intention to fulfill one's obligations. A total absence of any intention to seek unfair advantage or to defraud another.

Graduated-payment mortgage (GPM): A fixed-rate mortgage that provides for reduced payments in the beginning of the mortgage, with payments increasing to a set level in later years. Sometimes called a graduated payment plan.

Grant: The operative word or conveyance in a grant deed. In general, the transfer of interest in real property by deed.

Grant deed: A voluntary written instrument transferring an interest in real property.

Gross income: Total income before any expenses are deducted.

Housing and Urban Development (HUD): The U.S. Department of Housing and Urban Development.

Impound account: An account into which a borrower deposits payments toward annual taxes and/or hazard insurance, usually at the insistence of the lender.

Income and expense statement: An itemized statement of income received from a property and the expenses incurred in its operation.

Income property: Property owned or purchased for the generation of income.

Installment loan: A loan that requires periodic payments until both principal and interest are completely paid.

Institutional lenders: Banks, insurance companies, or other commercial lenders that provide real estate loans.

Interest-only note: A promissory note that requires that only the interest be paid during the term of the note, with the principal **amount due in a lump sum at the end of the term.**

Interim loan: A short-term loan usually made while a borrower is waiting for a subsequent term loan to be granted.

Judgment: A final determination in a court or competent jurisdiction to an action or proceeding.

Judgment lien: A statutory lien ordering the payment of a sum of money, created by recording an abstract or a complete judgment.

Land: Real estate without any improvements attached to it.

Land contract of sale: Also known as a conditional sales contract and a contract of sale, whereby the title remains in the name of the seller until the buyer fulfills certain conditions of the contract.

Lease option: A lease allowing the tenant the right to buy the property if and when certain conditions are met.

Legal description: A description that legally describes real property or the interest being conveyed. Usually accomplished by lot/

track, metes and bounds, or U.S. Government survey type or legal description.

Leverage: The concept of utilizing other people's money to achieve the full benefits of the ownership of real property. Yield from the property use of leverage can be extensive in real estate transactions.

Lien: A charge, hold, or claim of another for the purpose of securing a debt or obligation.

Liquid assets: Assets that are readily convertible to cash.

Liquidate: To convert property or other assets into cash.

Liquidated damages: The amount of money agreed upon in a contract is payment or compensation for a breach of contract, thus eliminating further legal action. A liquidated damages clause is often a part of a deposit receipt or offer to purchase.

Listing: A written contract between an owner and an agent or broker authorizing the agent to sell, lease, or rent the owner's property in exchange for compensation.

Loan: Delivery of something of value with the expectation of repayment or return. Money given to another in expectation of return of the principal amount plus interest for a given period of time.

Lot split: The legal division or splitting of a parcel of land into more than one parcels of land.

Maintenance: The ongoing painting, cleaning, and repair work done to property and equipment to keep them productive, useful, and in good repair.

Margin: The amount that the lender adds to the index to determine the rate on an adjustable-rate mortgage (ARM) when it adjusts.

Market data approach: A method used in appraisal that determines the price of a home or other real property by comparing it with other property similar to the subject property that has recently sold.

Market value: The price for a property that a willing buyer and a willing seller would agree upon when neither is under abnormal pressure.

Maturity: The date at which time a note becomes due and payable; the same concept is valid with regard to when legal rights become enforceable.

Mechanic's Lien: A statutory lien to secure payment for persons contributing labor and/or material toward improvements upon real property when the compensation was not paid in a timely manner.

Metes and bounds: Measurements, angles, boundaries, and distances used in describing land parameters.

Mortgage: A two-party security instrument pledging real property as security for the performance of an obligation.

Mortgagee: The creditor or lender who takes a lien on the subject property in return for expected performance on the obligation by the mortgagor.

Mortgagor: The debtor or borrower who executes a mortgage, has possession of the property used as security, and promises the performance or payment of the obligation.

Multiple listing service (MLS): An organization that allows member real estate brokers access to information on all properties listed in an area governed by that service.

Negative amortization: Payment terms under which the borrower's payments do not cover the interest due. The deferred interest is added to the principal balance.

Negotiable: Capable of transfer between parties by endorsement of the holder in the ordinary course of business.

Negotiable instrument: An instrument that contains an unconditional promise or order to pay a certain sum of money, payable at a definite time or on demand, and payable to order or to bearer.

Negotiation: The process of creating a meeting of the minds between two or more parties in order to reach an agreement.

Net income: The amount of money from income property that remains after expenses and charges have been deducted.

Net lease: A lease that requires the tenant to pay all the costs of maintaining the building, including the payment of taxes, insurance, repairs, and other expenses normally paid by the owner.

Net listing: A listing that states the minimum amount the seller is to receive and stipulates that any amount above that specified minimum amount goes to the broker as commission.

Net worth: That which remains after subtracting liabilities from assets.

Notarize: Provide proof of execution of a document by means of notary public certificate or acknowledgment.

Notary public: A public officer authorized to administer oaths to attest or certify certain types of documents, to take depositions, and to perform certain other civil functions.

Notary seal or stamp: The official seal of the notary public or other authorized official.

Note: A common reference to a promissory note.

Notice of default: A recorded notice of a trustor's failure to perform his or her obligation under the trust. It is the initial step in non-judicial foreclosure.

Notice of intent to sell: States intent to sell a defaulted property at public auction to the highest bidder. Must be posted and published according to specific regulations.

Notice to quit: Notice given by a landlord to a tenant to pay rent within three days or vacate the premises. This term also is used after a foreclosure to give notice to tenants to vacate the premises and give possession to the new owners.

Obsolescence: A loss of value or property due to its being out-moded.

Official records: The books in which all documents filed in the County recorder's office are recorded that impart constructive notice of matters pertaining to real property.

Open-end mortgage: Sometimes called an open-end deed of trust, it is a provision that allows for additional loan advances to be funded to the borrower while keeping the same security and security documents.

Open listing: A listing given by a property owner that states that the first agent to secure a buyer on the terms and conditions agreeable to the seller will be paid a commission.

Option: A choice, right, or consideration to do or not do a certain thing, either now or sometime in the future, such as to lease or buy a property.

Optionee: The person who acquires or holds a legal option; the person who has a choice.

Optionor: The person who grants an option and is bound by the decision of the optionee during the lifetime of the option.

Owner's equity: The value held by the owner that represents the difference between the market value and the existing liens on a property.

Ownership: The exclusive right to use and enjoy the property.

Parcel: Any area of land contained within a single description.

Performance: The fulfillment of an obligation or promise.

Personal property: Anything that is movable and not attached to real property. Anything that is not real property.

Policy of title insurance: A contract indemnifying against loss resulting from a defect in title or outstanding liens on the real property that is insured.

Power of attorney: A document authorizing a person known as the attorney-in-fact to act on behalf of another. To be directed in real estate, the power of attorney must be specific and recorded.

Prepayment clause: A clause within an agreement permitting payment of a debt prior to a due date; may be with or without a penalty.

Prepayment penalty: A provision inserted into a note whereby a penalty is to be paid by the borrower in the event that the note is paid off before the due date. Most prepayment penalties expire at the end of five years into a term.

Private mortgage insurance (PMI): Insurance written by a private company that protects the lender against losses if the borrower defaults.

Probate: A period of time during which the court has jurisdiction over the administration of an estate of a deceased person.

Promissory note: A document promising to pay a sum of money at a specified time in the future; an IOU.

Proration: Dividing something according to relative time and amount of use.

Purchase money loan: A loan originated at time of purchase for all or a portion of the purchase price.

Purchase offer: A written document used to secure a firm offer to purchase property and provide a receipt for the buyer's earnest money; also known as a purchase agreement or deposit.

Real property: Land and whatever is attached, growing or affixed to the land.

Realtor: A real estate licensee who is a member of the National Association of Realtors and who has agreed to abide by the ethics and standards of that organization.

Reconveyance: A document that returns the bearer legal title to the owner upon fulfillment of all obligations under the deed of trust.

Record: To give public notice of a document by placing the document on file with the county recorder.

Recorder's office: The government office that publicly records deeds, mortgages, trusts and all other legal documents as part of the public record process.

Recording information: The book and page numbers of the official records where the document is entered; the file number (sometimes called the document or instrument number) is assigned by the county recorder and the date and time of recordation are noted on the document.

Refinancing: The process of taking out a new loan on property already owned; paying off the existing financing, and retaining the cash balance, if one exists.

Renegotiable-rate mortgage: A mortgage whose interest rate may be renegotiated periodically, typically every three to five years.

Request for reconveyance: Written instructions from the beneficiary to the trustee to issue a reconveyance deed to the trustor because the loan obligation has been satisfied.

Right of way: A right granted by an owner to another person or entity to pass over or through the owner's land.

Sale contract: An agreement entered into for the purchase and sale of real property. Also known as a purchase agreement or deposit receipt.

Secondary financing: Mortgages or trust deeds that are secondary in priority, or subordinate, to first mortgages and trust deeds; also known as junior liens.

Secondary money market: The market where existing secured notes are bought and sold. This is accomplished at the institutional and private level.

Seller carryback: Any situation in which a seller acts as a lender, holding or carrying back a part of the purchase price on a note.

Statement of identity (S of I): A questionnaire used by title companies to help establish the identity of a person in order to protect the title from liens on persons with similar names; also known as a statement identification.

Subordination agreement: A provision allowing a new agreement to move into superior position of priority over an existing or concurrent agreement.

Sweat equity: Labor or services put into improving real property and used in place of money to gain title.

Takeout loan: A long-term loan that pays off and takes the place of the short-term construction loan.

Taxes: As applied to real property, a charge assessed against the value of the real property to pay the cost of governmental services.

Term: With regard to lending, the length of time of the contract.

Terms and conditions of sale, contract of sale: A distinction must be made between a contract of sale in the legal concept of the purchase agreement and the contract of sale as used in the real estate profession, as an alternative method of financing. During the life of the contract, the contract of sale is unique in that possession and equitable interest is delivered to the vendee (buyer) and the vendor (seller) retains title to the subject property. Therefore, it is necessary to set forth specific areas to rights and responsibilities, as well as to identify the consequences for the violation of said agreements during the term of the contract.

Time is of the essence: A standard clause in real property contracts that indicates that punctual compliance is required.

Title: The basic rights of enjoyment and possession or interest in property; also used to describe a document that furnishes proof of ownership.

Title insurance: Indemnification from loss occasioned by defects in the title to real property or to an interest in real property.

Title policy: An insurance policy or contract indemnifying against loss resulting from a defect in title to the interest or lien in the real property thus insured.

Title search: The examination or research in the history of title to a specific property in order to develop the chain of title.

Transfer tax: Tax levied by the county, city, or state on the transfer of title of real property.

Trust deed: A three-part security document conveying bare legal title to be held in trust as security for the performance of an obligation; also known as a deed of trust.

Unlawful detainer: An action brought for recovery of possession of property from a person who is in unlawful possession. This is the action that is taken by a property owner to regain possession of real property from a renter or lessee.

Usury: Charging an interest rate higher than that allowed by law.

The United States Veterans Administration (VA): The Veterans Administration was established in 1930 by Congress' authorization to "consolidate and coordinate government activities affecting war veterans." The Veterans Bureau, the Bureau of Pensions of the Interior Department, and the National Home for Disabled Volunteer Soldiers became bureaus within the Veterans Administration. Brigadier General Frank T. Hines was named as the first Administrator of Veterans Affairs.

Valuation: An opinion of an asset's worth. Not necessarily a formal appraisal.

Variable-rate mortgage: Any real estate loan in which the interest rate varies over time according to a prescribed formula or set of conditions; usually changes in economic conditions, also known as an adjustable-rate mortgage.

Voluntary lien: A lien created by choice.

Warranty: An assurance or promise that certain defects do not exist or will be corrected.

Wraparound mortgage or deed of trust: A deed of trust or mortgage that "wraps around" or secures payment of a senior or prior deed of trust; also known as an all-inclusive mortgage.

Zone: An area, region, or district officially designated for specific types of use.

Zoning: Governmental regulations controlling the use of property according to specific areas within the community.

Set a goal to review this terminology section every few days until you have mastered every definition. I always use the analogy that for the investor, learning the terminology of real estate is like "pool safeing" children at a very young age. Children may go on to learn the backstroke, the butterfly, and many other more complex strokes, but if they have not overcome their fear of water, they will never feel comfortable and will never be good swimmers. If new investors are afraid to talk to sellers because they "might say something wrong," they also will probably never be successful. Like the swimmer, you must first get into the water before you can learn to swim.

You have completed a very basic overview of the direction in which you are headed. Now we move step by step through the specific actions that you will take to become a successful real estate investor.

Part II

The Components Necessary for Immediate and Long-Term Real Estate Wealth

4

How You Make It All Work

The Benefits You Will Achieve Through Real Estate Investment

Most of you reading this book are doing so because you have recognized the tremendous opportunity that is available in real estate investing. Many of you have stood on the sidelines and watched as your friends, relatives, or acquaintances have bought and sold real estate with much success, and maybe you have finally reached the point where you have said to yourself that you are no longer going to be only a bystander. You have made the decision to get into the game as a participant.

There are many different reasons why investors are drawn to real estate. Primarily, there are five aspects of real estate investing that make it so appealing: income, depreciation, equity, appreciation and leverage. Notice that the first letters of each of those words spell *ideal,* which is certainly appropriate when you think of real estate investment. I have never forgotten this acronym that I learned from my first real estate broker, Bill Elliott, nearly 30 years ago. Let's take a moment and look at each aspect individually.

1. *Income:* There are several types of income that can be generated from real estate. They include income from rents, income from

options, income from sale of notes, income from fees that you can legally collect if you are licensed or unlicensed, and income from actual sales of the property. Also, revenues can be generated from refinancing the property when there has been an equity increase.

2. *Depreciation:* Depreciation is the declining value of the property that is allowed as a tax write-off, even though the value of the property may be increasing through appreciation.

3. *Equity:* Your equity in a property, in most cases, will increase due to appreciation in the property's value. With respect to rental property, you will experience equity buildup as the renters are making the payments.

4. *Appreciation:* Appreciation will occur at different rates depending upon several factors, including type of property, local and national economic conditions, and condition and location of the property.

5. *Leverage:* When you are using someone else's money to your benefit, that is leverage. When you own a real property and you are using money borrowed against the property from a bank or other outside source, you have tenants making the payments on the property and the appreciation you experience is on the full value of the property. That is great *leverage.* No other investment offers the tremendous leverage advantage that is available in real estate.

In addition to the benefits listed above, many other tax benefits are allotted the real estate property owner such as write-offs and deductions for closing costs, capital improvements, repairs on income properties, and most importantly, interest on loans secured by real property.

Is There Risk Involved?

Although there are many advantages to real estate investing, every person who considers real estate as an investment should remember that there is a certain risk involved, as with any other investment. If you look at the history of real estate values, it is quite astounding. Properties that sold in the 1950s, in locations such as New York City and Los Angeles, for $30,000 to $40,000, now have values in excess of $1 million dollars. However, that long-term view is often misleading in that although values have continued to increase overall, there have been times when values were static or even declined in many areas across the country.

In the 1970s, real estate values grew dramatically and the write-offs that were available to the investor were astounding. Hundreds of thousands of new investors jumped into the real estate market and it was near frenzy. People were buying and selling as fast and furious as they could and often the buyers were significantly overpaying for properties. I have always deemed that period of time as "the greater fool than I era." By that I mean the buyers were out there in the market saying, "I know that I'm a fool for paying this much for this property, but I know that a greater fool than I will come along tomorrow and pay more."

Unfortunately, many of those investors got caught at what I call the "apex of fooldom." Interest rates rose to over 20 percent and property values in many areas declined drastically. Foreclosures were commonplace. Many investors who had little or no equity in properties found themselves upside down, owing more than the properties were worth, and they simply walked away, leaving the lenders to dispose of the properties.

An additional consequence of that time period was that many of the so-called real estate seminar gurus, who taught the "no money down" theories as gospel, found themselves eating their words and for several years it appeared that the "good old days" of low-down, high-return real estate investing had come to an end.

In 1986, the government decided that it was time to control, to a certain extent, the ability of investors to achieve the dynamic returns from real estate that had been so prevalent in the past by reducing the tax benefits of real estate ownership. In the minds of the legislators, the new laws would safeguard against the blatant misconduct of the get-rich-quick type of investor who could know nothing, build nothing, and help nothing and still make substantial profits while putting nothing back into the marketplace.

In other words, the government legitimized the real estate investment business. I personally believe that this move by the government was a very positive shift toward making the real estate investor a true professional and that since that time many of the accidental profiteers have faded from the landscape. In today's market, a quality real estate investor can make more money than ever before because many of the uninformed, unethical, out for a free ride types are no longer in their way.

Often in seminars I am asked, "What can I do right now to become very good at investing and make a lot of money very quickly?" My answer usually is rather disconcerting for the questioner. I usually say, "What you need to do is hurry up—and be patient." Real estate investment offers so many different types of opportunities that it is sometimes a mistake to just hurry up and make a lot of money. Instead, your goal *must* be to make as much money as possible, in the shortest period of time as possible, and keep as much of that money as possible. To help you better understand that concept, let me give you an example of an investor who was *not* in tune with this concept.

A few years ago I met a young man in Raleigh, North Carolina, who was very aggressive and very determined to create a great deal of money in the shortest period of time possible. His motivation was purely to make $1 million by the time he was 25, four years from the time we spoke. He indicated that he was not interested in long-term investments, he had no interest in write-offs, and he wanted all of his assets to be as liquid as possible. He had no plan beyond generating the money that he wanted.

As I progressed through the training program, the only areas or topics that interested this young man were the sections on buying with no money down, selling notes at a discount, the process of short-term flipping of properties for resale, and double escrowing for immediate return. Although the man was a licensed real estate agent, he had no notion of the concept that real estate investing should be a combined effort toward short-term revenue gains and long-term investment strategy.

In only two years, by utilizing the techniques that he had learned in our seminar, that young man generated revenues of over $400,000. Unfortunately, he also had no write-offs and tax liabilities of nearly $200,000. He had most of his cash tied up in two major development purchases that were ongoing and he still lived in a rented house. He had purchased several personal items such as a truck, two cars, a boat, a motorcycle, and two wave runners, all on leases or credit purchases and his debt service was nearly $10,000 per month.

Although it appeared to most of his friends and coworkers that this young man was well on his way to achieving his goal of making $1 million before he turned 25, in actuality he had set a course for failure that could not be reversed. When the local real estate market suffered a slight, short-term decline due primarily to layoffs at two major employers, the young man's bubble burst as rapidly as it had been inflated. The two big deals that would have achieved the generation of the $1 million that the man had set for a goal fell apart within days of each other and could not be resurrected.

Ultimately, most of his personal toys were repossessed since the man had little income, no savings, could not make the payments, and their resale values had dropped considerably below their market values due to the normal high depreciation on those types of personal property. Less than a year after the peak of his investment ventures, the young man was broke, had several lawsuits pending against him, and was forced to file bankruptcy.

Now, you may be thinking that this is not a story that I should share with you in a book proclaiming the many advantages of real estate investment. I do so only to make you understand one very important aspect: *Successful real estate investing is a two-part process:*

1. Generating income
2. Building long-term wealth

To be successful in real estate investment you should set your goals to achieve both: income generation and creation of long-term wealth.

Can You Save Your Way to Wealth?

Most of you have had a savings or checking account that drew interest. I would imagine that most of you, at one time or another, have had a Christmas club or some similar account that was for a specific purpose. And, possibly you were disappointed when you withdrew the money for the intended purpose and found that the returns had been very minimal on your investment.

As an example, if you were to save $200 per month at a 6 percent return for one year, you would have an interest return of only $67.11 on your total $2,400 investment. Even if you had put the entire $2,400 in the bank at the beginning of the year and you had drawn interest on the total amount for the entire 12 months, your return would have only been $148.03. Not so great, is it?

Worse yet, when you look at the same investment over a 20-year period, you may be even more shocked. Think about this: At $200 per month you would have deposited $48,000 into that account over the 20-year period. If the return on your deposits averaged 6 percent, about twice that of a typical return in the 2004 market, you would have in your account approximately $112,645. If you subtract the $48,000 that you invested, your return is $64,645. Now, if we take into consideration the reduction in the value of the money that you have invested and the value of the return due to inflation, even at its lowest levels, about 4 percent per year, the spending power of your $112,645 has been reduced to $50,682. That means that what would have cost you $50,682 today will cost you $112,645 in 20 years! Could that be possible?

Think about it. If we use 20 years of history, 1984–2004, and look at the cost of particular items, then and now, you will begin to better understand this concept. Here are some examples:

	1984	2004
Ford, F-150 Pick-Up	$ 11,000	$ 21,000
Mid level Mercedes	30,000	56,000
Chevrolet Camaro	13,000	25,000
Paperback novel	4	7
Four average car tires	177	341
Movie ticket	3	6
Median home price/California	$114,260	$376,260

Shocking, isn't it? So now that you have had your rude awakening, let's talk about what it is going to take for you to succeed over the next 5 or 10 or 20 years.

Hopefully, you are beginning to understand how important it will be for you to set specific goals for both income and long-term investment gain. If you are in your thirties or forties or older, most of you are wishing that you had purchased numerous properties in the last 20 years and never sold any of them. The rents could have virtually paid for the properties and you would now be sitting on millions of dollars of equity, as well as hundreds of thousands of dollars in income. But, as the old adage says, "Today is the first day of the rest of your life."

You now understand one of the most important aspects of this training course: *From today forward you must never pass up an opportunity that will bring you closer to achieving the financial success that you desire.*

What It Takes to Be Successful in Today's Market

Someone asked me not long ago to draw them a picture of the perfect real estate investor. In other words, from my experience and years in the field, what traits appeared to be the most prominent in self-made, successful real estate investors?

For the most part, the answer was fairly simple. Successful real estate investors have many of the same traits that successful people in other industries possess. Qualities such as determination, desire, perseverance, knowledge, dedication, optimism, commitment, vision, creativity, and drive seem to run consistently through most success-oriented individuals. However, I have found one main difference between successful real estate investors and many other successful people. That difference is: *There are very few highly successful real estate investors who did not begin and maintain their line of business with a solid basic knowledge of the market in which they chose to work, a strong set of specific but flexible goals, and most importantly, a workable, effective plan to achieve those goals.*

Few business ventures that generate a great deal of money or benefit are ever quick and easy. Success in the real estate investment industry is no different, and for the most part, it can certainly be more equated to a marathon than to a sprint. There is no magic wand that can be waived over your head to make you know everything that you need to know and be able to do everything that you need to do. It is a process or a journey, not a destination.

I read many years ago that a bee will pollinate in excess of 3,000 flowers per day. Think about that for a moment. There is no doubt that if bees had the minds of humans and could comprehend what they had

Table 4.1   Appreciation of Real Estate Investments*

Year	Accumulated Properties	Appreciation Per Year	Accumulated Appreciation	Total Property Values End of Year
1	$ 500,000	$ 25,000	$ 25,000	$ 525,000
2	1,000,000	50,000	75,000	1,075,000
3	1,500,000	75,000	150,000	1,650,000
4	2,000,000	100,000	250,000	2,250,000
5	2,500,000	125,000	375,000	2,875,000
6	3,000,000	150,000	525,000	3,525,000
7	3,500,000	175,000	700,000	4,200,000
8	4,000,000	200,000	900,000	4,900,000
9	4,500,000	225,000	1,125,000	5,625,000
10	5,000,000	250,000	1,375,000	6,375,000
11	5,500,000	275,000	1,650,000	7,150,000
12	6,000,000	300,000	1,950,000	7,950,000
13	6,500,000	325,000	2,275,000	8,775,000
14	7,000,000	350,000	2,625,000	9,625,000
15	7,500,000	375,000	3,000,000	10,500,000
16	8,000,000	400,000	3,400,000	11,400,000
17	8,500,000	425,000	3,825,000	12,325,000
18	9,000,000	450,000	4,275,000	13,275,000
19	9,500,000	475,000	4,750,000	14,250,000
20	$10,000,000	$500,000	$5,250,000	$15,250,000

*Appreciation assumption: 5 percent per year; number of properties purchased: 4 per year; average property values: $125,000.

to face each day, they would probably never get out of bed in the morning. But instead the bee just crawls out of the hive and 3,000 times or more moves from flower to flower, day after day, and ultimately gets the job done. The road to becoming a real estate multimillionaire is very much like that of the honeybee: It is not difficult if you are willing to accept the fact that you must simply move, one step at a time, toward achieving the goals that you will set.

Use Table 4.1 to help you visualize how dramatic and how quickly you can create wealth in real estate investment.

5

Establishing Yourself as a Professional Investor

When you actively begin searching for properties to purchase and contacting the owners of those properties, you will begin to function as a real estate investor. It will be important that you not only have the knowledge, but the tools necessary for you to succeed. The knowledge that you obtain from this book gives you basically everything that you need to begin your real estate venture. However, there well be a few additional tools that you need to acquire if you are to achieve a high degree of success.

Getting Organized

Undoubtedly, the most forgotten part of becoming a professional investor is all of the things that you must do to get yourself organized *before* you begin making contacts. You noticed that I emphasized *before* you begin making contacts. It is critically important that you have your tracking sheets, contact forms, and any other follow-up material available before you begin your prospecting, marketing, or contacts with potential individual sellers. Once you start your contacts, you will be amazed at the volume of response that will be necessary on your part to keep up with all of the properties and sellers that will become a part of your everyday business.

Too often, new investors start off thinking that they need some potential business before they ever need to begin getting organized. That type of thinking is a big mistake and can cost you dearly down the road when you lose a deal, or deals, because you failed to do the proper follow-up, simply because you were disorganized or you had no tickler or reminder process in place. Some of the things that are absolutely necessary for you to have in place are detailed here.

A Place to Work and Make Calls

Sometimes when you're starting out, your kitchen table and your wall telephone will be the only tools that you can afford. There is nothing wrong with beginning that way, but you will soon understand how important it is for you to have a location set up for you to work where you have all of your tools and organizational materials easily accessible. A desk or table and a small filing cabinet are two very good investments if you can afford to make them. If you are not inclined to buy a desk from a retailer, check garage sales and thrift stores and you will find many desks, tables, and filing cabinets at pennies on the dollar compared to the cost of new furniture. If you would like to check prices on different types of desks and tables, try the following web sites:

www.Staples.com
www.OfficeMax.com
www.SamsClub.com

If space is a problem and you do not have the ability or resources to be able to set up a permanent workspace, I suggest that you purchase a couple of cardboard filing boxes that can become your own mobile office. Later in the book when we have you set up your call sheets and contact information, we will cover in detail what materials you should always have with you wherever you might be.

One of the most successful real estate investors that I have ever met has been buying and selling real estate all over the United States for nearly 15 years and he does so, 90 percent of the time, while traveling the country in his motor home. His coach is equipped with a desk, small filing cabinet, computer, satellite Internet connection, fax machine, and a couple of cell phones.

Date Book or Planner

Make sure that the planner you choose is large enough, preferably 8½ by 11 inches, to allow you space for notes and other information that you will need to collect. If you are high-tech-oriented, a PDA or Palm Organizer is an excellent tool to use. One nice feature about the electronic organizers is that you can transfer information back and forth between your computer and the Palm or PDA simply by uploading. Also, some of the PDAs actually have telephones, Internet capabilities, and digital cameras built into them. However, these electronic gadgets are somewhat expensive and an old-fashioned day planner will do the job until you want to spend the money for something more extravagant. You may want to check the following web sites for different types of date books, planners, and PDAs.

www.Staples.com
www.OfficeMax.com
www.SamsClub.com
www.PDAStreet.com

Telephone

It will be almost essential that you have unlimited access to a telephone. If you can afford to do so, you may want to consider having a second line installed in your home. That way you will be able to have an answering device on that line with a message that is recorded to best answer calls that will come from potential sellers and buyers. If you have children in the house, it is even more important to have a separate line that will only be answered in a professional manner.

Mobile or Cell Phone

Although not absolutely necessary, a cellular phone is an invaluable asset for an investor. Much of your work will be done in the field, and a cellular phone will save you an enormous amount of time. As you might imagine, there will be many times that you will find a property that will interest you and you will not want to drive back to your office or your home before you make contact with the property owner. Remember, you may be in competition with other investors who are interested in the same types of properties and often the first buyer or investor to make contact with the property owner will get the deal. As you will begin to see, there are many reasons and situations why the phrase "Time is of the essence" is included in nearly every real estate purchase agreement. The quicker you can make the contacts, the more deals you can put together. You may want to check the following web sites for different types of cellular services and mobile phones that are available in your area:

www.Verizon.com
www.ATTwireless.com
www.Nextel.com

Computer and the Internet

A computer, with Internet access, is one of the most important tools in the world of investment today. Although, you can certainly succeed without a computer, this tool makes your job much, much easier. There are many ways that a computer helps a potential investor. Letters, flyers, brochures, spreadsheets, follow-up and organization pages, and even business cards can all be created and printed from a computer and low-priced printer. In addition, with Internet access, the computer becomes a tremendous prospecting tool that will save you a great deal of time.

The complaint that I hear from some of my seminar attendees is that they don't want to spend the time learning to use the computer when they believe that they can spend the time making contacts with potential sellers, and there is some truth to that argument. However, I will tell you that the minimal amount of time that it will take for you to learn a few functions on the computer is time well spent and it will come back to you 100-fold in financial return within the first year of your investing career.

If you are truly starting your investment career on a shoestring and cannot afford to purchase a computer, there are many alternatives that you can consider. Possibly a friend or family member has a computer that you can use. If you live in an area that has one, many public libraries now have computer and Internet access. Also, in many cities there are access locations such as Internet cafes and computer coffeehouses that offer computer and Internet access for a small fee. Even some of the larger printing organizations such as Kinko's and Pip offer the equipment and online access that will help you in your business.

Several months ago I received a letter from a former seminar attendee who told me that she used the computers and Internet access at a local Kinko's store in San Diego to put her first two no-money-down deals together, before she could afford to buy her own computer. She indicated that although it was a bit of a drag to have to go to the store to use the computer to do her property searches, it paid off in the end. The second home that she purchased, painted and repaired and put back on the market ultimately sold to a person that she had met at the Kinko's print store. The sale generated for our former student a $32,000 profit. It seems that she had met her potential buyer while the buyer was using the store computers to look for homes to purchase.

If you are thinking that this is just a coincidence, think again. This is just another affirmation that business and deals are everywhere if you are paying attention to everything and everyone around you.

The Microsoft Office Suite of programs will provide you with professional software, Including: Word, Excel, Access, Power Point, Publisher, and Front Page. These programs will enable you to produce professional quality letters, contracts, flyers, news letters, spreadsheets, presentations, databases as well as web site development and interaction. Microsoft Publisher makes a nice complement to the Office Suite products. Publisher will enhance all of your document production and provide brochure, flyer and news letter templates which will easily allow you to incorporate graphics. If you would like to do some price comparisons on computers and software that are available in today's market you may want to try the following web sites:

www.DealTime.com
http://shopper.CNet.com
www.Pricescan.com
www.Pricegrabber.com
www.nexttag.com

How You Will Represent Yourself

There are several ways that you can represent yourself when you make contact with potential sellers. Business cards, flyers, postcards, oversize bonus postcards, and brochures are only a few of the methods that we recommend investors use to get their names out to potential sellers and buyers.

Business Cards

"Do you have a card?" How many times a day is that question asked? Probably, thousands, if not hundreds of thousands, of times a day. It is interesting to me that people will work in the business world for many years, utilize business cards every day of their business life, and not have cards for their own real estate investment business. Business cards are not very expensive, usually $20 or less for basic cards, and are a very useful tool if they are created and used properly. The two cards below are examples of business cards that are used by successful investors. You will note that both of these cards are very simple and are designed to say exactly what you want people to know... that you are interested in buying real estate.

When you design your business cards, you need to keep in mind that they should be very simple and should give people the exact message that you want them to receive and that is *call me!* Make sure that you

keep a good quantity of your business cards in your car, your house, your office, and your wallet or purse, and do not be stingy handing them out. Often, the best deals will come from the person you felt was the most unlikely to respond. Give cards to everyone with whom you come in contact, every day.

Begin making a list that you will entitle "My 100 Best Prospecting Affiliations." These are people who can help you to find investment properties or sellers who may be flexible and accommodating. Where will that list come from? Let's get your mind moving in the right direction: Think about where you might go and whom you might be able to give cards to as you conduct your daily activities. Here are just a few ideas: post office, mini-mart, pharmacy, grocery store, gas station, hairstylist, church, dry cleaner, pet store, restaurant, feed store, hardware store, and even the local pub. As you can see, you probably come in contact with 25 to 100 people in any given day so, as I said, it will be important for you to have a good supply of business cards and be very free at handing them out.

Other ways to get your message out will be to place your business cards and other prospecting material on bulletin boards and any other location that allows the posting of that type of material. I once purchased a property from a person who had seen my card on the bulletin board at a local tack and feed store. The seller told me that she had called me because it said on my card, "I will buy your house." She also indicated to me that there were several real estate agents' cards on the bulletin board, but none of them indicated that they were interested in buying property and she was not interested in listing the property for sale.

Don't be afraid to ask the owners or managers at your local stores if they will allow you to leave a stack or small holder of cards on their counters. You can even offer the clerk, manager, or store owner some type of remuneration if you happen to make a deal with someone who picked up the card in that location. However, make sure that you always track those referral situations and properly take care of the people to whom you have made promises. In many instances, people will never ask for any type of payment, but if you happen to make a deal and you can track where it came from, be sure to take care of the people who have helped you.

Although it is always good to deal with local businesses, you may have to resort to ordering business cards from a supplier that offers you the best deal. Remember that you want a good-quality card, but you also need a substantial quantity. Also, remember that there are special formatted pages that can be purchased at your local stationery store that will allow you to print your own business cards out of the computer. Although most of these cards are not of especially high quality, they will get the job done until you can afford something better.

The following are a few web sites that can print business cards, flyers, and brochures and seem to offer very good prices:

www.printingforless.com
www.theallineed.com
www.business.com
www.overnightprints.com

Flyers and Brochures

Flyers and brochures are another very inexpensive way to help promote the prospecting side of your investment business. Similarly to business cards, flyers and brochures give you the opportunity to get your message out, but allow you more space for information and personal design. Again, like business cards, flyers should be simple and to the point. Both flyers and brochures can be designed and printed on a computer, but if you have no access, you might ask at your local print shop how much they would charge to design a very simple handout-type flyer. In most cases, the cost will be minimal and once you have the design, you can reprint it again and again. Figure 5.1 illustrates a flyer that has proven to produce excellent results for investors.

Flyers and brochures can be distributed in the same manner as business cards. Once again, keep a good supply of your flyers and brochures and don't be miserly at handing them out. My goal is to receive four to

FIGURE 5.1   An example of a flyer that has produced excellent results for investors.

five calls from every 1,000 brochures and to put together one deal from those calls. Remember, if those 1,000 flyers cost you $30 to $50 and you put one deal together, it is money well spent.

As I said about business cards, it is best to have your flyers and brochures printed in your local area; however, from a cost standpoint you may need to print outside the area until you have generated some money. The same web sites listed above in the business card section can be used to identify flyer and brochure printers.

Web Site

More and more it has become commonplace for real estate professionals, as well as professional real estate investors, to have an informational web site. As you progress into your career, you may decide that this is one of the ways you will market your investment business. Web sites can be developed at a nominal cost and many times will give you the opportunity to answer questions of potential buyers and sellers with whom you would like to do business.

If you're considering a web site, or will do so in the future, take the time to look at the following examples of sites that have been well developed and have proven to produce positive results:

www.fasthomeoffer.com
www.Ibuyhouses.com
www.IbuyMIhouses.com

It Is a Numbers Game

This entire chapter has been dedicated to ways that you can help potential sellers and buyers to know and to find you when you begin to make contacts in the market. Keep in mind that the investment business, like many others, is a numbers game.

Many, many new investors never have the perseverance to be able to hang in there long enough to even put their first deal together. It is imperative that you recognize the fact that, on the average, out of each 100 potential sellers that you contact, only two to three of those potential sellers are actually potential deals. With that in mind, you begin to realize how important it is for you to distribute as much marketing material as possible.

Whether it is flyers, brochures, newspaper ads, or business cards, every item that identifies you as an investor is another potential opportunity for you to find the perfect buyer or seller for whom you are always searching.

6

Analyzing the Marketplaces

As it is with nearly any business, it is critical that you have a good understanding of the marketplace in which you have decided to work. As you begin to search for properties, your time will become more and more valuable and it will be critical that you spend your hours prudently. Your decisions about properties and your actions to make offers must be done quickly and efficiently for you to become successful and reach your goals.

What Is the Process?

As I have discussed previously in several sections of this book, it is important to have a detailed and specific plan when it comes time to begin searching for the areas in neighborhoods in which you are interested, as well as the properties that you'll ultimately purchase. The process of finding the right properties at the right price involves a simple five-step method that if followed exactly will produce outstanding results:

1. Find the area (see Figure 6.1).
2. Find the properties that might be for sale (see Figure 6.2).
3. Identify and go after the sellers who have the properties you want (see Figure 6.3).
4. Make an offer, work through negotiations, and get an accepted offer (see Figure 6.4).
5. Close the transaction and make the move (see Figure 6.5).

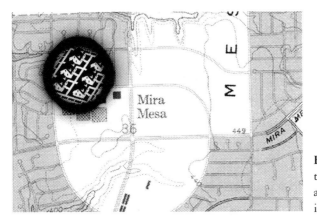

FIGURE 6.1 A map to help you zero in on an area for real estate investment.

FIGURE 6.2 A group of properties that might be for sale.

FIGURE 6.3 Zero in on the properties that you want.

FIGURE 6.4 Get an accepted offer, and go to contract.

FIGURE 6.5 Close the deal and make the move.

Finding the Best Areas, Neighborhoods, and Properties

Most new investors start off like the young lady in Albuquerque that I told you about earlier in the book, looking for low-end properties. There are several reasons that most of these investors choose this route. First, there are usually more less expensive properties in the marketplace. Second, most investors have the conception that sellers with higher-priced properties might be more difficult to deal with and less apt to make a good investment deal. Third, and the most common reason is *fear*. New investors, for the most part, are afraid that if they make a mistake on a more expensive investment, they may not be able to recover as quickly as they might with a less expensive property.

As you begin to look at properties as potential investments, I suggest that you divide the potential investments into five categories:

Level 1: Low-end, cheap, and maybe needing a lot of work
Level 2: Moderately inexpensive
Level 3: Mid-level
Level 4: Expensive
Level 5: Very expensive

Figure 6.6 will help you to remember the levels.

The example that I provided for you earlier in the book about the young Albuquerque investor should have shown you that there will be many transactions where your success depends not on the size or price of the property, but on the type of transaction that you can structure. However, for the most part, I have found that beginning investors seem to be better served starting their investment careers with Level 2, moderately inexpensive properties.

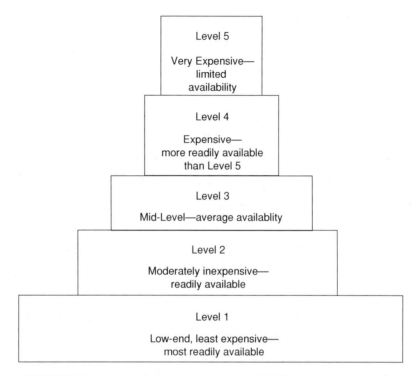

FIGURE 6.6 Levels of price and property availability.

There are a number of reasons why Level 2 properties seem to work out best for new investors:

1. Level 2 properties are easy to find.
2. Level 2 properties tend to have the most comparables.
3. Level 2 properties are usually owned by sellers who must deal with common personal and economic problems such as job loss, bankruptcy, and divorce.
4. Level 2 properties in need of basic, cosmetic repairs are usually easy to locate.

5. Level 2 properties often have sellers who can be flexible and accommodating for a buyer.
6. Level 2 properties have a higher turnover rate than most other levels.
7. Level 2 properties provide opportunities ranging from one- to four-family occupancy, often decreasing the cost per unit and thereby increasing the income and sale potential for the investor.
8. Level 2 properties have very good long-term wealth-building potential, as well as short-term income possibilities.

My rule has become: At least 50 percent of the properties on which I make offers and ultimately purchase will be Level 2. As you have seen by previous examples in the book, there are many exceptions to the Level 2 rule, but if you can become very competent in purchasing and working with Level 2 properties, you will probably be able to achieve any level of income and wealth building that you desire.

What Are the Most Common Mistakes?

One of the most common mistakes made by new investors is to buy a dilapidated, Level 1 property that requires an enormous amount of work to bring it to a state where it can be rented or sold. The fixer-upper syndrome that was very popular in the 1970s and 1980s got a lot of people into trouble when they realized, after they had purchased a property, that they themselves could not do much of the work on a property that was severely run-down. Structural damage, major termite or water damage, foundation repair, roofing repair, electrical problems, and plumbing repair are just the few of the areas with which many investors in Level 1 properties must deal.

If an investor in a Level 1 property has the experience, ability, and time to do the repairs, this type of real estate can generate enormous profits. However, if the investor does not have those specific abilities, the profits can be greatly depleted and the value of the investment can drop dramatically.

If your goal is to generate a monthly income and you are going to work full-time in the real estate business and you have the abilities to do major repairs, Level 1 properties may work for you. However, if you are looking for long-term wealth or a better retirement from your part-time real estate investment, my suggestion is that you work more with Level 2 and Level 3 properties.

Another common mistake of new investors is to try to make a killing on every property they buy. Many of these investors are out to make their whole fortune or retirement on one deal and they try to buy the biggest, highest-priced property that they can get their hands on. Many times that approach ends up in disaster because the investor doesn't have the ability and experience to ultimately make the deal work.

Making the Right Choices

Earlier in the book I discussed the importance of investors having a solid knowledge of an entire area before they start making the decisions about which neighborhoods they were going to invest in. It should go without saying that if in an overall area, unemployment is increasing, employers are laying off workers and closing their businesses, and the general economy in an area is declining, that might not be the best marketplace for a new investor to be working. There may in fact be some great purchase opportunities in that type of market, but the term that you might have to hold the properties to make them worthwhile may preclude you from being able to purchase and hold on.

Once you have found an overall area or marketplace in which you are comfortable working, you will need to begin systematically looking at the neighborhoods that will offer you the most opportunities. The type of properties and the amount of anticipated return will be predicated primarily by the goals that you have set for yourself. If you are looking to purchase, maintain, and rent out 30 to 40 investment properties over the next five-year period, growing your monthly income to a reasonable level, let's say $10,000 to $15,000, as well as growing your potential long-term net worth to $1 million or more, you will need to identify enough market areas and neighborhoods that will support those goals.

Tracking Your Research—Developing and Using a Property Search Log

Developing and using a property search log is the most important step in beginning your area and property searches. After you have chosen the area(s) in which you are interested in investing, you will begin looking at specific properties, probably first on the Internet and then in person. What you must remember is that your search for the right properties will be ongoing. You must not forget that you may view 50 or 60 or even 100 properties before you make offers. For all of the properties that you view that are potentials, it will be critical for you to have detailed information pages and photographs so you will be able to remember all of the aspects of those individual properties. The fact is, after you have seen only about 10 properties, they will all begin to blend together in your mind.

Your Property Search Binder—The Layout and What Is Included

Obtain a three-ring, 8½ by 11, two-inch binder with pockets on the inside front and back covers. This binder does not need to be anything fancy, but if you choose to spend a little extra money, you may find it is easier to work with a zipper-type binder that can be completely closed so not to lose any documents. You will place in your property search binder: log pages, dividers (optional), listing information pages, maps, property brochures, and other information, plus a highlighter and a couple of pens or mechanical pencils.

Several copies of your property search log should be available at the front of your binder and when you begin to search for individual properties, you will maintain copies of the comparative market analysis forms (see Table 6.1) that you will complete for each area or neighborhood in which you are looking for a property. The sample property search log pages shown in Table 6.2 are an excellent format for almost any type of property search. These log pages can be easily laid out in a Word program or can be hand-drawn on 8½ by 11 pages. Blank log pages can be placed in the back of the binder and dividers can be used if you want to separate cities, areas, or neighborhoods. Each page, as it is completed, should be placed in the binder for future reference. Photographs that are taken of each property can be attached to the back of each log page with a glue stick or adhesive tape. Maps of areas can be attached to the dividers for each neighborhood or area. A great place on the Internet to print maps is www.mapquest.com. This site allows you to zoom in or out for as much detail as you desire.

As you begin to use your property search log, it will be important for you to record the information as soon after you view the area or individual properties (either on the Internet or in person) as possible. Do not wait until the end of the day and try to remember all of the information about the properties that you have seen.

Photographs of every property are very important when the time comes for you to make a decision about which property or properties you will consider for actual offers. Try to make it a habit to take, or print if working on the Internet, at least two photographs of each property that you *believe* might be worth considering for investment.

Table 6.1   Comparative Market Analysis Form

Date:_____   Competative Market Value: $_____
For: _____   Probable Sale Price: $_____
Address:_____   Seller's Acknowledgment:_____
Prepared By:_____

Note: List prices and sale prices add 000 to each number shown.
   Sq. Ft. is price per square foot rounded to the nearest dollar.

Address/ Features	Bed Rms	Bath	Sq.Ft.	Age	Fam. Rm.	Din. Rm.	Fire- Place	Pool	Gar.	List Pr.	Sale Pr.	Sq. Ft.	Days on Mkt.	Trms	Date Sold	Remarks

Table 6.2 Sample Property Search Log Page

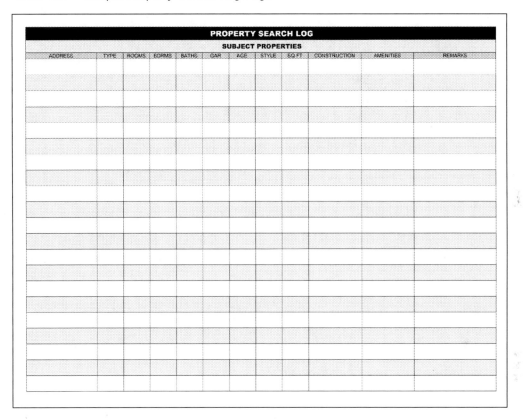

Finding the Areas

Now that you have a tool that allows you to keep track of the areas, neighborhoods, and properties that you view, it is time to begin your search for the areas that you will consider. If you currently reside in the general area in which you are considering investing, there is a pretty good chance that you already know what areas and neighborhoods you will consider, as well as the approximate prices of homes in those particular neighborhoods. However, many buyers do not have that advantage; therefore, this book addresses the search process from the beginning, assuming the potential buyer has no knowledge of the areas.

The Internet

Once again, using the Internet for your initial search for areas and neighborhoods will save you a great deal of time and will provide an enormous amount of information. As I also indicated previously, in most cases, you will *not* need to register on most of the sites to obtain the information that you need, so *do not do so* unless you want to start receiving continual calls, letters, and e-mails from the agent/broker with whom you register. Remember, all you are looking for in the beginning is a general overview of the areas and neighborhoods, possibly information about the schools, hospitals, or other services, a basic idea of the types of homes, the price ranges of the properties that you want to see, and a few photographs of the homes in the areas. Much more information is offered on some of these sites, such as videos and virtual tours, but you probably won't get into much of that until you choose the areas in which you are interested in buying.

Do You Have Adequate Internet Service?

It is important to note that if you are one of the many Internet users who are on a dial-up connection and you do not have DSL, cable modem, or some other type of broadband connection, you will probably be in for a slow and rather arduous task. As you know, when sites appear that have many photographs or graphics, the pages load very slowly. If you do not have a broadband service and it is offered in your area, I suggest that you get it, even if it is only for the times when you are buying or selling a property. If no service is available in your area and/or you do not want to spend the additional $40 to $50 per month for the service, you do have some other choices.

If broadband is not available, don't be too concerned. You just may have to move through the information that you want a little more slowly than you would like.

TERRY'S TIP: If you do not have high-speed service, borrow a friend's service, find an access location such as an Internet cafe or a business like Kinko's that offers that service for a small hourly fee, or go to the local library if they offer high-speed access—whatever you need to do to gain access to a broadband service before you start your search.

Later in the book, we will discuss using search engines for one task or another when you are using the Internet. You have numerous choices with regard to the specific search engines that are available on the Internet. My two personal favorites are Google and Yahoo, but if you are getting the results that you want, use the search engine with which you are the most comfortable.

TERRY'S TIP: When you find pages on sites where there are areas, properties, or other information in which you are interested, make sure that you click your Favorites button and save those pages for future reference. However, name those pages so you can find them easily. If your browser provides a Folder option, put the properties into separate folders under that area name.

How You Search Is Up to You

Every investor is different when it comes to the information he or she will want to obtain when beginning a search for properties. If you are looking only for potential quick-turnover properties, you will be less interested in the overall living amenities. However, if you're planning on keeping the properties for mid-term or long-term investment and you want to see the highest appreciation and increase in rental income, then those same area, neighborhood, and overall living amenities will be much more important.

Some of the amenities in which the longer-term investor would be interested are: schools, hospitals and available medical care, golf courses, horse facilities, etc., but many investors are just looking for nice neighborhoods that will appreciate and that will afford a good rental income. Regardless of your personal and property requirements, the goal of every investor should be to become a knowledgeable and professional buyer in a reasonably short period of time. There is no better place to achieve that goal than on the Internet.

General Information—City and Area Comparisons

There is no doubt that the population base in the United States is in a state of flux. Much of the workforce is transitioning not only from job to job, but from city to city and from state to state. Additionally, the retirement population is growing every year.

Fortunately, it has become much easier to obtain general and specific information about not only the real estate market in an area, but also all of the other factors such as climate, health, economy, crime rate, and much more. With the proper web addresses and a simple click of your computer on the Internet, you easily can learn nearly everything that you would like to know about an area and never leave the comfort of your home.

Now, I am sure that you are thinking that there are 80 million web sites out there and web surfing is more work than fun and you are absolutely right. So, we have done the work for you. Using the following information and some tremendous web sites, you will probably be able to retrieve any and all data that you desire. We start with a site that we believe is the best overall area comparison resource on the web.

Sterling's Best Places

There are several sources on the Internet that can help you with general area comparisons, but no site that we have found is as complete and easy to use as *Sterling's* Best Places, www.bestplaces.net. Make sure you go to .net and not .com. This site offers you the opportunity to compare 3,000 or more cities in many topic areas including housing, costs of living, crime, economy, health, schools, and climate. At the time this book was being prepared, several other topic sections were being developed and added to the site.

One of the nice features of this site is the unique Find Your Best Place to Live comparison tool that allows you to input preferences in areas such as Climate, Economy, Housing, Education, Health, Crime, Recreation, Arts and Culture, and Transportation and then have the calculator display the cities that best meet your criteria. Sample comparisons of Los Angeles and South Burlington, Vermont, are shown in Figure 6.7 (crime rates) and Tables 6.3 (cost of living) and 6.4 (climate).

Sterling's Best Places can be a tremendous help if you are thinking of moving to an area with which you are unfamiliar. This site is fast, easy to use, and very reliable. We highly recommend *Sterling's* Best Places at www.bestplaces.net.

Other Information Sources

Another site that offers area and city comparisons is www.Monstermoving.com. However, this site does not offer as many cities or as much information as *Sterling's* Best Places.

Chambers of Commerce and City Sites

Many individual cities and areas have web sites to provide area information. However, the quantity and quality of the data vary dramatically from site to site. When searching for these sites, it is best to use a search engine such as Google or Yahoo and be specific in your search criteria, as shown in Figure 6.8.

HOME	CITIES	CRIME	CLIMATE	COST OF LIVING SALARY CALC.	FIND YOUR BEST PLACE	SCHOOLS	ABOUT US
Crime in Cities		Crime in MSAs	Compare Cities	Sort			Crime notes

Home > Crime > Compare (Choose states) > Compare (Choose cities) > **Crime statistics**

South Burlington, VT and Los Angeles, CA

- 2001 FBI Uniform Crime Reports (released 11/02)
- Crime rates higher than the national average are displayed in red.
- Click for raw crime numbers

Crimes per 100,000 population	Natl. average	South Burlington, VT	Los Angeles, CA
Population	114,967	14,619	3,713,238
Violent crimes murder, rape, robbery & assault	506.1	95.8	1,353.0
Property crimes burglary, larceny & auto theft	3,617.9	6,553.2	3,509.0
Murder	5.5	0.0	14.8
Forcible rape	32.0	0.0	39.3
Robbery	144.9	41.0	418.2
Aggravated assault	323.6	54.7	880.8
Burglary	728.4	499.4	657.7
Larceny-theft	2,475.3	5,841.7	2,053.1
Motor vehicle theft	414.2	212.1	798.2
Arson	32.2	n/a	n/a

FIGURE 6.7   Crime rate comparison of Los Angeles and Burlington, Vermont. (From the *Sterling's Best Places* web site.)

Table 6.3 Cost of Living Comparison of Los Angeles and Burlington, Vermont

Compare Costs of Living

- To maintain the same standard of living, your salary of **$1,000,000** in Los Angeles, CA could decrease to **$871,637** in Burlington, VT.
- Stated another way, it's **12.8% cheaper** to live in Burlington, VT than in Los Angeles, CA.
- Where applicable, numbers worse than the national average are displayed in red.
- Need more detail? Click to compare 3,000 cities in 100 categories.
- Sources - BLS Consumer Price Index, Census Bureau, NAHB, surveys

Cost of Living Indexes	Natl. average	Los Angeles, CA	Burlington, VT
Overall 100=national average (lower = better)	100.0	130.1	113.4
Housing comprises 31% of overall COL	100.0	164.3	124.2
Food and groceries comprises 16% of overall COL	100.0	116.1	104.9
Transportation comprises 10% of overall COL	100.0	117.2	103.4
Utilities comprises 8% of overall COL	100.0	121.2	129.6
Health comprises 5% of overall COL	100.0	117.2	117.3
Miscellaneous comprises 30% of overall COL	100.0	111.1	105.3
Housing	Natl. average	Los Angeles, CA	Burlington, VT
House purchase cost median home value - Q3/00	$128,500	$200,000	$136,000
Home appreciation 12 months ending Q3/00	7.2%	8.6%	9.5%
Property tax rate tax rate per $1000 valuation	$15.65	$11.00	$20.70
Other Costs	Natl. average	Los Angeles, CA	Burlington, VT
Sales Tax Rate total local, county, and state sales taxes	5.75%	8.25%	5.00%

Source: *Sterling's* Best Places web site.

Table 6.4 Climate Comparison of Los Angeles and Burlington, Vermont

SOUTH BERLINGTON, VT

Climate Quickview	Year	Jan	Feb	Mar	Apr	May	Jun	Jul	Aug	Sep	Oct	Nov	Dec
High temperature (avg.) degrees F	54	26	28	38	53	67	76	81	78	69	57	44	31
Low temperature (avg.) degrees F	35	8	10	21	33	44	54	59	57	49	39	30	16
Days warmer than 90 deg. degrees F	6	0	0	0	Tr	Tr	1	3	1	Tr	0	0	0
Days colder than 10 deg. degrees F	49	17	14	6	Tr	0	0	0	0	0	0	1	10
More temperature info													
Precipitation (avg.) inches	34.1	1.8	1.8	2.2	2.7	3	3.5	3.5	4	3.2	2.9	3.1	2.4
Snow (avg.) inches	78	19	16	13	4	Tr	0	0	0	Tr	Tr	7	19
Days with some precip.	155	14	11	13	12	14	13	12	13	12	12	14	15
More precipitation info													
Days with thunderstorms	22	Tr	0	Tr	1	2	5	6	5	2	1	Tr	Tr
Humidity (4 pm) % relative	59	65	61	58	52	51	54	53	56	61	61	68	69
Windspeed (avg.) knots	10	11	10	10	10	10	9	9	9	10	10	10	11

LOS ANGELES, CA

Climate Quickview	Year	Jan	Feb	Mar	Apr	May	Jun	Jul	Aug	Sep	Oct	Nov	Dec
High temperature (avg.) degrees F	70	65	66	65	67	69	72	75	76	76	74	71	66
Low temperature (avg.) degrees F	55	47	49	50	53	56	59	63	64	63	59	52	48
Days warmer than 90 deg. degrees F	5	0	Tr	Tr	Tr	Tr	Tr	Tr	Tr	1	1	1	Tr
Days colder than 10 deg. degrees F	0	0	0	0	0	0	0	0	0	0	0	0	0
More temperature info													
Precipitation (avg.) inches	11.3	2.6	2.3	1.8	0.8	0.1	Tr	Tr	0.1	0.2	0.3	1.5	1.5
Snow (avg.) inches	Tr	Tr	0	0	0	0	0	0	0	0	0	0	0
Days with some precip.	34	6	5	6	3	1	Tr	Tr	Tr	1	2	4	5
More precipitation info													
Days with thunderstorms	1	Tr	Tr	1	Tr	Tr	Tr	Tr	Tr	Tr	Tr	Tr	Tr
Humidity (4 pm) % relative	64	60	62	64	64	66	67	67	68	67	66	61	60
Windspeed (avg.) knots	8	8	8	9	9	9	9	8	8	8	8	8	5

Source: *Sterling's* Best Places web site.

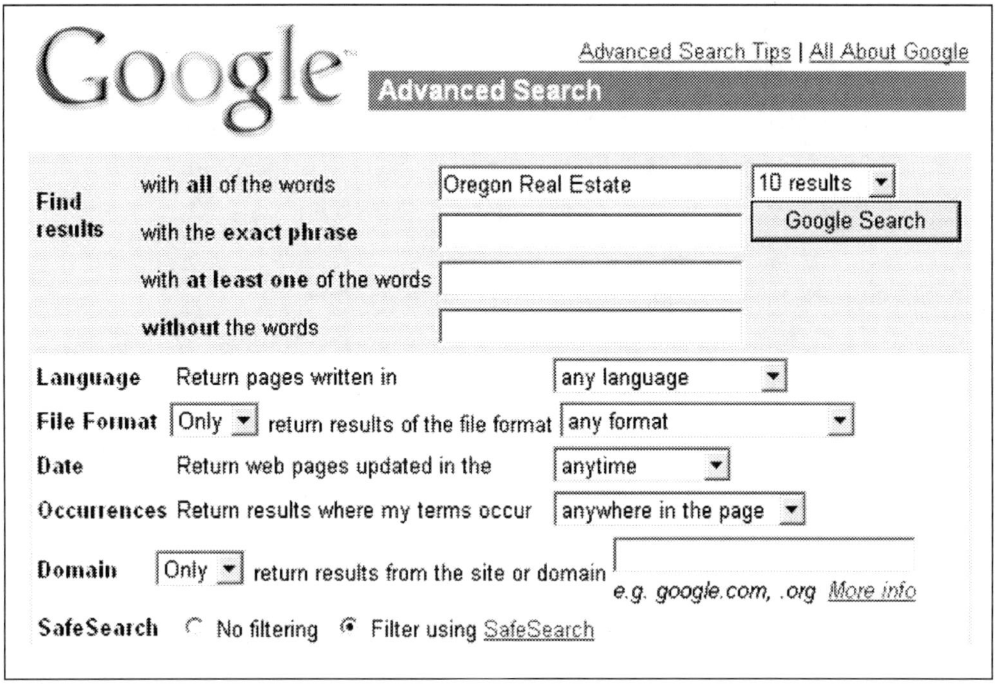

FIGURE 6.8   Use of specific search criteria when using a search engine. (From Google.)

Some Other Great Sources for Information

Although you can go direct to area agencies such as chambers of commerce, and city and county information agencies, most of the information that they provide is somewhat jaded and tends to paint a very rosy picture of the area. As an example, one brochure that we recently obtained stated that the violent crime rates for a particular city had continued to decline for four consecutive years. When we researched the crime comparisons, using the methods detailed above, we discovered that although crime reports had declined for four consecutive years, that city still had the highest crime rate for any area within a 100-mile radius. It is important that you temper the value of information provided by subjective sources.

Population Connection

This web site, www.populationconnection.org (see Figure 6.9), offers information about cities that seem to be particularly, as they put it, "Kid Friendly." Actual projects involving children and schools that have been successfully implemented are shown in detail.

The Internet Site That Has Changed the Real Estate World

Once you are satisfied that you have obtained all of the information that you need to make a decision about an area, it is time to start look-

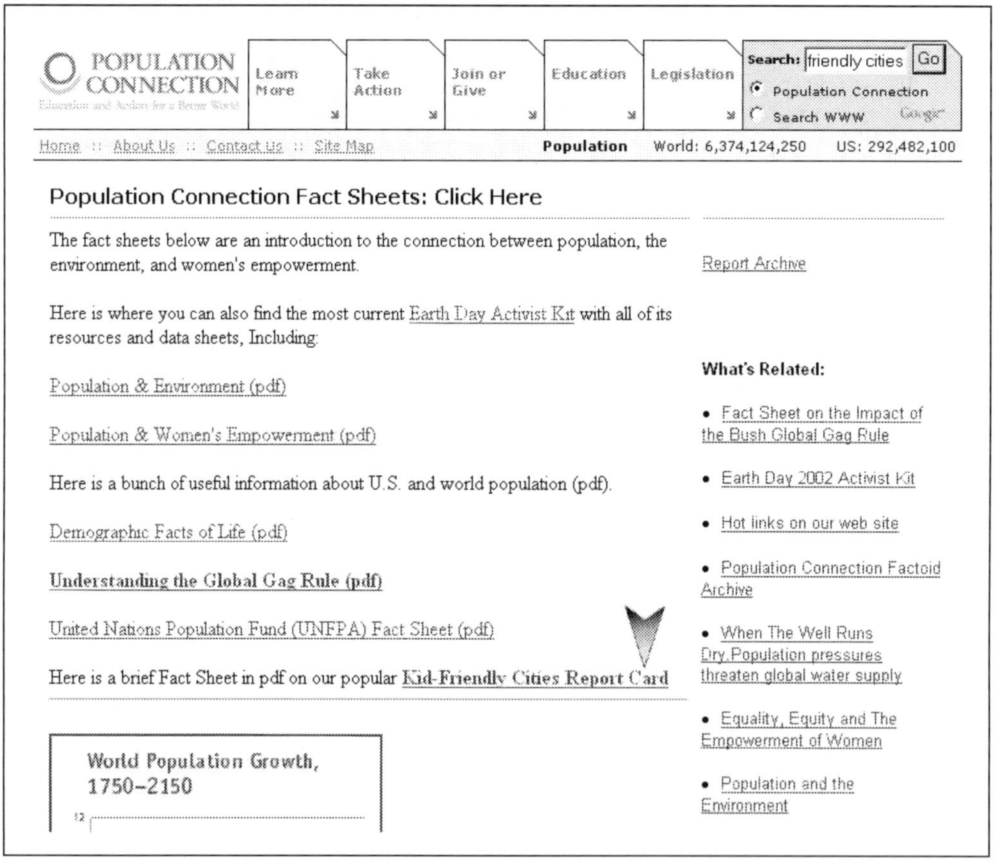

FIGURE 6.9   Sample page from the Population Connection web site. (From Population Connection.)

ing at neighborhoods and specific properties. My suggestion is that you begin your search for neighborhoods and ultimately individual properties on the Internet at www.Realtor.com. On a national scale, this site contains more information and properties than any other. At the time this book was written there were nationally over 2 million properties, shown on this site and the diversity, quality, and quantity of data is not available at any other web site.

Although sponsored by the National Association of Realtors, this site allows nonlicensed, nonaffiliated users to obtain an enormous amount of information without forcing the user to be contacted by, or become affiliated with, a Realtor until the user is ready to do so. In addition to the millions of properties for sale shown on this site, there is also a wealth of information available regarding schools, specific neighborhood amenities, financing, moving and storage, and neighborhood resident demographics, plus many links to other information sources.

Also, you will note as you begin to use the site that it has been constructed to operate very quickly, even with a slow-speed, dial-up connection. Additionally, in most cases, the agents and brokers that are shown on the specific listed properties are the actual listing agents and brokers of record, and later in this book you will learn why that information could save you money on your purchase.

TERRY'S TIP: As you look at the sites and specific pages throughout this section, keep in mind that the names, numbers, and information sources are continually changing. Therefore, when you begin your own search, there will be some differences between the specific information that will be displayed on your computer and what is shown in this book. Use the site addresses in this book as a guide to take you to the most current and accurate data available.

What About the Schools or Other Demographics?

Many buyers want to find information regarding schools and other demographics in an area before they begin looking for specific properties. www.Realtor.com offers that information in a more easily accessible format than any other resource that we have found.

The following discussion guides you through the process and ends in accessing school information. First, click into www.Realtor.com and you will see a page similar to that shown in Figure 6.10. On the left side of the home page, under Homebuying Tools, click on the site menu title line Neighborhood Tour. This will take you to a page where

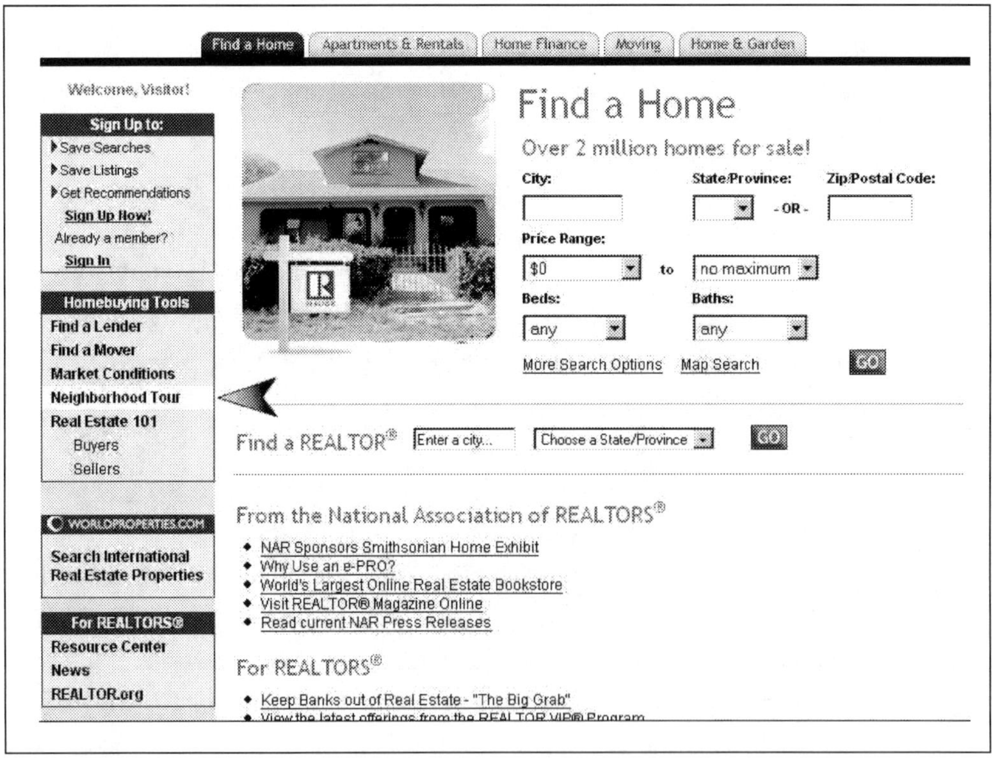

FIGURE 6.10   Home page for www.Realtor.com with arrow indicating a click on Neighborhood Tour. (www.Realtor.com.)

Home > Cities & Neighborhoods > Find a Neighborhood

* Find the best neighborhoods for you

* Find neighborhoods like your own

* Find neighborhoods near a given address

  Look for neighborhoods near your new job, kids' school, etc...

  Address: [   ]
     City: [Grants Pass]
    State: [Oregon   ▾]
   Radius: [21 ▾] miles (go) ◄

* Research a specific neighborhood

  Enter the ZIP code and learn about the area. (U.S. ZIP codes only.)

  ZIP code: [   ] (go)

Home > Cities & Neighborhoods > Find a Neighborhood

FIGURE 6.11 Page on www.Realtor.com where you can select a city and state and a radius within which to search. (www.Realtor.com.)

you may identify the area in which you are interested (see Figure 6.11). Fill in the city and state. Also, choose a Radius. That means the number of miles around the city that you want to include in your search. Then click on "go." You will see a graphic page similar to that shown in Figure 6.12. In section 1, map is broken down into county and zip code designations and the main highways are displayed. You may use the Zoom feature for more or less detail in the map. As you zoom in, you will see much more detail of the streets and roadways.

TERRY'S TIP: If you zoom in on the area to approximately the second level of magnification, you will note that hospitals are also shown on the map.

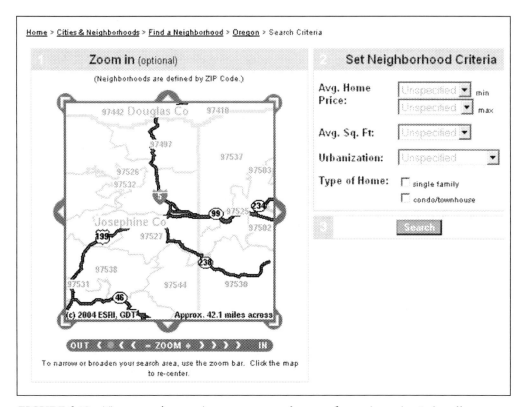

FIGURE 6.12   The next web page gives you a map and a zoom feature in section 1 that allows more detail of streets and roadways. (www.Realtor.com.)

In section 2 of this page, Set Neighborhood Criteria, you may input minimum and maximum Avg. Home Price, Avg. Sq. Ft., Urbanization, and Type of Home. Figure 6.13 illustrates the criteria used for this example, with an urban single-family home indicated.

Figure 6.14 shows the Search Results; three neighborhoods by name and zip code are shown. The Percentage Match also is shown (see Figure 6.15). Clicking on the first area at the top, Grants Pass, OR 97527, you will see the first Neighborhood Summary, which includes About the schools and Average Home Qualities (see Figure 6.16). Also, toward the middle of the same page, you will see a section entitled Dominant Lifestyle Profiles (Figure 6.17). As you can see, there are a variety of factors that make up the Lifestyle Profiles for that particular area.

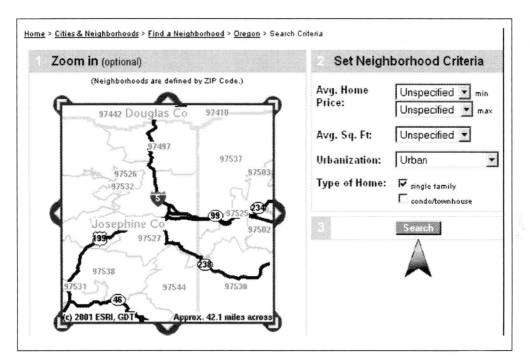

FIGURE 6.13   Choices made in section 2 of the web page indicate a search for an urban single-family home. (www.Realtor.com.)

Home > Cities & Neighborhoods > Find a Neighborhood > Oregon > Search Criteria > Search Results

Search**Results**

3 neighborhoods found!
Equally matching neighborhoods are displayed in ZIP code order.
Change your criteria to refine your matches.   Map your results

Neighborhood name & ZIP code (click on any neighborhood to read more)	Percentage Match to search criteria	Compare (check up to ten)
Grants Pass, OR 97527	73%	☐
Wolf Creek, OR 97497	40%	☐
Merlin, OR 97532	40%	☐

3 neighborhoods found!
Equally matching neighborhoods are displayed in ZIP code order.
Change your criteria to refine your matches.   Map your results

Home > Cities & Neighborhoods > Find a Neighborhood > Oregon > Search Criteria > Search Results

FIGURE 6.14   The choices made on the web page in Figure 6.13 resulted in three neighborhoods. Grants Pass, Oregon, was the next choice, leading to the web page in Figure 6.16. (www.Realtor.com.)

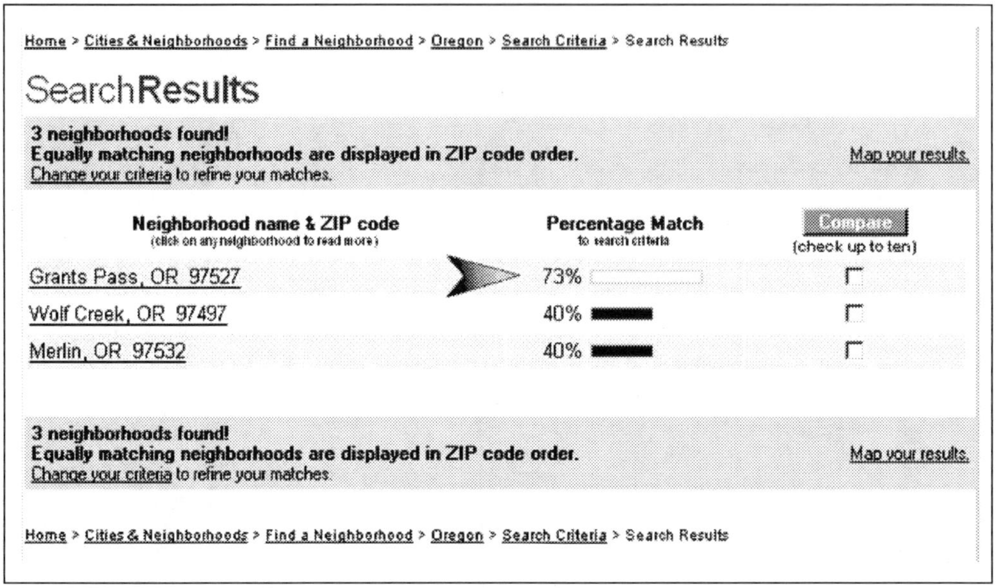

FIGURE 6.15   The web page of Figure 6.14 also shows the percentage match with the choices made on the web page shown in Figure 6.13. (www.Realtor.com.)

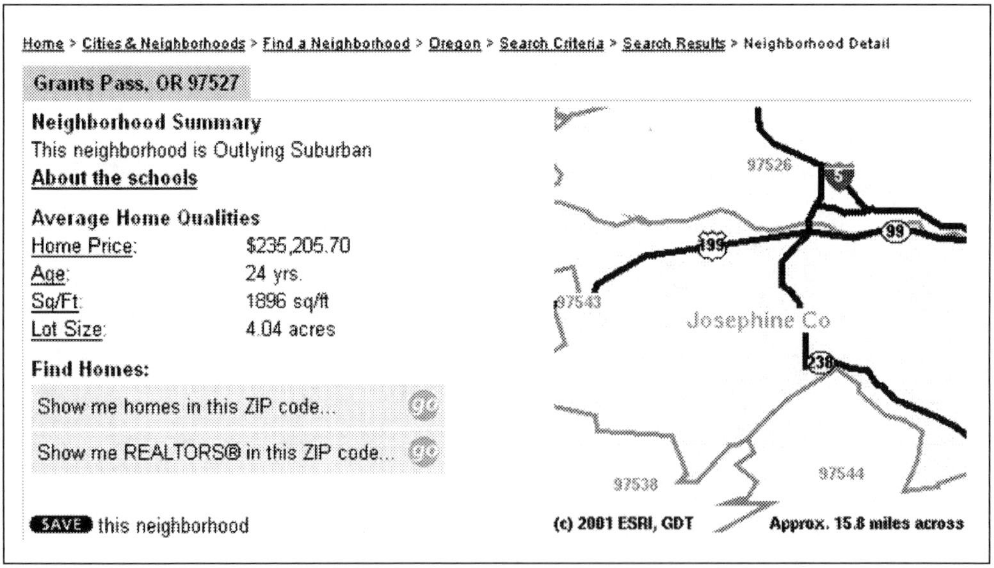

FIGURE 6.16   The top part of the web page for Grants Pass, Oregon. (www.Realtor.com.)

Dominant Lifestyle Profiles   A variety of factors make up the Lifestyle Profiles

37.76% of residents in this area fit the following profile:
Demographic:
Median age is 37.6 years.
Half of the householders are over 55.
Mostly couples with no children at home and singles are increasingly common.
Socioeconomic:
Median household income is $24,900.
Represents a 3.7 percent share of consumers.
More than 40 percent of the households are receiving Social Security income.
Two-thirds of the adults have completed high school.
Wages and salaries are not the only source of income.
16 percent are self-employed -- in farming or other business.
Residential:
Almost 70 percent of the homes are owner-occupied; more than 10 percent of the housing is vacant.
Average home value is 60 percent lower than the national average.
Single-family houses account for almost 75 percent of the housing.

18% of residents in this area fit the following profile:
Demographic:
Median age is 35.6 years; slightly older with more householders aged 35-44 and fewer under 25 years.
Seventy percent of households are couples, compared to 55 percent for the U.S. national average
Family size is average, 3.1 persons per family.
Socioeconomic:
Median household income is $33,300.
Represents almost 8 percent of U.S. households and a market share of almost 7 percent.
Almost 35 percent of households earn less than $25,000, but very few are below the poverty level.
Unemployment, 5.2 percent, is below the national average.
Most of the work force is employed in manufacturing or farming.
Thirty percent commute to a different county or state to work.
Residential:
Most homes were built after 1970.
More than 15 percent are mobile homes, which is twice the national average.
Homes are owner-occupied and valued at 30 percent lower than the national average.
Single-family and mobile homes predominate.

12.27% of residents in this area fit the following profile:
Demographic:
Median age is 35.6 years.
Born and raised in the same state, not inclined to migrate to a different county.
Most of the households are couples with school age or adult children living at home.
Socioeconomic:
Median household income is less than $25,000.
Dependent upon manufacturing and sustained by farming.
55 percent of the adult population (age 25+ years) have completed high school.
Most commute long distances to work.
Residential:

FIGURE 6.17   The middle part of the web page for Grants Pass, Oregon, showing the format of demographic data. (www.Realtor.com.)

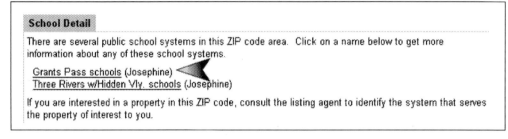

FIGURE 6.18   The top part of the web page resulting from clicking on About the Schools on the web page in Figure 6.16. (www.Realtor.com.)

To continue, click on About the schools, the information that you are seeking. This takes you to a page that displays a section called School Detail (Figure 6.18), under which you will see the actual school and district information provided by The School Report that is produced by the Homestore.com family of companies, an affiliate of Realtor.com (Figure 6.19). Clicking on Grants Pass schools will take you to the detailed information about these schools including names of schools and districts, number of students, number of students per teacher, number of administrators per student, state average comparisons, SAT scoring and state comparisons, etc. (Figure 6.19)

Toward the bottom of the page are the names and addresses of the schools in the area (see Figure 6.20). Also, at the top right of the page (Figure 6.19) is a line that reads, "Data Provided by The School Report. Click here for a complete, free report for your county." By clicking on that line you will see the actual report provided by the National School Reporting Services, Inc. (Figure 6.21). You will also be given an opportunity to request a free, in-depth detailed report of the county (Figure 6.22).

As you peruse the information, you may use your browser's Back button to return to previous pages and/or identify new areas for you to examine. This school information can be invaluable in your neighborhood search. And, most importantly, you can search thousands of areas from the comfort of your own home, before you go out and start driving around.

Back to Home | Find a Neighborhood Start | New Search | Search Results | 97527

School**Detail**
Grants Pass School Area

Data Provided by **The School Report**.
Click here for a complete, free report for your county.

School Area Information

Grants Pass School Area		**OR State Average**
County & State	Josephine	---
School Area	38001700	---
District Type	Public	---
District Name	Grants Pass	---
Total Students	5234	---
Avg Student to Teacher Ratio	21:1	16:1

Elementary Schools

Grants Pass School Area		**OR State Average**	**National Average**
Avg Elementary School Enrollment	384	---	---
Avg Class Size (first grade)	27	23	19

Middle Schools

Grants Pass School Area		**OR State Average**	**National Average**
Avg Middle School Enrollment	675	---	---
Avg Class Size (eighth grade)	30	22	23

High Schools

Grants Pass School Area		**OR State Average**	**National Average**
Avg High School Enrollment	1580	---	---
Avg SAT Math	527	510	510
Avg SAT Verbal	511	510	504
% students attending 4-year colleges	27%	35%	43%
% students attending junior colleges	41%	26%	27%

FIGURE 6.19 Web page giving detailed information about Grants Pass, Oregon, schools. (www.Realtor.com.)

Public Schools

Elementary Schools	Middle Schools	High Schools

Elementary Schools

Allen Dale Elementary School
2320 Williams Highway
Grants Pass, OR 97527
Grades: K-5
Students: 402
Contact: Liz Swinea
Phone: 541-474-5760

Redwood Elementary School
3163 Leonard Road
Grants Pass, OR 97527
Grades: K-5
Students: 366
Contact: Doug Reinhart
Phone: 541-474-5775

Riverside Elementary School
1200 SE Harvey Drive
Grants Pass, OR 97527
Grades: K-5
Students: 361
Contact: George Blue
Phone: 541-474-5780

Highland Elementary School
1845 Highland Avenue
Grants Pass, OR 97526
Grades: K-5
Students: 417
Contact: Linda Wells
Phone: 541-474-5765

Lincoln Elementary School
1132 NE 10th Street
Grants Pass, OR 97526
Grades: K-5
Students: 385
Contact: Dan Smith
Phone: 541-474-5770

Parkside Elementary School
735 SW Wagner Meadows Drive
Grants Pass, OR 97526
Grades: K-5
Students: 373
Contact: Diane Mease
Phone: 541-474-5777

Middle Schools

South Middle School
350 West Harbeck Road
Grants Pass, OR 97527
Grades: 6-8
Students: 627
Contact: Aaron Anderson
Phone: 541-474-5750

North Middle School
1725 NW Highland Avenue
Grants Pass, OR 97526
Grades: 6-8
Students: 723
Contact: Jim Fletcher
Phone: 541-474-5740

High Schools

Grants Pass High School
830 NE 9th Street
Grants Pass, OR 97526
Grades: 9-12
Students: 1580
Contact: Dave Currie
Phone: 541-474-5710

Back to Home | Find a Neighborhood Start | New Search | Search Results | 97527

FIGURE 6.20   Bottom of the web page of Figure 6.19 with names and addresses of Grants Pass schools. (www.Realtor.com.)

THE SCHOOL REPORT®

Josephine County, OR School Districts

The School Report
Review below and **CLICK HERE** to get a FREE In-depth Detailed Report. Your report will include SAT scores, % of students going on to college, awards and recognition, and much more.

NOTE
If you were previously viewing HOME LISTINGS, Please use your browser's BACK BUTTON to return to the last listing you viewed.

Locator Map
To locate a school district on a map, click the name of the district in the table below.

Josephine County, OR Districts	Total Student Population	Average Elementary School Population	Student Teacher Ratio	Average Class Size - Grade 1	Average Class Size - H.S. Math	Computers in Elem. Classroom
Grants Pass	5234	384	21	27	28	K
Three Rivers w/Hidden Vly.	2407	216	15	20	29	K
Three Rivers w/Illinois Vly	1299	460	16	22	26	K
Three Rivers w/N. Valley	2110	284	18	22	26	K

Review below and **CLICK HERE** to get a FREE In-depth Detailed Report.

Your report will include SAT scores, % of students going on to college, awards and recognition, and much more.

FIGURE 6.21   The School Report requested from the web page shown in Figure 6.19. (www. Realtor.com.)

| Find a Home | Apartments & Rentals | Home Finance | Moving | Home & Garden |

THE SCHOOL REPORT®

The data provided in The School Report® is the result of diligent research and our investment in solid data collection techniques. By filling out this form you will find valuable information that can be particularly helpful if you're moving within the next six months.

View your detailed report instantly by clicking on "Create My Reports."

Please select up to 3 school districts in
Josephine County, OR below

Create My Reports | Start Over

FIGURE 6.22   Web page enabling you to get an in-depth report on schools in Josephine County, Oregon. (www.Realtor.com.)

Making Personal First-Time Contacts

Although the Internet will save you great deal of time on your overall analysis of areas and neighborhoods, you will need to do some face-to-face or telephone contacts before you make the decision to start searching for properties to purchase in an area.

TERRY'S TIP: It is my suggestion that when you begin your investing, you would be better served to stay somewhat within your own area, say within 25 miles or so of your home. However, don't be afraid to journey outside of your own neighborhood.

Some of the local people that you may consider contacting will include real estate brokers, police departments, local businesses, postal or other delivery people, anyone working in the area, and any other investors with whom you might be able to make contact—in other words, anyone who might have information that is relevant to investment in the area.

These people might provide the answers to some relevant questions:

1. Do you live or work in this area? If so, does it appear to be a nice area?
2. Does there appear to be any particular crime problem in the area?
3. Would you consider living or investing in this area?
4. Are there a lot of properties for sale in the overall area or in particular neighborhoods? If so, why do you think that is?
5. Are there neighborhoods within the area that appear to be improving or declining more than the others?

If you decide that you want to contact some of the residents in the area, I would suggest that you avoid simply going door-to-door. Many people are reticent to open their doors to strangers, and your goal is to establish good working relationships with the people in the area if you are going to own property there. Sometimes it is best to visit local yard sales, area events, and area retail stores and stop and talk to people who are working in their yards or on their vehicles on a sunny afternoon.

The best way to start a conversation is to explain that you are thinking of buying property in the area and want to know what they think of the area. There are some questions that will help you and that most people do not mind answering:

1. Do you like living in the neighborhood?
2. Are there a lot of rentals in the area or are most of the properties owner-occupied?

3. Do you have any idea what the properties are worth in the area? (Give an example: three-bedroom, four-bedroom, etc.)

4. Would you consider buying a rental property in this area?

5. What do you like most about the area?

6. What do you like least about the area?

7. Do you know anyone in the area who is thinking about selling? (Remember, you are looking to find flexible, accommodating sellers and if you can get a referral from a neighbor, it is often better than a cold call.)

If you are nice, polite, and professional, most property owners and residents of the area will be more than happy to talk to you and you will be able to develop a tremendous amount of information in a very short period of time.

What About Unique Properties?

After many years of traveling the country and working with many, many real estate investors, I have found that the only uniqueness that is universally positive is when the unique aspect of the property creates an unusually high demand. For example, if 9 out of 10 of the homes in the area have two or three bedrooms and 1 out of 10 of the properties have four bedrooms, that four-bedroom property will usually be in greater demand than the other properties in the area. Even if the four-bedroom property is essentially the same square footage as the other properties, the four-bedroom seems to always have a higher sale and rental value.

Another example that is becoming more and more prevalent is the duplexes that are being constructed in areas that are populated primarily with single-family residences. Each half of the duplexes can be purchased separately, creating a reduced cost per unit, and often those units will rent at a rate nearly comparable to the single-family homes in the area. Also, if an investor can purchase both sides of the duplex, he or she might consider living in one side and using the other side as a rental.

In some cases, uniqueness can create problems with a property as an investment:

1. A two-bedroom home in an area where almost all of the properties are three bedrooms or more.
2. A property that is substantially smaller or larger than most of the properties in the area.
3. A property that has a history. (Don't laugh, I have seen properties sit on the market for sale or rent for weeks and months when they have a history attached. Crimes, deaths, strange occurrences, and even local legends can create problems for a property owner.)
4. A property that is substantially different than the rest of the area. (If you are investing in an area like Brentwood, California, where nearly every home is substantially different, this might not be a problem. However, if you are buying in a tract in San Antonio, Texas, it may create a big problem.)

A smart investor will always keep in mind that in an area of comparably priced properties, the nicest property in the neighborhood will become a victim of *regression*, which means that its value will be pulled down by the lesser-value properties. The least cared for and least valuable home will become a product of *progression,* which means its value will be pushed up by the nicer, more valuable homes.

After you have spent the time to identify the areas and neighborhoods in which you would like to invest, it is time to begin the search for those specific properties and the flexible, accommodating sellers. It is nearly showtime, but first, in the next chapter, we teach you how to properly inspect the properties.

7

Understanding Comparable Values *Before* You Begin the Property and Seller Searches

What is Most Important?

Each time that you *buy* a property, you must do so with *selling* in mind. Although, you may buy 20, 30 or 100 properties before you ever sell one, you want to always be sure that you are as *property liquid* as is possible. By property liquid I mean that every property you own could be easily liquidated or sold in nearly any market and in a short period of time.

We have previously discussed the importance of location with regard to potential property purchases, and we delve more into the importance of location later in the book, but as you will learn in this chapter, pricing and terms are often the key factors that override the importance of location.

In a later chapter, we discuss in detail methods to value an income-producing property, but it is important that you understand compar-

117

able values and comparable sale pricing as a stand-alone method of valuation before you begin to look for potential properties to purchase. In most cases, comparable values and comparable sale pricing are the primary methods of valuation that new investors use to begin their investment careers.

The Factors of Comparable Values and Comparable Sale Pricing

Appraisers and real estate evaluators use many different factors when they are establishing the market value of properties, but without a doubt the most important component of pricing is Comparable Sales, often called "comps."

The five most important elements that a professional real estate appraiser will utilize when determining the value of property by comparable sales are the date the property was sold, comparable neighborhood or area, comparable amenities in the home and on the property, comparable size of the home, and comparable quality of the home.

In the same way that professional appraisers use comparable sales to establish the value of a property, professional investors and real estate professionals will use exactly the same information to determine a property's value. Once you understand and know how to read and utilize comparable sales data, you'll be able to consistently determine proper valuation on properties and it will become a fairly simple and quick process.

Once again remember that price will not always be the most important factor in your purchase of a particular property. There may be times that you will be willing to pay market value, or more, for a property if the terms are good enough. It will depend upon the willingness of the seller to be flexible and accommodating.

Conducting a comparative market analysis is a fairly simple process if you understand that all you are doing is comparing like properties with like properties or properties with *somewhat* the same amenities in *somewhat* the same areas.

As a professional investor you always will be looking for the best deal that you can get on the best property that is available to you. If you are saying to yourself that it is only common sense always to get the best deal possible, you are right. However, most people do not understand enough about pricing, in all aspects of the products that they buy, to be able always to get the best deal possible. To explain this, I will first use an example that does not relate to real estate. Think about this question for a moment: Do new-car dealers, who pay the manufacturers exactly the same amount for their cars, all sell their cars for exactly the same price? The answer is no.

Second question: Do you sometimes have to shop, dealer to dealer, to be able to get the best possible price? That answer is obviously yes. The car pricing market is essentially based on the same theory as the real estate pricing market. For the most part, it is a "willing buyer, willing seller market." Of course, the theory can only go so far in that, once the car dealers and property sellers are priced too far above the market, even the most uninformed buyers will recognize that they are overpaying and they will stop purchasing from a dealer that is gouging its customers. So it is with real estate.

Also, when finance rates are very low for automobiles, dealers have a tendency to keep the prices of their vehicles in the higher range because buyers are often more concerned with their down payment and monthly payments than they are the actual price that they are paying for the vehicle. But, even in fast-moving markets, prices can vary a great deal from dealer to dealer. Again, real estate is very much the same way.

Consequently, it is important that you know that most dealers will "price match" with other dealers. In other words, if one dealer will sell you a car for a certain price, most of the other dealers will beat or match the price to be able to make the deal, if you can prove, usually with written paperwork, that another dealer has made you that better offer. Again, that same concept may apply when you are negotiating an offer on a property.

Keeping all of that in mind, think about how important it is to know the comparable sales prices of real estate when you are looking to purchase a property. Quickly pinpointing the exact price, within a small price range, that you are willing to pay for a property is one of the most important lessons that you must learn. Understanding comparable sales pricing will give you the ability to deal more successfully with agents, brokers, and sellers.

How to Learn Proper Comparable Sale Pricing

Before you go out and sign up at your local college to become a certified real estate appraiser, let me assure you that nearly everything you will ever need to know about pricing for investments you will learn from the rest of this book and in the on-the-job training that you will receive in the next two to six months because comparable sales pricing is really *very easy*. So, stay tuned—you are on the fast track.

Common Fallacies of Comparable Pricing

Some fallacies concerning comparable pricing exist within the real estate community:

1. *Comparable properties must be in the exact neighborhood of the property that is being evaluated.* In fact, appraisers often use properties for comparables that are several miles from a subject property, but that are in similar types of neighborhoods and have similar amenities and similar sale prices.

2. *Comparable properties, homes, and apartments must be the exact same age as a subject property.* Again, properties that have similar values and similar amenities and are in similar locations can often be used as comparables, even when the subject property is considerably newer or older than the comparables.

3. *Listing prices on comparable properties can be used as comparable sale prices.* Remember, sellers can list their property for any price, as far above or below the actual market value as they please. Therefore, listing prices are often irrelevant for use in establishing comparable values. However, no matter how askew to the actual sale market they may appear, listing prices will become important when you are selling properties.

How Properties Are Compared

If you look at the comparative market analysis form in Table 7.1, you will see how several comparable properties can be compared to establish the market value for a particular property. As you probably noted, having the proper market sales information made the sales analysis quite simple. However, you are probably thinking, "Where in the world am I going to obtain this market information?"

Real Estate Brokers and Agents and Title Companies

Earlier in the book we talked about developing an investment team or team of professionals. One of the very important and integral players on your team will be one or more licensed real estate agents or brokers. Although you will be purchasing many for-sale-by-owner properties, you also have the opportunity to purchase properties that have been listed by brokers. One of the easiest ways for you to obtain the com-

Table 7.1 Comparative Market Analysis

Date: 01/30/04   Competitive Market Value: $ 196,000
For: Bob and Mary Jones   Probable Sale Price: $ 194,000–198,000
Address: 590 Madrone Drive   Seller's Acknowledgment Joe Smith
Prepared By: John Johnson

Note: List prices and sale prices add 000 to each number shown.
      Sq. Ft. is price per square foot rounded to the nearest dollar.

Address/ Features	Bed Rms	Bath	Sq.Ft.	Age	Fam. Rm.	Din. Rm.	Fire- place	Pool	Gar.	List Pr.	Sale Pr.	$per Sq Ft	Days on Mkt.	Terms	Date Sold	Remarks
Subject Prop																
590 Madrone	3	1.5	1500	18	X	X			X	196	191	130				
Sold																
603 Madrone	3	2	1700	18	X	X	X		X	207	205	120	45		1/15	
891 Orchard	3	2.5	1750	10	X	X			X	208	205	117	60	Oc2nd	1/11	
23 Peach	4	2	2000	10	X	X	X	X	X	220	215	107	20		12/20	Grt Pool
For Sale Now																
505 Madrone	3	1.5	1500	18	X	X	X	X	X	200	-	133	15			Very nice
990 Oak	4	2	2100	15	X	X	X		X	225	-	107	36			
1233 E. 22	3	2	1700	10	X	X			X	210	-	123	41			
Expired																
446 Hall	3	1	1400	25	X				X	190	-	135	180			Off mkt
1011 E. 17th	4	2	1900	22	X	X	X		X	235	-	124	209			rented

parative sales data that you will need on an ongoing basis is too establish a good and trusting relationship with a licensed real estate agent or broker.

Another way to obtain the sales data is from title companies. Again, it is important that you establish a working relationship with a title company that will be able to help you not only with the closing of your transactions, but also with the comparable sales closing data. Many of the major title companies, such as First American, Land America, Fidelity, and Stewart have member services whereby the closing sale information can be obtained online. These services can be invaluable and tremendous time savers. If you are a professional investor and a good customer, those companies can make information available to you online.

It can be difficult and time-consuming to determine sales prices of properties if you do not have access to the sales data from a licensed real estate agent or from a title or escrow company. However, it is possible to search sales data through the county records. If you feel that you cannot or do not wish to establish a working relationship with a real estate professional or a title company, contact your local county recorder's office and ask them what the procedure is for you to be able to search sales data on an ongoing basis.

Depending on the particular market in which you are investing, there may be many or few comparable properties that have sold. The difficulty in proper pricing usually only occurs when markets are slow or you are purchasing a unique property, and the sales prices for comparable properties that have sold in the past six months cannot be found.

Understanding the Nuances of Pricing

It is important for you as an investor to understand what aspects affect the downward or upward motion of pricing in your particular investment area. There can be national, regional, local, or even neighborhood factors that will positively or adversely affect the pricing of entire areas or only individual properties. When you look at the history of pricing, you will begin to better comprehend and appreciate the sometimes volatile pricing that occurs in different markets.

Looking back 30 to 40 years to the late 1970s, the market was so "hot" for sellers that they were listing their properties as much as 10 to 20 percent or more above market value and receiving not one, but several full-price offers. In some cases, properties sold considerably above list price when buyers would get into bidding wars with their offers.

However, within a few years, as we moved into the 1980s, interest rates rose dramatically from 6 and 7 percent, to over 20 percent. As you might imagine, the buyer pool, those buyers who could qualify for incredibly high payments, all but dried up. Consequently, property prices were pushed down dramatically. In many areas across the United States property values declined 20, 30, and 40 percent or more. Many of the sales that occurred during that period of time often involved some type of creative financing that often proved to be problematic for both the sellers and buyers. That very difficult time in history created the perfect willing buyer, willing seller market more succinctly than any period previously, except possibly the Depression years in the 1930s.

As we moved into the late 1980s and on into the 1990s, the market began to stabilize. In 1993, mortgage rates dropped dramatically and real estate purchases began to increase again. However, an anomaly had been created that was difficult for most economists to understand: Rates were low and prices were down, but sales of properties were only increasing slightly from the very difficult years that had just passed.

It became evident that two factors were playing a very negative role in this market that had stymied the experts:

1. It was true that lenders had reduced their rates to some of the lowest percentages in history; however, at the same time, they had implemented much more stringent qualifications for the buyers, primarily due to the heavy losses that they had incurred over the past few years due to the very weak economy. In other words, it was very difficult for the average buyer to get a loan.

2. The borrowing public was extremely uneasy with regard to what seemed to be only a slight break in the economic difficulties, and they were waiting to make major purchases until the economy showed signs of a more stable recovery. In other words, people were afraid to buy property or make any kind of large commitment.

In the mid-1990s, interest rates for mortgages had risen to over 10 percent and real estate purchases were at a minimum. Although the lenders were easing some of their stringent qualifications for the buyers, the properties fell under even more scrutiny. The attitude of the lenders was that if there is even the slightest chance that we, as the lender, are going to end up owning the property, through foreclosure or some other process, we are going to be very sure that it has enough value to cover the amount that is loaned against it!

During that time, comparable sales information was analyzed very carefully and more than any time in history the "like for like" rule was stringently enforced. If no "exact comps" could be found, sellers often found themselves with an appraisal that came in at a lower price than the offer that they had received from the buyer. That time became a very strong buyer's market and it was not uncommon to see offers to sellers that were 10 to 30 percent or more below the asking price.

Also during that period, a new pricing technique was first incorporated by numerous real estate salespeople around the country. The technique was called range pricing and it involved using floating listing prices. As an example, a home might be offered at a list price "ranging" between $200,000 and $220,000 based on the type of offer that was presented to the seller. If a buyer came in with an offer that required the seller to pay more closing costs, fees, etc., the upper range price would apply. If a buyer were to offer the seller a flat-out, quick-close, cash deal, the price might be in the lower range. Variations of range pricing still exist in today's market; however, when interest rates are low and many buyers can qualify, the need for creative pricing declines.

As you begin to work in the real estate investment market you will begin to see how the changes in the overall national economy, as well as in neighborhood economic conditions, will affect the value of the properties for you as an investor. You always must try to have as much factual data as possible when you make your decisions about purchasing property, but it is equally important to learn to use your own personal insight or gut hunches when you make those decisions. It will not take long to develop a real sense for the deal. Before long you will inherently know if it's good or it's bad, most of the time.

What About Using Appraisals?

For the most part, I have three words to say about using appraisals, "Don't do it." That is, of course, unless you are in a situation where it is absolutely necessary. The main reason that you would want to order an appraisal would be if a bank or mortgage lender is requiring the appraisal for a loan.

There are times when it is necessary to use an appraisal to identify or confirm the value of the property. However, when you are purchasing as an investor, in most cases you should be able to determine the value of the property as it applies to your interest as an investor. In fact, obtaining an appraisal may cloud the issues and many times will slow down the transaction.

Many sellers who want to obtain a full-blown appraisal before they establish a potential list price are in no hurry, do not have any pending problems, and generally will move slowly and be difficult to work with. If you do your homework, obtain the comparable sales information, inspect the property properly, and generally examine all aspects of the potential sale and property features, you will not need to spend the $400 to $600 usually charged for an appraisal. Let's face it. In some cases, you will be making lowball offers for properties where sellers are facing personal or economic difficulties and your goal will be to solve their problems as efficiently and effectively as possible, but at the same time, get the very best deal that you can for your benefit.

Sometimes, an appraisal does nothing but clutter the issues in the seller's mind. I'll give you an example. A few years ago, I made an offer on a property in southern Arizona. The home, on a nice five-acre parcel, had been a rental for several years and was quite run down. The structure needed paint, a new roof, new carpet and floor coverings, replacement windows, a massive amount of yard work, and generally a professional cleaning top to bottom.

I had previously worked with a maintenance man who had moved to that same area and who could complete all of the work necessary on the home, and he was willing to do so at no labor cost to me if he could be a 30 percent partner in the property. Since I did not live in the area, he also agreed to manage the property for free.

When I made my offer to the seller, I indicated to him that I was willing to purchase the property as is and that he would not need to do any work to the property or even order any inspections. My offer was very simple: $4,000 cash to the seller, buyer to assume existing $56,000 loan, property as is, and buyer responsible for all closing costs.

The comparable sales data for the area indicated that property would be worth approximately $90,000 after all of the work had been completed. The seller, a former real estate agent, became quite indignant when I presented my offer and in no uncertain terms told me where I could "stuff it."

I made several attempts to explain to the seller that by the time he had all of the work completed, would probably net about the same amount that I was offering, but he would have no part of it and stated that he would order an appraisal, have the work done, and ultimately come out with a lot more money than I was offering.

I have one very stringent rule: *I do not concern myself with any property on which I have not been able to make a deal—period!* I have found that if you worry about the deals that you don't get, you can drive yourself crazy, and it is a very short ride. Forget them, move on, and don't look back—you will be a lot happier and live a lot longer. That property was no different—I just wrote it off and moved on to the next deal.

However, it was very interesting that about a year after the incident, I received a letter from that seller—an apology of sorts—explaining what had happened with the home. He said that he had let his emotion overcome his best judgment and that he felt obliged to tell me that he should have taken my offer. His story was as follows: Immediately after he had received my offer, he had ordered an appraisal from a local bank that he had worked with when he was selling real estate in a local brokerage. The appraisal came in at $87,500, lower than he expected, and required a new roof, home inspection, termite inspection, much general maintenance work, and several permits that had never been obtained when additions and changes had been done to the property. The seller paid to have all of the required work done, $16,400; for a new roof, $5,800; for the landscaping (also called on appraisal), $4,400; and paid $2,300 standard closing costs for the area.

The property sold four months later for $88,100. Because the buyer wanted to use the existing appraisal and avoid the cost of a new valuation, and because the bank would not increase the loan amount to coincide with the sale price, the seller ended up reducing the sale price to the original appraisal of $87,500. The bottom line was that after eight months, a great deal of anxiety, and an outlay of cash, the seller came out with a net of $2,600 in his pocket, $1,400 *less* than he would have netted if he had accepted my offer. Worse yet—the seller had suffered a slight heart attack that he believed was the result of the stress that the sale had put on him. The last line of his letter was classic: "Being that I am 58 years old, you would think that I would have learned to keep my ego in check and my 'big mouth shut,' long before now. Not! This was a tough lesson to endure so late in life, but one that I will not forget."

If you are wondering if my partner and I would have fared any better with the property, keep in mind that of the $26,600 in repair costs, only about $6,000 was actual material hard costs. The rest was labor, which my maintenance partner would have done himself, giving us a $34,000 equity when the work was completed. Also, because we planned to keep the property for a period of time, the rent, a minimum of $750 per month, would have given us a $200 per month positive cash flow. Also, it is interesting to note, that the same property resold two years after our potential deal for $123,000.

With regard to the original appraisal issue, with a willing buyer and willing seller, there is a very good chance that the appraisal would have come in higher than the original $87,500. However, the seller's impatience to identify the exact valuation of the property probably cost him several thousand dollars and a whole lot of grief. It is almost always best to order an appraisal only after a buyer has been identified and an offer has been tendered.

Your Pricing Will Be Based on Inspections and Comps

Comparable pricing for your own investment purposes will be based upon your knowledge of the area, comparable sales prices, and your ability to properly inspect the property that you are considering for purchase. As your knowledge base grows, the time frame to process those three factors will decrease significantly and you will be able to move quickly from deal to deal with great confidence.

Remember, as I have said previously in this book, you *will* make mistakes, but hopefully those mistakes will be small and easily overcome. And, if you do not deviate a great deal from the processes and systems that you are learning in this book, you never will have a problem that will be insurmountable.

8

Using Income to Value Investment Properties

Get Rid of the Emotion—Now!

For most of my life I have been involved with owning, riding, breeding, and training horses, and good horse people always laugh at the cliché that goes something like, "The beginners always want to buy the *pretty* ones," and how true that is. Most people who go out to buy their first horse are not looking for great bloodlines or the overall performance aspects of an animal as much as they are seeking a horse that really appeals to them visually. It is, for the most part, an emotional decision. Unfortunately, many people who make that first equine purchase without considering all of the nuances of the animal, often are disappointed.

It goes without saying that emotion usually has a great deal to do with any decision that we make. However, when it comes to valuation of potential investment properties, you must try to take as much of the emotion out of your decisions as possible. Have you ever driven past a property and said to yourself, "I would really love to own that house someday." Sight unseen you are making an emotional decision with regard to a property. It could be structurally unsound, it could have major plumbing or electrical problems, or it could be infested with termites, but in your mind that little voice that we all have in our brains is saying, "I want it," and your judgment probably would be clouded should you ever have the opportunity to purchase that property.

Another common example of emotion in the real estate industry is evident when sellers are very attached personally to their property and cannot realistically and objectively look at their home and be willing to recognize that the general buying public may not view it with the same warm, fuzzy feelings that they feel. The consequence is that most of those emotion-based sellers have a tendency to overprice their properties.

Unfortunately, real estate is not like the stock market, where you can get a quote today and know exactly what a stock is worth. It has often been said that valuation is in the eyes of the beholder and I suppose that is true to a certain extent. However, there are limits to the upper and lower valuations that can be easily identified if proper value analysis techniques are applied.

Valuation Methods Used by Appraisers

There are primarily only three valuation methods used by appraisers. Those methods are the comparable sales analysis, reproduction cost analysis, and net income analysis approach.

In most cases, as a buyer or investor you will utilize the comparable sales analysis and the net income approach. For smaller investment properties such as single-family homes or duplexes, there are usually enough comps to allow for proper valuation. However, when you move into larger investments such as multi-unit apartments and commercial properties, finding effective comps can be a problem and therefore valuation must be made by using the net income analysis approach.

The reproduction cost analysis is almost always included in a professional appraisal, but with the increasingly high building costs in today's market, that method is often unreasonable for an accurate valuation. When using this valuation process, the cost to rebuild the structure on the property is added to the value of the land, and then an amount for actual physical depreciation is deducted to arrive at the overall valuation. Often the difficulty with this type of valuation analysis is the subjective nature of the portion of the valuation that is deducted for the physical depreciation or wear and tear on the property.

The net income analysis approach will be the most effective technique you will use to evaluate your potential investment property purchases when the comparable sales analysis approach cannot be used.

The Two Most Used Valuation Methods in Detail

Comparable Sales Analysis—Multi-unit

We discussed in a previous chapter how to use comparable sales analysis (CSA) when there are comparables that are similar to the property that you are valuing. When you are considering properties such as multi-unit residential apartments, commercial buildings, or industrial properties that are producing rental income, you still may use the CSA approach but in a slightly different manner.

You may compare the selling price per unit of an apartment or office by dividing the sale price by the number of income-producing units. In other words, if a 10-unit apartment sold for $500,000, approximately $50,000 per unit ($500,000 ÷ 10 = $50,000), and you were comparing an eight-unit apartment, the basic CSA valuation would be approximately $400,000 for the apartment.

Another similar method is to compare the sale price per square foot by dividing the selling price by the total square footage. If we were to use the same apartment selling for $500,000, with a total square footage in the building of 10,000 square feet, that equates to $50 per square foot. Using the CSA approach, if you were valuing an 8,000-square foot comparable apartment, the value would be $400,000 (8,000 × $50 = $400,000).

Another method of comparison would be to use the gross income multiplier (GIM). To determine the gross income multiplier (Table 8.1), divide the sale price by the annual gross income generated from the income property. For example, if a property selling for $500,000 had a gross annual income of $55,556, the gross income multiplier would be approximately 9.00 ($500,000 ÷ $55,556 = 9.00). If you were valuing a comparable property that had a gross income of $44,445, using the gross income multiplier method you would value the property at approximately $400,000 ($44,445 × 9.00 = $400,005).

Net Income Analysis Approach

The net income analysis approach (NIAA) to valuation will be used in most cases when you are valuing a property that has four or more units. As indicated by the title, this method determines the value of property based on the *net* income that property produces. For this type of valuation process net income is determined to be the total amount of annual income produced by the property, assuming that there is no loan.

There will be occasions when you will purchase an investment property in which rents have not been raised for several years. The reasons for these lack of increases are usually that the owners have allowed the property to become run down, renters have stayed in the property for a long period of time and the owners felt obligated not to raise the rents, and additional construction in the area of similar units has kept the rents at a lower level. If you purchase a property with the intent to refurbish the units, most probably you will be able to increase the rents, which in turn may increase the net income valuation of that property.

An example would be a six-unit apartment that I purchased for $210,000. Comparable sales properties in the area had sold for between $260,000 and $304,000. The average rents for those properties units ranged between $285 and $315 per month. However, the property that I purchased was quite run down and had an average monthly rent per unit of only $220, or approximately $15,850 per year. If I had paid all cash for the property, my return would have been about 7 percent per year. However, I put only $6,500 down on the property and my cash flow after making all mortgage payments was approximately $4,000 per year. My actual return on cash investment was about 62 percent per year ($4,000 ÷ $6,500 = 62 percent). However, I knew that it would be difficult to keep the units rented or resell the property unless improvements were made.

Within 60 days after the purchase, I had painted all the units, replaced nearly all of the refrigerators and ovens, painted the exterior of the building, replaced the shrubbery, and resurfaced the parking area at a total cost of approximately $14,000. When I rerented the units, the rents were at $315 per month. The annual increase in rental income was approximately $7,500.

After the improvements, my total cash outlay was $20,500, but my cash flow had increased to over $11,000 a year. After owning the property for approximately 18 months I resold it for $310,700, netting approximately $80,000 plus the $13,000 realized in cash flow for a total of $93,000. After deducting the $20,500 invested in the purchase and refurbishing of the property, the net gain was $72,500.

As you can see, even on a rental property as small as six units, it does not take a great deal of rent increase to boost the annual net income and thereby increase the sale value of a property. Even a small rent increase of $15 per unit, in a 50-unit complex, equates to a $9,000 per year income growth. Keep in mind that in most investment properties that you purchase, the rents will not be maximized at the time of purchase and you will have the opportunity to increase the net income of the property immediately upon purchase.

Analyzing Cash Flow

Whether you are thinking of purchasing a single-family residence or a 100-unit apartment, it is important for you to analyze the cash flow to determine if you can legitimately afford to own the property. Cash flow analysis is really a pretty simple process. Table 8.1 is a form that makes the process even simpler, but it is important that you understand each segment of the procedure for two reasons. First, there will come a time when you will want to get a loan for a property, and it will be important for you to be able to intelligently explain to the loan officer how you arrived at the value of the property by using the cash flow analysis process. Secondly, when you decide to sell the property, it will be equally as important to be able to explain the cash flow to the potential buyer.

If you look at the cash flow analysis form as I go through each of the following segments, it will be easy for you to follow the process. I will include an explanation of each item. We use for this example a six-unit apartment. The determination of cash flow is broken into three segments: income, debt service, and expenses.

Income

1. *Estimated annual gross rental income.* This is determined by multiplying the monthly rents by the number of units and multiplying that figure by 12 months ($350 × 6 = $2,100 × 12 = $25,200).
2. *Other Income.* Other income includes any income that the property produced such as from vending machines, washers and dryers, pay telephones, rented parking spaces or garages, video games, or any other additional income-producing items ($143 × 12 = $1,716).

Table 8.1   Cash Flow Analysis

Gross Income:
> Estimated annual gross rental income _____
> Other income _____
> Total gross income
> Less vacancy rate allowance _____
> Effective gross income _____

Debt Service:
> First mortgage _____
> Second mortgage _____
> Third mortgage _____
>
> Total debt service _____

Expenses:
> Taxes _____
> Insurance _____
> Water/sewer _____
> Garbage _____
> Electricity/gas _____
> Maintenance _____
> Pest control _____
> Snow removal _____
> Yard care _____
> Licenses _____
> Advertising _____
> Supplies _____
> Management (off site) _____
> Management (on site) _____
> Accounting/legal _____
> Bonds and assessments _____
> Miscellaneous _____
> Telephone _____
> Pool _____
> Elevator _____
> Budget for replacements _____
>
> Total expenses
>
> Net operating income _____

Cash Flow: _____

3. *Total gross income.* This figure is the total amount of income produced by the property. It is determined by adding annual gross income to other income ($25,200 + $1,716 = $26,916).

4. *Vacancy rate allowance.* Vacancy rates will vary area to area and it will be important for you to research the vacancy rates in the areas in and around the neighborhoods in which the properties you are interested in buying are located. A typical acceptable vacancy rate would be 3 to 5 percent. One note: If a multiunit property has an extremely low vacancy rate, 1 percent or less, it probably means one of two things. First, the rents have not been raised for a considerable period of time, or second, the demand for that type of rental property is exceedingly high in the area. In either case, it is probably a good scenario for an investor. The vacancy rate figure is determined by multiplying the estimated annual gross rent income by the vacancy rate allowance ($25,200 × 3% = $756).

5. *Effective gross income (EGI).* This figure is the total gross income less the vacancy rate allowance ($25,200 − $756 = $24,444).

Debt Service

6. *First mortgage.* This is the annualized total of the payments on the first mortgage ($11,790).

7. *Second mortgage.* This is the annualized total of the payments on the second mortgage.

8. *Third or other mortgages.* This is the annualized total of the payments on all other mortgages on the property.

9. *Total debt service.* This is the annualized total of all mortgage payments on the property ($11,790).

Expenses

10. *Taxes.* This includes all property taxes charged by the county or city. It does not include the personal income tax of the owner.

Property taxes are usually assessed on the value or the most recent sale price of the property. In some areas a personal property tax is assessed by the county or the city and is assessed on the value of the personal property that is located on the property and is the property of the owner. This might include furniture, free-standing appliances, or video game machines. Property taxes are assessed at different rates across the country. For this example, we will use an assessment rate of 1.3 percent on an assessed value of $210,000 ($210,000 × 1.3 percent = $2,730).

11. *Insurance.* In most cases, your insurance will include a liability and fire policy. In some areas, you may want to consider earthquake, flood, or other types of specific coverage policies. For our example, we have included only liability and standard loss insurance ($1,240).

12. *Water and sewer.* For nearly every rental unit, except possibly commercial and industrial properties, the owner usually pays for the sewer and water. When you begin to purchase larger units, such as commercial office buildings, you may start using triple net leases where the lessee will be responsible for all utilities and expenses. For this analysis we have shown that the owner pays the sewer and water ($744).

13. *Garbage.* In most cases, for single-family homes or duplexes, garbage collection fees will be the responsibility of the renter. However, for complexes with four units or more, a large collection dumpster is usually provided by the owner ($780).

14. *Electricity and gas.* If the property has few units, such as a single-family or duplex, it is common for the renter to pay most of the utilities, including gas and electricity. However, with larger units often the owner will pay for the utilities that are used in the common areas. This usually will include parking areas and laundry rooms. For this example we have included a small amount for the electricity to cover the outdoor lighting ($336).

TERRY'S TIP: When you purchase a property; you should keep in mind that if the sale price is higher than the current assessed value of the property, there is a good chance that the property taxes will increase. This increase probably will take effect when the transfer occurs and the grant deed is recorded. Consequently, the new owner will receive a tax bill that may include not only the increase in taxes for the upcoming year, but also a supplemental tax bill covering the increase from the date of the sale recording to the end of the tax year.

15. *Maintenance, pest control, snow removal, and yard care.* Again, for smaller units the yard care may be the responsibility of the renter, but for larger units the owner is usually responsible. Maintenance can be a difficult item to determine when you are purchasing a property. It may relate directly to the amount of deferred maintenance that has been incurred and the cost of labor in your particular area. If the previous owner has maintained good maintenance records, it will help you to determine the future costs ($1,850).

16. *Supplies.* For larger units this might include paper items for public bathrooms, pool chemicals, etc. With smaller units, there may be no supply costs.

17. *Management.* Management might include a resident manager who may receive a small amount of rental deduction for a small complex or free rent and a salary for a larger complex. Also, an additional fee might be included if an off-site management company is used. If you plan to manage your property, collect rents, do the maintenance, etc., there may be no management fee.

18. *Accounting/legal.* Again, for smaller units there may be very little expense for legal and accounting work. However, when you get into larger complexes, these fees can be considerable.

19. *Bonds and assessments.* When they exist, bonds and assessments are always recorded against the property, and it is important that an investor understand these expenses because they can be quite costly. Some assessments have no payoff or end date, and the owner of the property must pay interest or a stipend on a bond or assessment indefinitely.

20. *Miscellaneous.* This expense covers any additional fees that might be incurred on the property. One of the miscellaneous items that should always be included is advertising. With larger complexes the advertising costs can be substantial, since ads may be run on an ongoing basis. Each time a unit is vacant, you may incur some cost for advertising to refill the vacancy.

21. *Total expenses.* This is the total of all expense items for the property, and it is determined by adding together all expenses, not including the debt service ($7,680).

22. *Net operating income* (NOI). This figure is the effective gross income less the total expenses ($24,444 − $7,680 = $16,764).

Cash Flow

23. *Cash flow.* This figure is determined by subtracting the total debt service from the net operating income ($16,764 − $11,790 = $4,974).

When you're looking at a property to purchase, the net operating income is critically important because you will use that figure, plus any increases in rents that you feel can be made, to determine how you will structure an offer to purchase the property.

The following is the purchase scenario that was used for the example above and on the cash flow analysis (Table 8.2). The owner of the property had experienced some health problems and had been unable to keep up with the maintenance on the six-unit apartment for approximately seven months. Two of the units were vacant and needed painting before they could be rerented. The owner was delinquent three months on the first mortgage payments and was becoming increasingly concerned about his credit rating. Additionally, he was behind on his property taxes by approximately $1,350. The total amount necessary to bring the mortgage current ($983 × 3 = $2,949), complete the deferred maintenance ($1500) and pay the property taxes ($1,350) was approximately $5,800.

When I spotted the property, it was apparent that it was falling into disrepair and I made contact with the owner. He indicated that he did not have the time nor the money to be able to bring the property up to standard, and he didn't feel that the property would sell in its current state. I made a purchase offer to the seller that he accepted with the following terms:

Sale price: $217,300

Down Payment: $0

Buyer to pay all closing costs: approximately $1,500

Buyer to clear delinquent payments and assume or take first mortgage "subject to" (8.8 percent interest; $117,300 balance)

Seller to carry a second mortgage for $100,000 at 5.1 percent, interest-only payments of $400 per month (nearly the same cash flow that he was receiving as owner), all due and payable after one year

Buyer to pay delinquent taxes

I negotiated with the bank to pay only the back interest on the delinquent payments and bring the loan current ($2,580). My cash outlay for the purchase was approximately $6,930 ($1,500 closing costs + $2,580 back loan interest + $1,500 deferred maintenance + $1,350 back taxes = $6,930).

However, because I was making a second mortgage payment to the seller, the cash flow was reduced to only $174 annually, or a 2.5 per-

TERRY'S TIP: When you own and personally manage smaller investment properties, 10 units or fewer, you will probably get to know the
renters and it may be wise to speak with them individually when you
have rent increases. An explanation from you personally about a small
increase in the rent to cover increasing expenses will often soothe the
ruffled feathers that are sometimes created by the increases.

cent return on investment before tax write-off. After raising each of the
rents by $20 per month, my cash flow increased to $1,500 per year,
increasing my return on investment to a respectable 21.6 percent.

At the end of one year, I obtained a new first mortgage loan for
$220,000 at 6.9 percent (paying off the seller), increasing the mort-
gage payment to $1,541 per month, but I was able to recover the cash
outlay for the purchase. The cash flow on the property is only about
$600 per year; however, the value has increased to just over $295,000.

Getting Caught Up in Analysis

Many first-time investors get caught up in the detailed analysis of
every property that they are considering for purchase. As I said at the
beginning of this section, analyzing the value of investment property
is really pretty simple. Take the income less expenses and determine
the cash flow, negative or positive. If it is a number that makes sense,
you may want to buy the property. One caution: Don't get greedy! If
you are going to try to make a killing on every purchase, you will not
be creating good win-win situations for both you and the other parties
to the transactions, and your tactics will probably come back to haunt
you in future deals.

9

Finding Great Bargain Properties Using Traditional Methods

When you began searching for the best bargain properties, you must remember that it will be equally as important to search for the most flexible, accommodating sellers. You will be looking for highly motivated owners who want to, or better yet *must,* sell a property that fits the qualifications that you are seeking. Keep in mind that because you are looking for a particular type of seller and a particular type of property, you'll probably need to look at numerous potential properties before actually making an offer.

There are many tried-and-true methods that you can employ to find the best bargain properties and the most accommodating sellers. You can do research of public notices to find foreclosures, bankruptcies, and possibly personal issues that affect sellers such as divorces, estate sales, deaths, and other legal notices. You also may work directly with attorneys, insurance agents, and real estate agents and brokers on more of a direct referral basis.

Another method that you can use is direct advertising, utilizing classified ads, brochures, and other direct contact methods such as letters and cards offering to purchase properties. You must always remember that even the best investment technique will be a numbers game. You must make a lot of contacts to find the very best deals.

What Success Levels to Expect

As a real estate investor, your job will be much easier if you can generate incoming calls from sellers rather than having to make many, many outgoing calls to people who may, or may not, be interested in selling their properties. The key to your success will be to generate as many leads as possible, in as little time as possible. Newspaper advertising is by far the best source for lead generation; however, there are many other ways that will generate good deals for you on an ongoing basis. The following breakdown will give you an idea of the approximate percentages of leads that are generated from the prospecting methods that produce the best properties and sellers with whom you will want to work:

1. 30 percent—Classified buyers newspaper advertising
2. 20 percent—Direct seller contacts—telephone, mail, or Internet
3. 20 percent—Real estate brokers and agents
4. 10 percent—Referrals from friends and associates
5. 5 percent—Ads placed by sellers
6. 5 percent—For-sale-by-owner signs
7. 5 percent—Bird-dog referrals
8. 3 percent—Other partner investors
9. 2 percent—Other sources

Investors will have the propensity to develop and use methods that work the best for them. When you begin to develop your own techniques, you'll certainly find that some methods work better than others and I encourage you to follow the path of least resistance that produces the best results for you.

Classified Buyer's Newspaper Advertising

Without a doubt, the easiest and fastest way to generate calls from property owners who are motivated to sell their property is to place ads offering to purchase real estate. These ads can range from two to five lines and when worded properly can produce amazing results. However, you must keep in mind that you are looking for very specific sellers who are flexible and accommodating and you're looking for specific properties that meet the guidelines you lay down for your own investment strategy. Knowing that only 2 to 3 percent of the contacts that you make will actually develop into a transaction, patience and perseverance must become two of your most prominent personal attributes.

If you decide that placing your own buyer's ads in newspapers is a method that you want to use to produce perspective sellers, it is important that those ads are simple and concise and portray exactly what you want to say as an investor. Some examples of successful buying ads are as follows:

> Cash paid for properties
> in the hometown area.
> Call today! 753-1747

Obviously, this ad will appeal to anyone who needs cash and who owns a property in a particular area.

> Need cash? I will buy your
> home today! No real estate
> commissions or fees.
> Call now! 753-1747

Again, this ad appeals to anyone who needs cash, but also clearly adds the advantage of the seller paying no commissions or fees.

> Do you have an assumable
> loan? If so, I will buy your
> property! Call today. 753-1747

This ad is more specific in that it identifies sellers who have assumable loans.

> Behind on your house payments?
> I will buy your home. Create cash
> now! Call now. 753-1747

This ad also clarifies the cash incentive but identifies sellers who have potential economic problems and have fallen behind on their payments. Many property owners who have economic difficulties will often fail to contact their mortgage holder when they become delinquent on their monthly obligations. Although they will not make contact with the mortgage holder, they will respond to an ad of this type because they see a possible cure for their problems without facing difficult negotiations with their mortgagor.

> Sell your property with no
> commission or fees. Call today!
> 753-1747

This very simple ad often gets very good results. If a property owner is thinking of selling but has yet to list his or her property with an agent or broker, the first inclination will be to avoid paying commissions.

> Need to sell your home fast?
> I will buy it today! Do not wait.
> Call today! 753-1747

This ad identifies sellers who have personal or economic problems. Of all of the ads shown, this particular ad seems to identify those problem-encumbered sellers more than any other. If a geographic area is experiencing some overall economic difficulty, this ad can generate a high volume of calls.

> I buy real estate! Private
> investor, not an agent.
> Homes or multiple units.
> Great prices paid!
> Call now. 753-1747

This is another high-response ad that identifies you as an investor, the type of properties in which you're interested, and clarifies that you are willing to pay a good price for the properties.

In the following chapters, you will learn dialogues and information-gathering techniques that will help you to respond to sellers who are calling in response to all types of advertising.

Ads Placed by Sellers

Responding to ads that have been placed by sellers is another method that can produce a good volume of transactions. Most sellers who place ads are, in fact, owners who want to sell their property and avoid paying the commission charged by a licensed agent or broker. Many of these sellers believe that their property will be so easy to sell that they will not need the assistance of a licensed professional. In most cases, this type of seller will end up listing their property with an agent or broker unless their property sells very quickly.

However, a few sellers who place ads to sell their properties do so because they have an economic or personal problem that can be solved by selling their property and they think that they will be able to sell their property quicker if they do it themselves rather than going through the broker listing process. Obviously, this type of seller can be good for you as an investor.

The Words of the Flexible, Accommodating Seller

When you begin searching for properties that are owned by flexible, accommodating sellers, you want to be sure that you are in tune with the terminology that identifies those property owners. As you begin to examine advertisements and MLS listings and talk to agents and brokers, you want to listen carefully for the following 18 words and phrases:

1. Desperate
2. Anxious
3. No/low down
4. Foreclosure
5. Must sell
6. Price reduction
7. Motivated
8. Wants fast sale
9. Exchange
10. Transferred
11. Below appraisal
12. Vacant
13. Flexible
14. Must leave area
15. Must have quick sale
16. Or best offer
17. Trade
18. Forced sale

In the following chapters, you will learn very explicit dialogues that you can use to make contact with sellers who have placed ads selling their own properties.

 TERRY'S TIP: One warning: Some sellers will list their own properties because they are aware of title, lien, or other problems that may crop up when the property is sold. These sellers may be trying to, for lack of another term, "pull a fast one" on a buyer and do not want licensed real estate agents involved in the transaction, since it is likely that those agents may recognize the problem areas and either refuse to accept the listing or they will be required to bring the problem areas to light before allowing the transaction to close.

Public Notices

Public notices are one of the best ways for you to identify flexible sellers who may have a problem. Notices of default, often called NODs, are posted in almost every newspaper across the country and provide tremendous opportunities for investors to identify sellers who may be in financial difficulty. However, once an NOD has been filed, contact must be made with the owner and the financial institution or the trustee as soon as possible for two reasons. First, once the NOD has been filed, the foreclosure process is usually in full swing. Second, when the notices are filed, plan on competing with a mass of investors who do nothing but work the foreclosure market. This is why it is better to find those sellers who have a problem *before* they have gone into foreclosure. Table 9.1 is an example of a trustee sale filed in a local newspaper.

Real Estate Brokers and Agents

One of the easiest ways for you to get started with your real estate purchases is to find a real estate broker or agent who understands creative methods of investment and is willing to work with you on ongoing basis, continually searching for the properties in which you are interested. You must find a knowledgeable agent or broker who may not necessarily want to work in the manner of most listing and sale brokers. By that, I mean the typical agent or broker is out in the market every day looking for listings that will sell easily and will not necessarily require any additional work on the part of the agent. Also, those same brokers and agents are looking for buyers who are easily qualified and can simply make an offer, get a loan, and close a purchase.

You'll have the opportunity, as an investor, to provide numerous transactions for any agent or broker who is willing to work in a more

Table 9.1   Sample Notice of Foreclosure

NOTICE OF TRUSTEE'S SALE

Trustee Sale No. <u>28-21764-2</u>
Title Order No. <u>3699 APN 036-231-013-0016</u>

YOU ARE IN DEFAULT UNDER A DEED OF TRUST DATED <u>08/10/1999</u>. YOU TAKE ACTION TO PROTECT YOUR PROPERTY, IT MAY BE SOLD AT A PUBLIC SALE. IF YOU NEED AN EXPLANATION OF THE NATURE OF THE PROCEEDINGS AGAINST YOU, YOU SHOULD CONTACT A LAWYER.

On <u>01/15/2004</u> at 01<u>:00PM, TIMEDOLLAR FINANCIAL CORPORATION</u> as the duly appointed Trustee under and pursuant to Deed of Trust Recorded on 08/10/1999, Instrument 2308317 of official records in the Office of the Recorder of GRANGER County, California, executed by: <u>WILLIAM D. FAULT AND ELIZABETH D. FAULT, HUSBAND AND WIFE, AS JOINT TENANTS</u>, as Trustor, <u>BENEHAMBRE MORTGAGE CORPORATION</u>, as Beneficiary, <u>WILL SELL AT PUBLIC AUCTION TO THE HIGHEST BIDDER FOR CASH</u> (payable at time of sale in lawful money of the United States, by cash, a cashier's check drawn by a state or national bank, a check drawn by a state or federal credit union, or a check drawn by a state or federal savings and loan association, savings association, or savings bank specified in section 5102 of the Financial Code and authorized to do business in this state). At: <u>THE TWENTY SECOND STREET ENTRANCE TO THE COUNTY COURTHOUSE, 474 G STREET, PARKER, CA</u>, all right, title and interest conveyed to and now held by it under said Deed of Trust in the property situated in said County, California describing the land therein: <u>AS MORE FULLY DESCRIBED IN THE ABOVE MENTIONED DEED OF TRUST</u>. The property heretofore described is being sold "as is." The Street address and other common designation, if any, of the real property described above is purported to be:
<u>23434 FRENCHIE ROAD, PARKER, CA 950091</u>
The undersigned Trustee disclaims any liability for any incorrectness of' the street address and other common designation, if any, shown herein. Said sale will be made, but without covenant or warranty, expressed or implied, regarding title, possession, or encumbrances, to pay the remaining principal sum of the note(s) secured by said Deed of Trust, with interest thereon, as provided in said note(s), advances, if any, under the terms of the Deed of Trust, estimated fees, charges and expenses of the Trustee and of the trusts created by said Deed of Trust, to-wit: $86,920.00 (Estimated) Accrued interest and additional advances, if any, will increase this figure prior to sale. The beneficiary under said Deed of Trust heretofore executed and delivered to the undersigned a written Declaration of Default and Demand for Sale, and a written Notice of Default and Election to Sell. The undersigned caused said Notice of Default and Election to Sell to be recorded in the county where the real property is located and more than three months have elapsed since such recordation.

DATE: 0 1/22/2004
TIMEDOLLAR FINANCIAL CORPORATION
P.O. BOX 80345 PARKER, CA 950091
For Sale Information: (242) 347-7738 Rodney Rascal, Trustee Sale Officer ASAP533372
PUB: Dec. 27, Jan. 4, 11

nontraditional manner. The problem that you will run into is that many real estate agents and brokers have never been trained and have never worked with any type of creative financing techniques. Unless you can find an agent or broker who is well versed in creative investing techniques, you may have to find someone who is willing to learn.

It is not uncommon for real estate agents and brokers to attempt to discourage you from making creative financing offers. You must keep in mind that licensed agents and brokers are in the business to earn commissions. If it appears to a broker or agent that his or her commissions might be affected in any way, possibly delayed or reduced, the broker or agent is going to be less apt to encourage the seller to take your offer. However, if you have structured your transactions properly, put together your offer in a manner that it is easily understood by the seller, and have been careful to make sure that it is a win-win opportunity for both you and the seller, often the offer will be accepted in spite of the agent presenting the offer.

Go with the Broker—You Want to Do What?

One very important action that you must employ as an investor or buyer, when you're working with a real estate broker or agent, is to include a stipulation that when any offer is made, you will have the right to accompany the broker or agent when the offer is presented to the seller. Many brokers and agents will react negatively to that request, and I have even had brokers and agents who have flatly refused my request to accompany them when the offer was presented. My reminder to them that it is the law in all 50 states of the United States that a buyer does in fact have the right to accompany the broker or agent when the offer is presented; this usually suffices to end the broker's disagreement. When you begin working with specific brokers or agents, you want to make sure that they understand that you will be loyal to them as long as they are willing to work with the techniques you may use when you are purchasing property.

When it does come time to accompany the broker to the presentation, make sure that you arrive early, wait for the broker or agent, and do not contact the seller until the broker or agent has arrived. When the broker introduces me to the seller, I usually say something along the lines of, "Thank you for allowing me to accompany Mr./Ms. Broker on this presentation." Always show respect for the broker or agent in the presentation, but make sure that your offer is presented properly. If you find that the broker or agent has not explained your offer correctly, do not be afraid to ask for the opportunity to clarify whatever portions of your offer that may have been misrepresented or misunderstood.

After you have presented a number of offers with one broker or agent it will become easier to present the offers properly and you'll probably develop a good working relationship when that real estate professional realizes that you represent the opportunity to earn numerous commissions.

Buyer's Brokers and Agents

In most real estate transactions, the real estate brokers actually will represent the sellers. Even if you as an investor have a broker or agent prepare an offer for you and present it to a seller who has his or her property listed with a different broker or agent, the broker or agent who has prepared your offer legally still has a fiduciary relationship with the seller. The reasoning behind this type of representation is that because the seller has hired his or her broker to represent the sale of the property and a commission is being paid to that broker, any agent who may present an offer for a buyer actually becomes a subagent of that listing broker and therefore also represents the seller. Of course, it is the responsibility of all licensed agents to deal fairly and honestly with all parties to the transaction.

This typical broker or agent representation can be circumvented if a buyer actually hires a buyer's broker and pays that buyer's broker a fee and that buyer's broker does not accept payment from the seller. This is not to say that a broker cannot receive a commission or fee from both the seller and the buyer; however, when that is the case, all of the commissions and fees must be disclosed to all parties to the transaction. It must also be fully disclosed to the seller when a buyer's broker represents only the buyer in a fiduciary relationship.

It will behoove you as a perpetual investor to find a buyer's broker with whom you can work on an ongoing basis. It will be important for this broker to understand that you are looking for specific types of properties and for specific motivated, flexible, and accommodating sellers. Once that broker has a feel for the type of transaction for which you are searching, he or she will always be able to keep you informed about what is available in the market. After you have closed two or three transactions with that broker, you will definitely become a preferred customer.

Some of the guidelines that you will need to lay down for your buyer's broker relate to both the types of properties and the types of sellers for which you are searching. You will want your buyer's broker to be looking for:

1. Any property for which the seller is willing to offer financing.
2. Any property that has an existing assumable loan.
3. Any property which the seller is highly motivated to sell for whatever reasons.
4. Any property with a mortgage that is 60 percent or less of the asking price.
5. Any property that appears to need a substantial amount of cosmetic work and that is owned by a seller who does not want to or cannot do the work to bring the property back to an acceptable state.

If you can find a buyer's broker who can bring you 10 or 12 properties per month that fall within the guidelines of the five areas listed above, you will have developed a good working relationship and you should be able to put together one or two transactions per month. If you do decide to use a buyer's broker, make sure that you use a written buyer's broker agreement. I cannot begin to tell you how many times I have run into agents and brokers who do not understand or do not want to work with creative investment offers and who will completely blow apart a potentially good transaction. It is very important that you search for a broker or agent with whom you can work who is well trained and willing to learn how to use creative investment offers.

Transaction Brokers

A few years ago the State of California began to recognize and differentiate between listing and selling brokers and a designation known as transaction brokers. In layman's terms, a transaction broker is nothing more than a middleman helping the buyer and seller to close a transaction. The transaction broker designation is now recognized in many states across the country.

If you find a seller who is uncomfortable working directly with you as an investor or buyer you may want to employ the services of a transaction broker. In that way, you may be able to alleviate some of the concerns of the seller, and the broker or agent will not be required to establish a broker fiduciary relationship with either party. In some cases, the transaction broker may also prepare the paperwork and assist in the closing of the sale.

Referrals from Friends, Relatives, and Associates

When you actively begin to search for investment properties, it will be critically important for you to let all of your friends and associates know exactly what type of properties you are looking for. It also will be important for you to continually remind those same people that you are in the real estate investment business and that you are willing to reward the people who might help you find the properties that you are interested in purchasing. A small "thank you" fee paid to someone who gave you a lead that eventually turned into a transaction will lead to many more deals being directed your way. Be sure you always take care of the people who take care of you.

If your friends, relatives, and associates have a basic understanding of real estate and the type of investment properties in which you are interested, it will save you a great deal of time in the long run—take a little time and educate them. The letter in Table 9.2 can be used as a handout to help clarify the type of properties that you want. Depending upon your personal investment interests, you can change the letter to fit your needs (make sure that contact information is included in this letter).

You also should use your business cards, flyers, and brochures as giveaway items for your friends, relatives, and associates contacts.

Direct Buyer Telephone and Mail Contacts

Direct buyer telephone and mail contacts include every type of contact generated from foreclosure and repossession notices, drive-bys, other legal and public notices, bankruptcies, auctions, estate sales, suits and liens, garage sales, or relocation services, or any other direct contact that you may make with sellers who may not have listed their property for sale.

For-Sale-by-Owner Signs

Although I spend a great deal of time in this book explaining ways that you can find properties and make contacts, most new investors seem to

Table 9.2   Investment Criteria Letter Request

Hello John,

Just a quick note to let you know I am in the market for investment real estate. I am interested in several types of properties, all of which should be in good rental neighborhoods:

Financially distressed—in foreclosure
Physically distressed—substantial deferred maintenance, but structurally sound
Single-family homes—three or four bedrooms, two baths, in the mid- to lower-end of the market
Duplexes
Triplexes
Four-plexes
Any property with a motivated seller who might have financial or other personal problems and have a need to sell

I am prepared to offer a variety of terms and payment options, including all cash.

I am offering a finder's fee at a minimum of $100 for any leads that produce a purchase for me.

I have enclosed a few business cards for you.

Feel free to call me anytime.

Best Regards,
Scott

enjoy and spend more time driving around in neighborhoods, looking for for-sale-by-owner signs, than any other method of finding potential investment properties. However, in actuality, only about 3 to 5 percent of the transactions that you put together will come from for-sale-by-owner properties found in that manner.

It is definitely worth noting that many run-down or dilapidated properties, the fixer-upper types, are usually spotted by the investor who has the time and inclination to spend a lot of time driving around an area. Many of the quick-return investments that require cosmetic work and can be put immediately back on the market will be found in

TERRY'S TIP: If you should have the opportunity to make a direct contact with an owner selling his or her own property, it is important that you identify yourself as a buyer *immediately* when you approach the seller. These owners are inundated with calls and contacts from brokers and agents from the moment they put their for-sale-by-owner sign up or they place their first ad offering their property for sale. If they believe that you are an agent or broker looking for a listing, you may not receive a very positive response to your approach. Make it clear to them that you are a buyer.

that way. Again, the actual dialogues that you will use to contact the owners of these properties are discussed later in the book.

Bird-Dog Referrals

Just the same as a bird dog works for a hunter, bird-dog referral people will work for you to "point out and scare up" potential deals. It seems that there are a few people in every area who know everything that goes on in their neighborhood. You want to be sure that you are always looking for these well-informed people who are willing to let you know when they see or hear of a property that may be for sale in their area.

Although I have put together a few transactions that were directed by bird-dog referral people, I have never had the success that one of my students in Alexandria, Virginia, told me that he had with an 80 plus-year-old neighbor in his area. The lady continually gave him top-notch referrals, resulting in over 20 transactions during a five-year period.

Look for people who are well entrenched in an area and are willing to help you find the type of transactions that you are seeking. Again, don't forget to properly reward these people. They can help you a great deal on a long-term basis.

Other Partner Investors

As you begin to establish yourself as an investor and you develop a good reputation, other investors will begin to seek you out and provide you with opportunities to become involved in their transactions. Sometimes, these partnerships or joint ventures can be a good thing. However, unless you are well acquainted with and know a person very well, I do not recommend that you jump into a joint venture transaction with a stranger.

It often is better to establish a referral network whereby you can refer deals to other investors and they can do the same for you. There will be purchase opportunities that you will not be able to take advantage of for whatever reason (too much capital required, too large an investment, too much work required on the property, etc.) and that you will want to refer to another investor who might be interested in that type of property. If you have established a good referral network with all levels of investors, you will make and receive referrals on a continual basis.

10

How to Maximize Your Use of Internet Investment Opportunities and Other Information

Saving Time Every Way Possible

As I have said many times in this book, the Internet is a tremendous tool that can save you a great deal of time and money when you begin searching for the investment properties that you want to buy. Listed, unlisted, and for-sale-by-owner properties can be found if you use the proper search techniques on the Internet. Granted, there are many, many investment properties that may be of interest to you that may never be found on the Web. However, remember that *time* will be your greatest asset or your greatest enemy and you must use it wisely.

Using the proper search techniques on the Internet can help you a great deal, not only in finding, viewing, and ultimately purchasing properties, but also in finding money to purchase your investments, equipment, materials necessary to make repairs, companies that do specific inspections, and other partner investors in the market. The best way for you to understand how valuable the Internet can be to you as an investor is to share with you a success story that I received from one of my students in Fresno, California.

Caroline had been buying and selling investment property successfully, on a full-time basis, for approximately four years. She used the Internet very little, primarily because she was extremely busy and had never found the time to sit down and become proficient on her computer. When she injured her knee skiing and was forced to have major surgery, she felt that it was the perfect time to learn to use the Internet. She wanted to keep her goal plan on track and being off her feet for nearly two months could have created a definite lull in her progress.

After the first week of recovery Caroline could sit comfortably at her computer and she began searching the Internet using a list of sites that we had provided for her in a seminar that she had taken about a year earlier. The following scenario, in her words, details exactly how Caroline was able to purchase, refurbish, and resell a property over a 120-day period and never leave her home, until the day she signed the final papers for her sale of the investment property.

Hello Terry and the HowUInvest.com crew:

I knew you guys would get a kick out of this story so I had to drop you a line and tell you that this Internet stuff is really the greatest. Coming from an old-school, rather hardheaded, staunch believer that I have to see, feel, and touch anything I am going to buy or invest in, this is really quite a revelation. I believe that I have found a new system that eventually will increase my success level a great deal.

After being bed-bound for nearly a week and on the verge of losing my mind, I finally turned on the computer and began browsing through some of the great sites that you recommended. www.realtor.com and www.bestplaces.net are truly amazing and I found several new areas both within my state and several other states that I plan to visit when I am fully recovered. There are many good investment areas that I would have never considered had I not taken this opportunity to check out some of the properties.

As you recommended, I started cruising around different sites and areas using the Google search engine and feeding in . . . For Sale by Owner . . . followed by several areas within approximately 50 miles of Fresno. On the fifth or sixth area that I put in as search criteria, I came across a site offering For Sale by Owner's, and I found over 75 properties that were located in the areas where I had interest. The site was www.HomesByOwner.com, which I later discovered was right there on your list of Best Sites.

Within three hours I had contacted several owners by telephone and had two potential properties lined up to view. I explained to both sellers that I was just out of surgery and that I might need to have someone else look at the properties, but I went ahead and set the viewing appointments.

I was thinking, what now? I couldn't walk or drive. So I called my neighbor, a school teacher, who happened to be off for spring break and who has always shown an interest in learning to invest in real estate. I told her what I was up to and asked her if she would be willing to view the properties for me, complete a basic inspection form and bring back a few photographs. I further explained that I might need more assistance if I got the deal together and I offered her a "piece of the action" if we could make it work. Long story short . . . she was ecstatic and couldn't wait to do whatever I needed.

When my neighbor got back from the viewings I was amazed. She had video taped both properties and had done a very good narrative while she was viewing each home. She had opened every cupboard, looked under every sink . . . I couldn't have done better viewing them myself.

After another conversation with both owners, it was apparent that only one seller was willing to be flexible on the sale terms. That seller needed $10,000 quickly, as he needed to leave the area for a job in Oregon and he was very motivated to sell. He made it clear that he didn't have time to do any work or clean up. But, he also knew that he couldn't get top-dollar for the property in its current condition.

The home and the property needed A LOT of clean up and several pick-up loads to the dump to get rid of a couple of tons of "clutter," mostly old car parts, that the owner explained had been left by his son when he moved out. The home and detached garage needed paint inside and out, some yard work, a new dish washer, a fence replaced and some sprinkler repair. The owner had an existing loan with a balance of $94,500 and he was asking $160,000 for the home.

When I called the owner back, I explained that I was interested in buying the property, but reiterated that I couldn't leave my home and asked if he could come to my house so we could talk about the details. Again, I was quite surprised . . . he agreed to be there in three hours.

Before he arrived, I:

1. Put together comparable sales. Because I have established a working relationship with my local First American Title Company, I have their *FastWeb* service, which allows me to access property ownership information, as well as recorded sale info. Ironically, I have had the online service for over two years and that was the first time I had used it. Previously, I habitually drove to the title office to get the info . . . what a waste of time . . . I had it at my fingertips and never utilized it. The upper end comps were between $175,000 and $180,000, the lowest comp $155,000.

2. Called two repair people that I use for repair work on properties that I purchase and own and was able to get one estimate to do the painting, repairs and hauling that we had identified would have to be done before the property could be resold. The total cost to do all of the work would be between $8,000 and $10,000.

3. Structured and wrote the offer that I was going to make to the seller. When the seller and I met, I made it clear to him that I intended to fix the property up and sell it as quickly as possible. I explained carefully about all of the work that I felt would be needed to sell the property and I agreed to allow him to share in the profits if by some miracle the property sold for more than $185,000, which I also made clear was highly unlikely. I also explained that I anticipated having the property sold in six months or less. I emphasized the fact that he was accomplishing what he had indicated to me that he needed immediately . . . he

would receive the $10,000 that he needed to move and he would not be required to do any work or clean up on the property and . . . he would receive the rest of the money from the sale in only a few months.

The owner accepted my offer, terms as follows:

Sale Price: $138,000

Down Payment: $10,000

Buyer to take existing loan, subject-to

Buyer to pay ALL closing costs - seller to net $10,000

Seller to carry second deed of trust for $33,500, no payments, 10% per annum, simple interest, all due and payable in one year or less

(As you suggest, I always include a payoff statement for each month, clearly showing the interest and principal payoff figures)

Close of escrow—10 days

Because my neighbor wanted to be a partner in the deal, she agreed that for 20% of the net profit, she would put up the $10,000 down payment. I only had to pay approximately $2,000 to close the purchase transaction. My repairman also agreed to put a demand into escrow for the work that he would do on the property if I would pay for materials, which were approximately $1,700. My total cash outlay would be about $3,700.

As you might imagine, my biggest concern with this transaction was the fact that I was nearly bedridden and would have to direct all of the work through my neighbor who had agreed to supervise the clean up and refurbishing that would be required to bring the property up to an acceptable salable state.

We couldn't have asked for a smoother deal, start to finish. All of the work, clean up and repairs were completed in less than 30 days and I had the property back on the market for $189,500. Although I did not have the property listed with an agent, I was presented an offer by an agent that had represented me on several other sale properties. After three counteroffers, I agreed to sell the property for

$179,200 and pay a 3% commission to the agent. The transaction closed in 43 days.

After paying all costs for repairs, title and escrow fees, commissions and other closing costs, as well as the second deed of trust and interest for three months, the net was $18,324. Out of that I paid my neighbor $3,665 and put $14,659 net, in my pocket.

Also, a couple of interesting nuances that occurred during this transaction were:

My repairman came to me and said that he needed to purchase a couple of power tools to be able to complete the work. He needed a flooring stapler and a roofing nailer and he wanted me to pay for them, approximately $900 for both items, and he would credit me for the tools out of what he would bill the escrow. On a pure whim, I went on the Internet, into eBay—Stanley Tools and was able to purchase the tools that he needed for less than $350, keeping my out-of-pocket costs down and saving the repairman $550.

I was able to find a salvage yard, online, that wanted many of the old car parts that included transmissions, rear ends and four-wheel-drive units that were strewn about the property and I was able to generate an additional $750 to our bottom line during the time that we owned the property.

The only time that I left my house was to sign the papers for the final sale of the property.

All I can say is "HOORAY" for the Internet and all it has to offer. From today forward it will save me a great deal of time and make a whole lot of money for me.

Thanks again for all your help and guidance and for turning me on to a TREMENDOUS new tool.

As you can see the Internet has a lot to offer. And for those of you who just can't quite bring yourself to make the move into the high-tech world, you are working harder than you need to. Start using the sites that we recommend and get into the new millennium—you will be amazed how easy it can be. In the rest of this chapter, we take you on an Internet tour of actual sites. Stay tuned—it is an exciting journey.

Search Engines

When you begin searching the Internet, you will want to find and utilize one or two search engines. That way, you will become comfortable with the screen layouts and you will save yourself time finding the information that you are seeking. For several reasons, we recommend www.Google.com. First, and most importantly, we find that Google simply provides better, more explicit results. Second, Google offers alternate types of searches for different types of information (see Figure 10.1).

Another good search engine is www.yahoo.com; however it can be a little more complex and it can be confusing to a new Internet user (see Figure 10.2). One nice feature about the Yahoo site is that it offers a complete real estate section that is discussed later in this chapter. Unfortunately, a great deal of the site is dedicated to advertisers and doesn't really provide the information that you will need to find the best bargain investments.

TERRY'S TIP: One point of information about the search engines: On some Internet service sites face pages you will see phrases such as "Search provided by Google" or "Search Google." We have found that the results that you will receive when using those dedicated searches will not generate the quality or quantity of responses that you will receive if you go directly to the www.Google.com site and then feed in your search criteria.

FIGURE 10.1 Home page for Google with arrow indicating a Web search. Blank box awaits key word(s) input. (www.Google.com.)

Finding Listed Properties

Until the last few years, unless you worked through any real estate licensee, it was very difficult to obtain the actual listing information on properties that were listed by real estate companies and/or that were included in the multiple listing services. However, with the advent and extensive use of the Internet, almost all of the listed property information can be obtained by the general public from the Web.

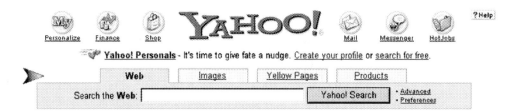

FIGURE 10.2 Home page for Yahoo with arrow indicating a Web search and blank box awaits key word(s) input. (www.Yahoo.com.)

When you begin your search for properties, it is best to again start your search on the Internet. However, I suggest that you avoid general searches. By that I mean using a search engine and typing in the name of a city or area and Real Estate. Most of the time that type of search will give you hundreds of real estate offices and agent sites, and it can be difficult to sort through much of that information. By going back to a site we talked about earlier, www.Realtor.com, you will be able to look at many properties listed by many companies. By utilizing the information taken from the Realtor.com web site, you will be able to continue and expand your search into the web sites for individual agents or brokerages.

Properties to Purchase

Open the home page of www.Realtor.com and fill in the information for City, State or Zip Code, Price Range, minimum to maximum, and desired number of bedrooms and bathrooms. If you wish to input more detail with regard to your search option criteria, you may do so by selecting More Search Options (see Figures 10.3 and 10.3A). This will give you a more complete option page (Figure 10.4) that includes Property Types, Property Features, Lot Features, Community Features, Financial Options, and as well as an MLS ID Search, if you happen to know a multiple listing service listing ID number on a particular property. (We discuss later in this chapter how you might obtain those MLS listing ID numbers.)

An Example Search

For this first exercise we will use only basic search options: City, State, Zip Code, Beds, Baths, and a wide Price Range, $100,000 to $250,000 (Figure 10.5). Once you have entered the search criteria, click the Go button.

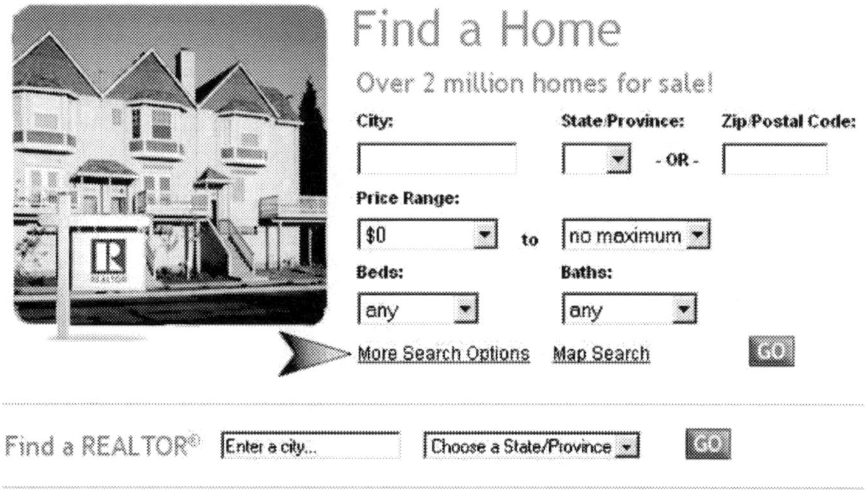

FIGURE 10.3 Home page to fill in—Realtor.com

FIGURE 10.3A Home page for Realtor.com (www.Realtor.com).

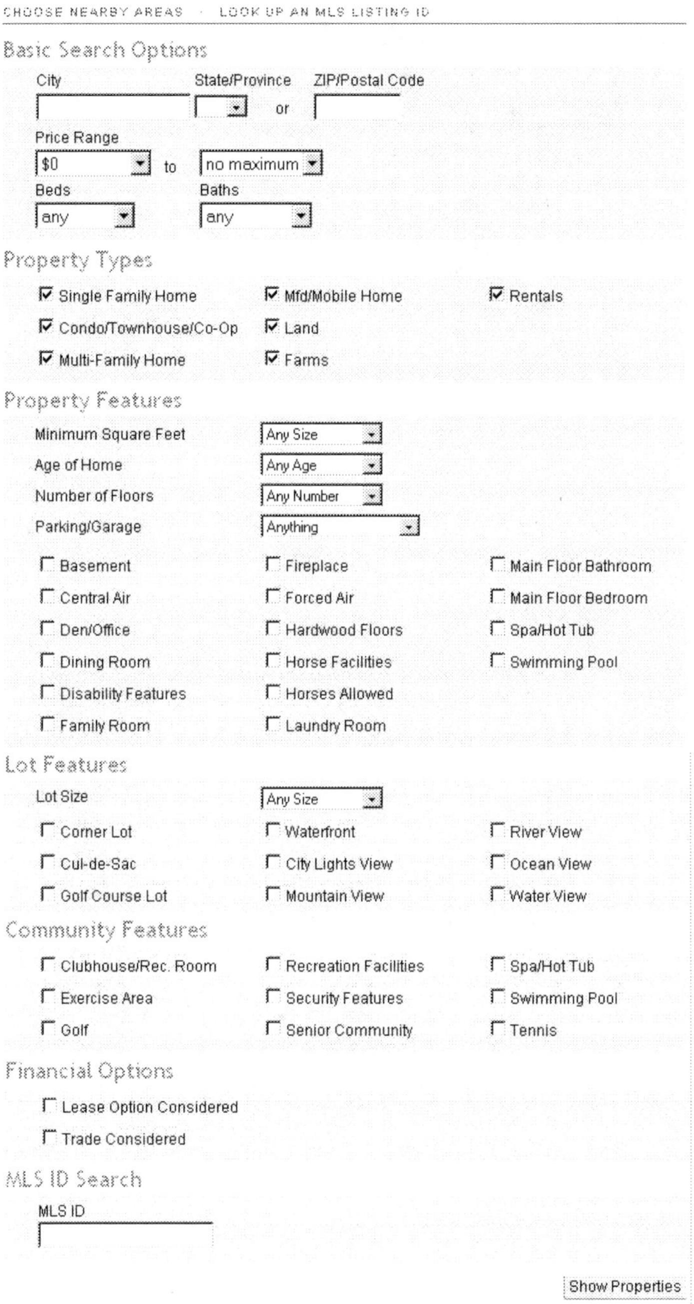

CHOOSE NEARBY AREAS · LOOK UP AN MLS LISTING ID

Basic Search Options

City   State/Province   ZIP/Postal Code

[ ]   [▼]   or   [ ]

Price Range

[$0 ▼] to [no maximum ▼]

Beds   Baths

[any ▼]   [any ▼]

Property Types

☑ Single Family Home   ☑ Mfd/Mobile Home   ☑ Rentals

☑ Condo/Townhouse/Co-Op   ☑ Land

☑ Multi-Family Home   ☑ Farms

Property Features

Minimum Square Feet   [Any Size ▼]

Age of Home   [Any Age ▼]

Number of Floors   [Any Number ▼]

Parking/Garage   [Anything ▼]

☐ Basement   ☐ Fireplace   ☐ Main Floor Bathroom

☐ Central Air   ☐ Forced Air   ☐ Main Floor Bedroom

☐ Den/Office   ☐ Hardwood Floors   ☐ Spa/Hot Tub

☐ Dining Room   ☐ Horse Facilities   ☐ Swimming Pool

☐ Disability Features   ☐ Horses Allowed

☐ Family Room   ☐ Laundry Room

Lot Features

Lot Size   [Any Size ▼]

☐ Corner Lot   ☐ Waterfront   ☐ River View

☐ Cul-de-Sac   ☐ City Lights View   ☐ Ocean View

☐ Golf Course Lot   ☐ Mountain View   ☐ Water View

Community Features

☐ Clubhouse/Rec. Room   ☐ Recreation Facilities   ☐ Spa/Hot Tub

☐ Exercise Area   ☐ Security Features   ☐ Swimming Pool

☐ Golf   ☐ Senior Community   ☐ Tennis

Financial Options

☐ Lease Option Considered

☐ Trade Considered

MLS ID Search

MLS ID

[ ]

[Show Properties]

FIGURE 10.4 Complete option page obtained by clicking on More Search Options on the Realtor.com home page in Figure 10.3. (www. Realtor.com.)

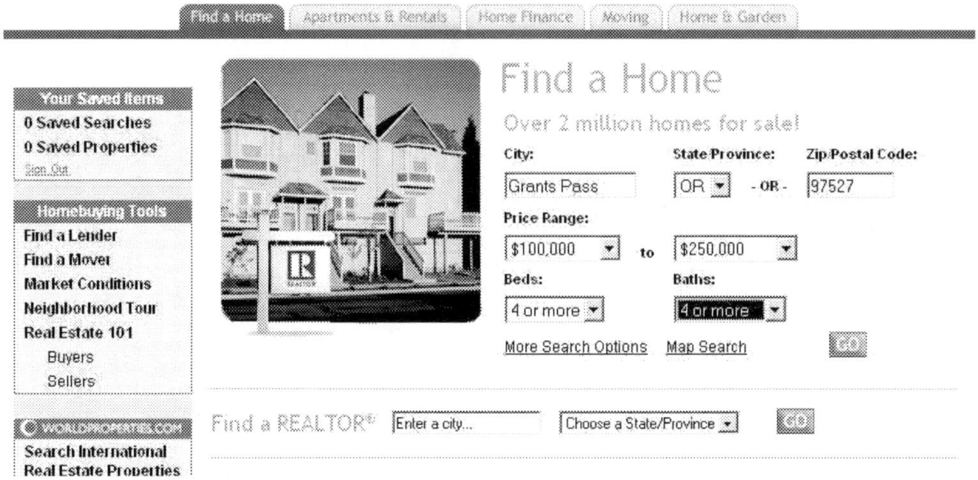

FIGURE 10.5 Realtor.com home page with basic search options indicated for our example search. (www.Realtor.com.)

The results shown will usually be two to four Featured Homes and just below those photographs, a section stating the total number of properties in that search criteria (Figure 10.6). Near that statement is a link to Show Properties. Before you activate this link you may want to view the page in its entirety. You will note that there is a line to choose more Search Options. You will probably want to use wide search option criteria on your first searches and then begin to narrow the options as you identify the areas in which you have the most interest.

Following the Search Options line, there is an option to limit the search to properties that offer Virtual Tours. Virtual tours are 360-degree viewing options that allow the viewer to completely scan individual rooms or areas. It probably is better to look at all properties rather than just those with virtual tours until you have identified specific properties in which you are interested.

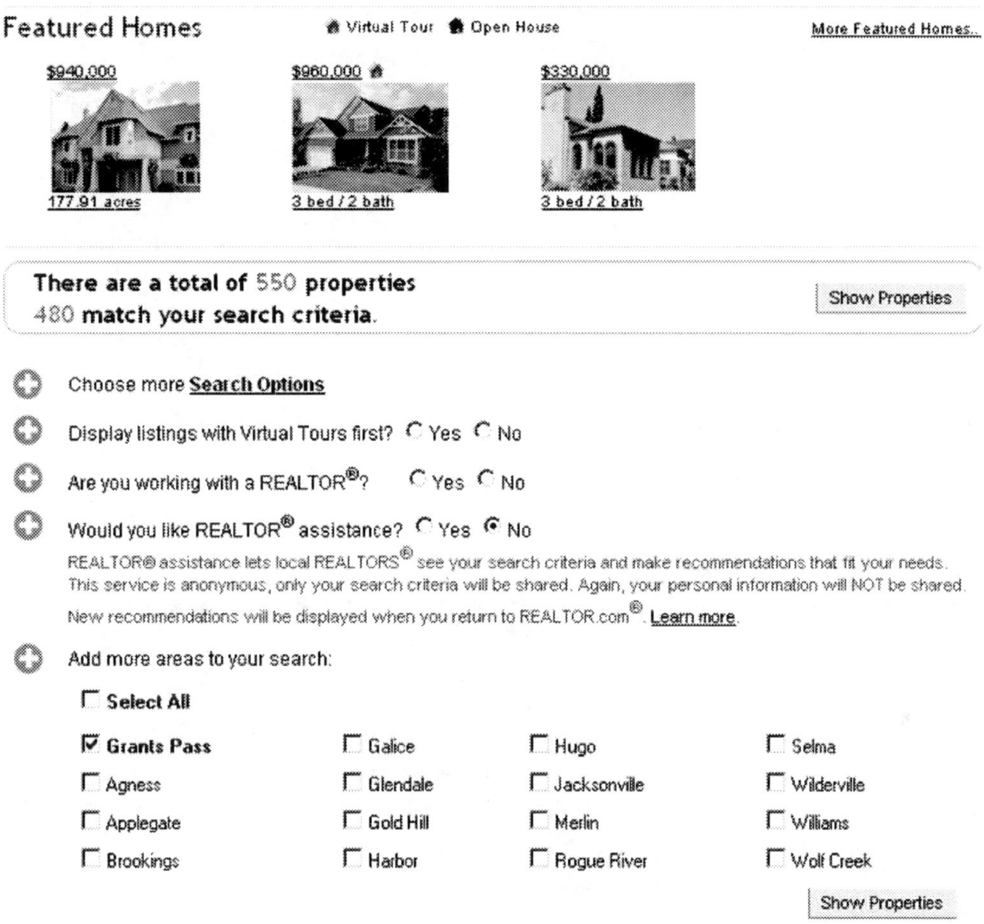

Featured Homes   🏠 Virtual Tour 🏠 Open House   More Featured Homes...

$940,000 $960,000 🏠 $330,000

177.91 acres   3 bed / 2 bath   3 bed / 2 bath

There are a total of 550 properties   [Show Properties]
480 match your search criteria.

⊕   Choose more **Search Options**

⊕   Display listings with Virtual Tours first? ○ Yes ○ No

⊕   Are you working with a REALTOR®?   ○ Yes ○ No

⊕   Would you like REALTOR® assistance? ○ Yes ● No

     REALTOR® assistance lets local REALTORS® see your search criteria and make recommendations that fit your needs.
     This service is anonymous, only your search criteria will be shared. Again, your personal information will NOT be shared.
     New recommendations will be displayed when you return to REALTOR.com®. **Learn more**.

⊕   Add more areas to your search:

     ☐ **Select All**

     ☑ **Grants Pass**   ☐ Galice   ☐ Hugo   ☐ Selma
     ☐ Agness   ☐ Glendale   ☐ Jacksonville   ☐ Wilderville
     ☐ Applegate   ☐ Gold Hill   ☐ Merlin   ☐ Williams
     ☐ Brookings   ☐ Harbor   ☐ Rogue River   ☐ Wolf Creek

                                                            [Show Properties]

FIGURE 10.6   After clicking on Go from the Realtor.com home page, four featured homes are shown. (www.Realtor.com.)

The next line indicates a need for Realtor® assistance. I suggest that you check No as there is an entire section on choosing an agent or broker in Chapter 2.

The last section on the page gives you the opportunity to select additional areas to be included in your search. If you click on the Select All option, be prepared for many hundreds or thousands of choices, depending upon the area. You are probably better off to search the areas individually in the beginning before you have narrowed your search criteria, using the advanced search criteria options. After you have completed the area choices, click on Show Properties at the bottom of the page.

The next page that comes into view will contain actual listed properties (Figure 10.7). Depending upon the site default display settings, you may see all types of properties including open land, single-family homes, etc., so you may want to use the menu item at the top, Modify Your Search, and clarify the types of properties in which you are interested (Figure 10.8).

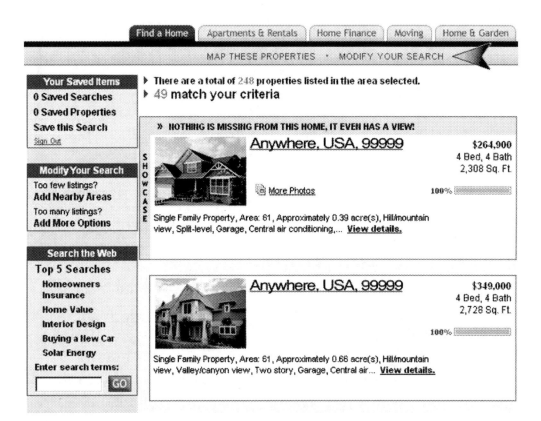

FIGURE 10.7   Realtor.com page of specific properties.

CHOOSE NEARBY AREAS · LOOK UP AN MLS LISTING ID

Basic Search Options

City   State/Province   ZIP/Postal Code
Grants Pass   OR ▾   or   97526

Price Range
$100,000 ▾ to $2,500,000 ▾

Beds   Baths
2 ▾   4 ▾

Property Types

☑ Single Family Home   ☐ Mfd/Mobile Home   ☐ Rentals

☐ Condo/Townhouse/Co-Op   ☐ Land

☐ Multi-Family Home   ☐ Farms

Property Features

Minimum Square Feet   Any Size ▾

Age of Home   Any Age ▾

Number of Floors   Any Number ▾

Parking/Garage   Anything ▾

FIGURE 10.8   Realtor.com search option page.

You will note that the number of properties is usually reduced dramatically when you indicate only one of the Property Types. With this particular search the number of properties was reduced from 194 to 103 (Figure 10.9).

As the pages of listings appear, you will see, on the left side, menu items that allow you to Sign Up Now and be able to save your searches and listings and obtain other recommendations (Figure 10.10).

From this page you may begin looking at actual listed properties. By clicking on the thumbnail photo, you will be directed to a listing page on Realtor.com (Figure 10.11).

▶ There are a total of 248 properties listed in the area selected.
▶ 18 **match your criteria**

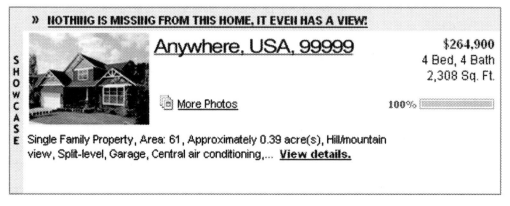

FIGURE 10.9   Realtor.com search results page.

FIGURE 10.10   Realtor.com sign up page.

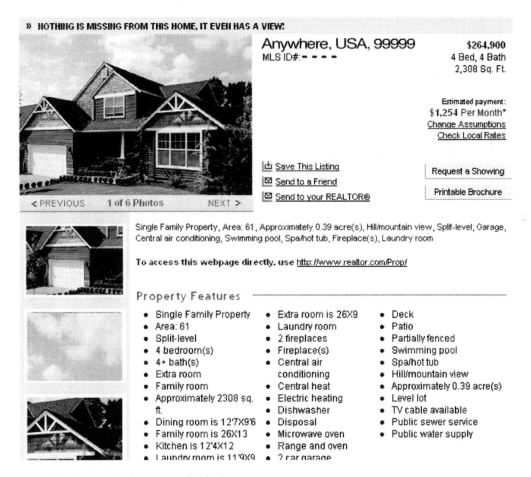

>> NOTHING IS MISSING FROM THIS HOME, IT EVEN HAS A VIEW!

Anywhere, USA, 99999
MLS ID#: — — — —

$264,900
4 Bed, 4 Bath
2,308 Sq. Ft.

Estimated payment:
$1,254 Per Month*
Change Assumptions
Check Local Rates

⬆ Save This Listing
✉ Send to a Friend
✉ Send to your REALTOR®

Request a Showing
Printable Brochure

< PREVIOUS   1 of 6 Photos   NEXT >

Single Family Property, Area: 61, Approximately 0.39 acre(s), Hill/mountain view, Split-level, Garage, Central air conditioning, Swimming pool, Spa/hot tub, Fireplace(s), Laundry room

To access this webpage directly, use http://www.realtor.com/Prop/

Property Features

- Single Family Property
- Area: 61
- Split-level
- 4 bedroom(s)
- 4+ bath(s)
- Extra room
- Family room
- Approximately 2308 sq. ft.
- Dining room is 12'7X9'6
- Family room is 26X13
- Kitchen is 12'4X12
- Laundry room is 11'9X9

- Extra room is 26X9
- Laundry room
- 2 fireplaces
- Fireplace(s)
- Central air conditioning
- Central heat
- Electric heating
- Dishwasher
- Disposal
- Microwave oven
- Range and oven
- 2 car garage

- Deck
- Patio
- Partially fenced
- Swimming pool
- Spa/hot tub
- Hill/mountain view
- Approximately 0.39 acre(s)
- Level lot
- TV cable available
- Public sewer service
- Public water supply

FIGURE 10.11   Realtor.com individual property page.

Although Realtor.com is one of the most informative sites on the Web, one of the issues that you will face when using that site, and many others, is that some of the search criteria that you input may not be recognized when you are given properties to view. As an example, you may input properties with 5 acres or more and many homes will be displayed that do not have the requested 5-acre minimum lots. As you begin to look at specific properties, you may want to go to the actual listing broker's web site by clicking on either the name of the brokerage or on a line that reads: Visit Website (Figure 10.12).

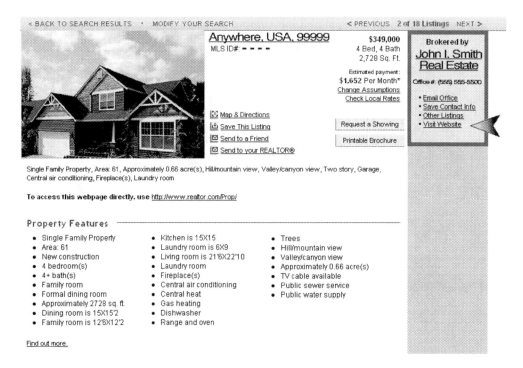

FIGURE 10.12   You can go to the listing broker's web site by clicking on the broker's name or the Visit Website line (arrow). (ww.Realtor.com.)

Some of the listings will not have links to the brokerages and you will need to utilize a separate search engine to determine if the office has a site, or if that fails and it is during business hours, you can call the company and ask for their web site address. Don't be too surprised if once in a while you hear, "we don't have a web site." There are still brokers with great listings that don't have web sites, but they are very quickly becoming the dinosaurs of the industry and they probably won't be around much longer. Also, keep in mind that many individual agents have their own web sites, and you may be directed there instead of to the company or brokerage web site.

The brokers' home pages of most of the sites to where you will be directed will look similar to a certain extent to the page shown below in

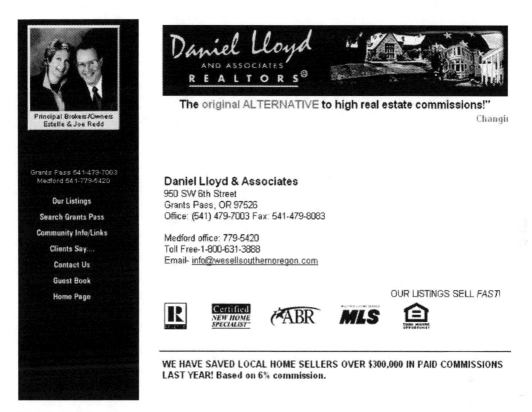

FIGURE 10.13   Home page of a broker in Grants Pass, Oregon.

Figure 10.13. You will be prompted to provide some specifics such as the area, town, city, or neighborhood in which you are seeking a property, the minimum and maximum price range, the number of bedrooms, and baths, etc., if you are looking for a home (the minimum acreage if you are looking for a horse property, ranchette, or farmland), generally in a range that will help the search process on the site. Again, you should use a fairly wide range on all of the information that you input while you are in the area search mode. You can narrow the parameters of your search at any time if you find an area in which you are interested. In the following pages, you will see several examples that will help you to understand the best ways for you to use these sites to determine the areas where you want to begin looking for a specific property.

The main reason that I suggest that you use a wide range of parameters, especially for price, is that when you are looking at neighborhoods you want to get a view of the *entire* area. If you are looking to buy a home valued at $200,000, you want that home to be surrounded mostly by properties valued at $200,000 or more. If you were to put into your search criteria properties that are priced between $100,000 and *$300,000* for the *same* search area, you might be able to see some of the inconsistencies, good and bad, that exist in the area with regard to the important concepts of regression and progression that were explained earlier in this book.

After opening the home page at www.Realtor.com, beginning at the page entitled Find a Home (Fig. 10.14), fill in the city around which you want a home. For this example we use Grants Pass, Oregon, Price Range Minimum: $100,000, Price Range Maximum: $300,000. You will note that Beds and Baths are left open since we are only looking for area information in this first search.

The first results (Figure 10.15) show that there are a total of 559 (this number will change on nearly every search) properties in Grants

FIGURE 10.14   Home page of Realtor.com with search criteria entered. (www.Realtor.com.)

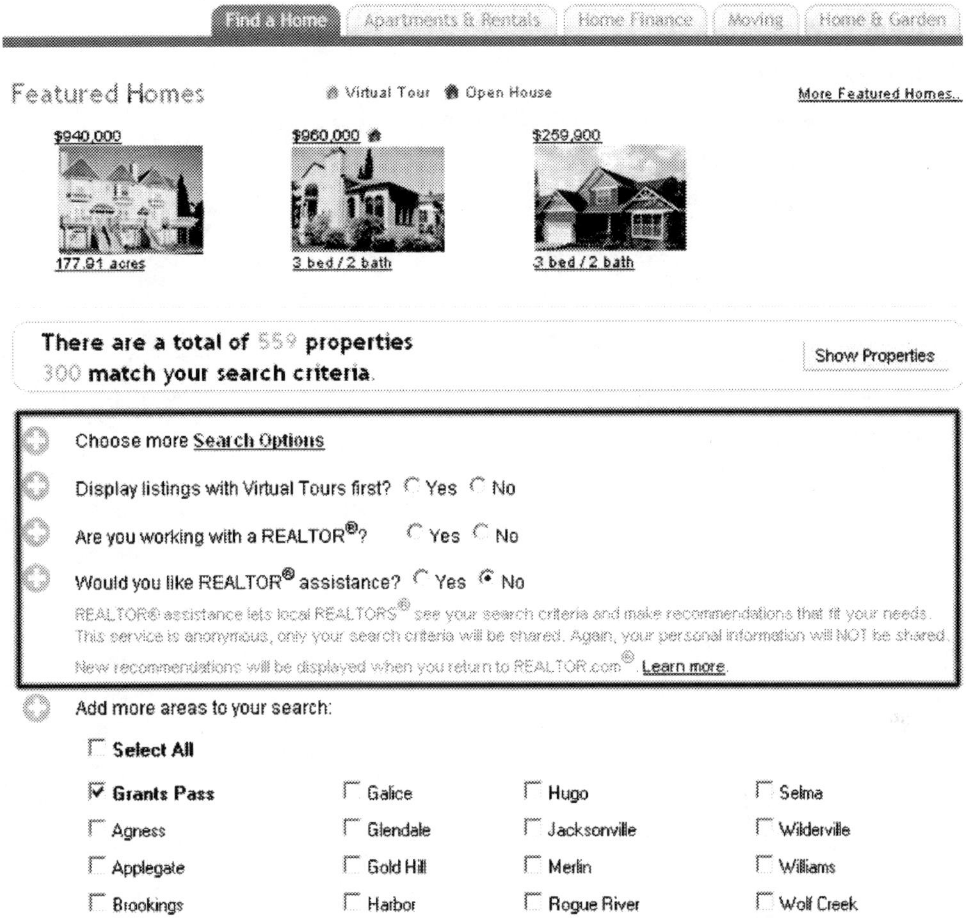

FIGURE 10.15   First results using the criterial input on the home page in Figure 10.14. (www. Realton.com.)

Pass, Oregon, and 300 meet the search criteria. Next, you are prompted to Choose more Search Options and Areas (optional).

Note that under the Search Options, I did not check for the properties offering Virtual Tours to show first. At this point, I want the pages to load only in the order of pricing, least expensive to most expensive, and I want them to load as quickly as possible. I also did not check Are you working with a REALTOR? and I checked No at Would you like REALTOR assistance? Figure 10.16 shows the basic search requested, which only includes the city of Grants Pass and five smaller areas.

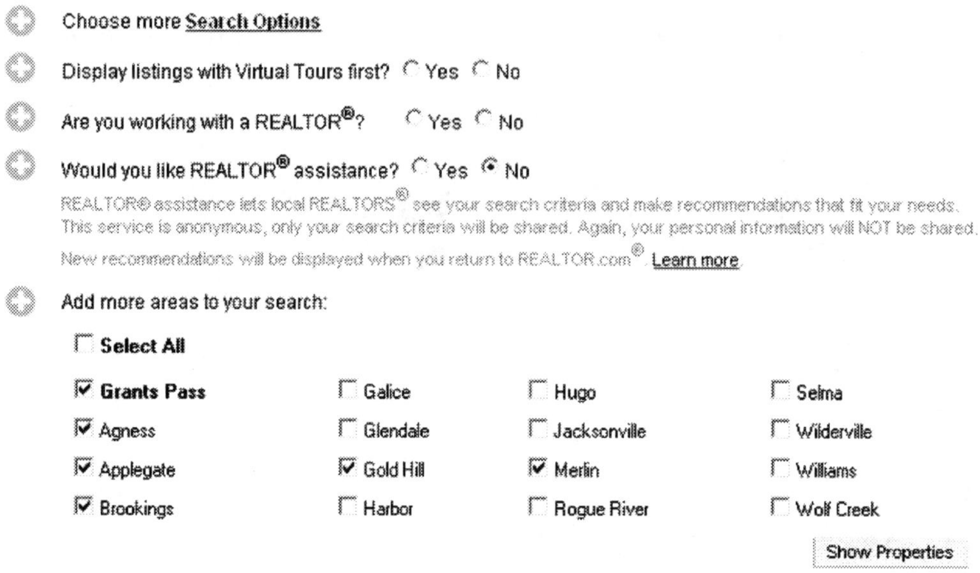

Choose more Search Options

Display listings with Virtual Tours first? ○ Yes ○ No

Are you working with a REALTOR®?   ○ Yes ○ No

Would you like REALTOR® assistance? ○ Yes ● No

REALTOR® assistance lets local REALTORS® see your search criteria and make recommendations that fit your needs. This service is anonymous, only your search criteria will be shared. Again, your personal information will NOT be shared. New recommendations will be displayed when you return to REALTOR.com® Learn more.

Add more areas to your search:

☐ Select All

☑ Grants Pass	☐ Galice	☐ Hugo	☐ Selma
☑ Agness	☐ Glendale	☐ Jacksonville	☐ Wilderville
☑ Applegate	☑ Gold Hill	☑ Merlin	☐ Williams
☑ Brookings	☐ Harbor	☐ Rogue River	☐ Wolf Creek

Show Properties

FIGURE 10.16   Search request from Featured Homes page indicating Grants Pass and five smaller surrounding areas. (www.Realtor.com.)

TERRY'S TIP: If you already know the areas or neighborhoods where you want to purchase or you have specific needs such as acreage for horses, a swimming pool, etc., fill in as much detail as possible on the Detailed Search Criteria. There may not be *any* properties in many of those areas that meet those specific needs and this will save you going back later and doing a second or third search of the same areas.

When you click the gray Search! button, the next page that you will see will be the actual properties that fit your search criteria. Note in Figure 10.17, under Search Results, it reads: "480 match your criteria." (Remember, the exact number will change with each search.) Four hundred eighty properties for only the five areas that we marked for our search! Now, you understand the problem that occurs when you use

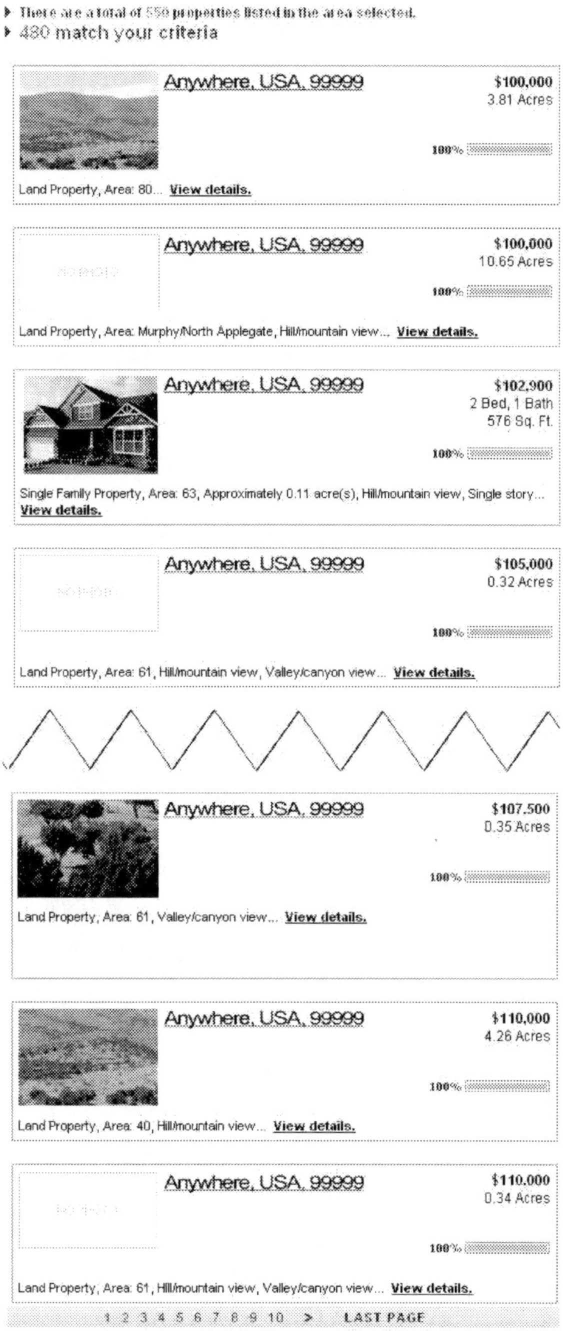

▸ There are a total of 550 properties listed in the area selected.
▸ 480 match your criteria

Anywhere, USA, 99999 $100,000
3.81 Acres

100%

Land Property, Area: 80... **View details.**

Anywhere, USA, 99999 $100,000
10.65 Acres

100%

Land Property, Area: Murphy/North Applegate, Hill/mountain view... **View details.**

Anywhere, USA, 99999 $102,900
2 Bed, 1 Bath
576 Sq. Ft.

100%

Single Family Property, Area: 63, Approximately 0.11 acre(s), Hill/mountain view, Single story...
View details.

Anywhere, USA, 99999 $105,000
0.32 Acres

100%

Land Property, Area: 61, Hill/mountain view, Valley/canyon view... **View details.**

Anywhere, USA, 99999 $107,500
0.35 Acres

100%

Land Property, Area: 61, Valley/canyon view... **View details.**

Anywhere, USA, 99999 $110,000
4.26 Acres

100%

Land Property, Area: 40, Hill/mountain view... **View details.**

Anywhere, USA, 99999 $110,000
0.34 Acres

100%

Land Property, Area: 61, Hill/mountain view, Valley/canyon view... **View details.**

1 2 3 4 5 6 7 8 9 10 >   LAST PAGE

FIGURE 10.17   One of the search request pages generated by the search initiated in Figure 10.16. (www. Realtor.com.)

wide search criteria. At 10 properties per page, that means that you have approximately 55 pages to view if you want to see all of the criteria results. Note that at the bottom of the Search Results page (Fig.10.16), there are page numbers. If you click on the higher numbers, you will be taken to the pages toward the end of the Search Results and the higher-priced properties.

TERRY'S TIP: If you spot a property that catches your eye, you can save that page into your favorites and you may also print the individual pages as they are displayed.

If you look at the Search Results page in Figure 10.18, you will note that by reducing the search criteria to one area, Merlin, the number of properties is reduced to only 20.

TERRY'S TIP: When you are searching for general area and neighborhood information, it is best to move through Search Results one area at a time. That will save you time in your analysis of the neighborhood and you will not need to look at each property listing to determine its area. However, when you are looking for specific properties, look at each one that might possibly interest you.

Yahoo.com

As I said earlier in this chapter, another informative site is www.Yahoo.com. You will note as indicated by the arrow on Figure 10.19 that Real Estate is usually always in the top searches for any year on Yahoo. When you click on Real Estate, you will be directed to a page (Figure 10.20) that gives you many search options including:

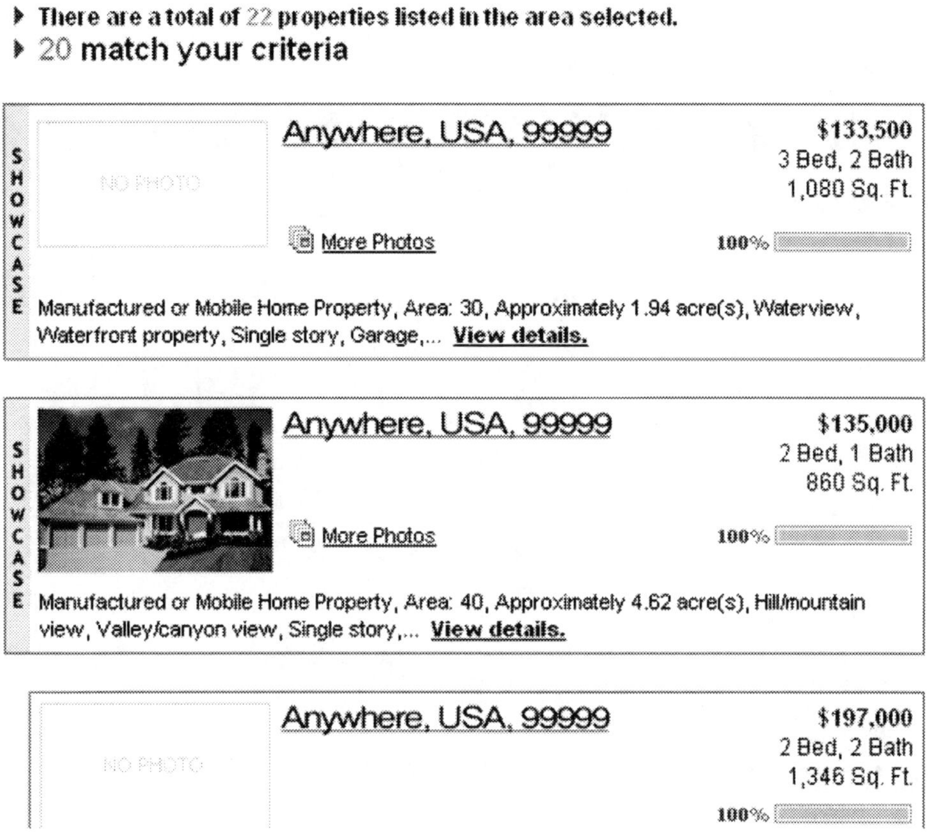

▶ There are a total of 22 properties listed in the area selected.
▶ 20 **match your criteria**

Anywhere, USA, 99999 $133,500
                                            3 Bed, 2 Bath
                                            1,080 Sq. Ft.

NO PHOTO

📷 More Photos   100%

Manufactured or Mobile Home Property, Area: 30, Approximately 1.94 acre(s), Waterview,
Waterfront property, Single story, Garage,... **View details.**

Anywhere, USA, 99999 $135,000
                                            2 Bed, 1 Bath
                                            860 Sq. Ft.

📷 More Photos   100%

Manufactured or Mobile Home Property, Area: 40, Approximately 4.62 acre(s), Hill/mountain
view, Valley/canyon view, Single story,... **View details.**

Anywhere, USA, 99999 $197,000
                                            2 Bed, 2 Bath
                                            1,346 Sq. Ft.

NO PHOTO

                                            100%

FIGURE 10.18   Search Results page with only the one area searched—Merlin, Oregon. (www.
Realtor.com.)

FIGURE 10.19   Real Estate is one of the top searches for any year on Yahoo. (www.Yahoo.com.)

FIGURE 10.20   Home page for Yahoo Real Estate. (www.Yahoo.com.)

Find a Home, Find a Rental, Mortgage and Insurance, Moving, Search For: Existing Homes, New Homes, and Foreclosures, as well as Advanced Search and Search Commercial Real Estate and Lender Information.

If you click on Find a Home, you'll be directed to a page that gives you the opportunity to search different types of real estate and toward the middle of the page provides a list of metro area MLS services that are available to the public. Note that not all MLS services across the country have partnered with Yahoo to offer the information on listings in their areas. However, it appears that the list of areas offering the information is growing every day.

One of the links on the Yahoo Real Estate page reads: "$199–499 Flat Fee Realtors Nationwide" (Figure 10.21). When you click that link, it takes you to a page that is entitled Realtor Flat Fee MLS Listing—Home Selling, which explains the discount selling program

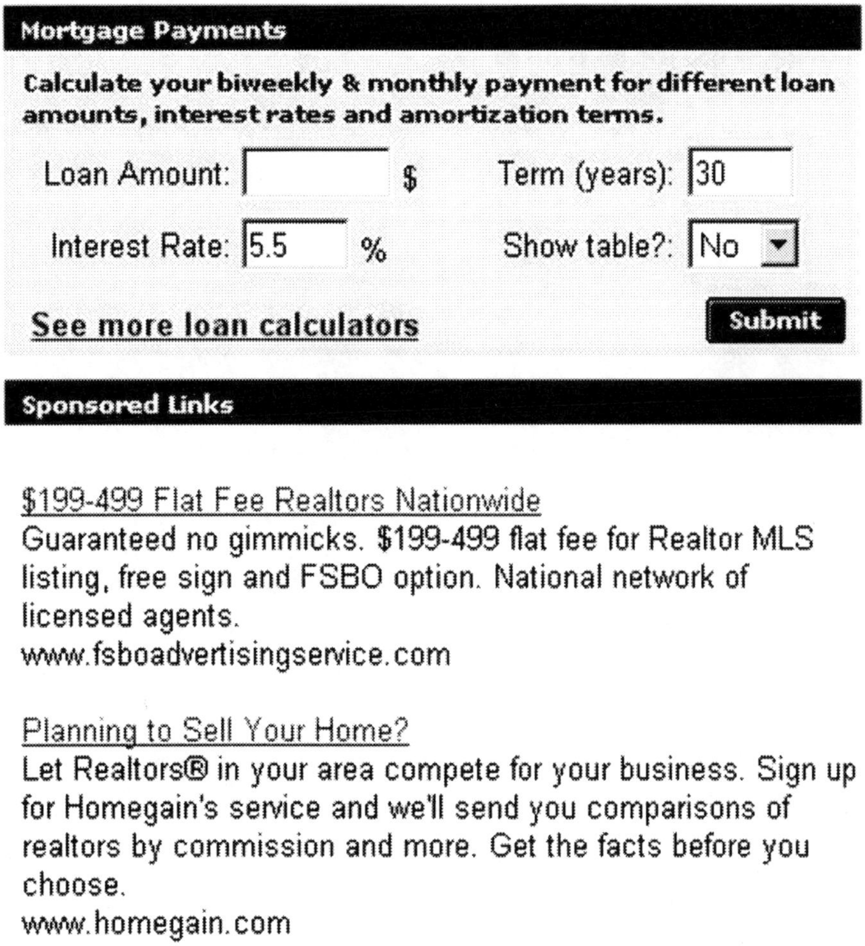

Mortgage Payments

Calculate your biweekly & monthly payment for different loan amounts, interest rates and amortization terms.

Loan Amount: [   ] $ Term (years): [30]

Interest Rate: [5.5] %   Show table?: [No ▼]

See more loan calculators   Submit

Sponsored Links

$199-499 Flat Fee Realtors Nationwide
Guaranteed no gimmicks. $199-499 flat fee for Realtor MLS listing, free sign and FSBO option. National network of licensed agents.
www.fsboadvertisingservice.com

Planning to Sell Your Home?
Let Realtors® in your area compete for your business. Sign up for Homegain's service and we'll send you comparisons of realtors by commission and more. Get the facts before you choose.
www.homegain.com

FIGURE 10.21   Detail of Yahoo Real Estate page. (www.Yahoo.com.)

that is available in many areas across the country. Since 1999, the Nationwide Network of Flat Fee List Homes in the Realtors MLS has offered a $199 to $499 listing service, and it is well worth your taking the time to look at that program. They also offer another program that is referred to as their Hybrid Marketing Method. When selling properties in the areas where these services are offered, a seller can utilize these programs and save a great deal of money as opposed to listing the property at a full brokerage fee.

Individual Broker Web Sites

At the time of this book printing it is estimated that 90 percent of the real estate companies in the United States have their own web sites. Also, approximately 55 percent of the individual agents or brokers that are employed by those companies also have their own web sites. As you might imagine, it is virtually impossible to find the exact web site addresses for all of these individual brokers and agents unless you use very specific search information and use a good search engine to locate the particular offices that you are searching for.

Many of the individual broker web sites offer the information on that individual broker's listings, and some of the sites will offer access into the MLS for that area. As I indicated earlier, it is often easier to move through the Realtor.com site than it is through the individual Broker sites. However, some of the brokers do not put all of their listings into Realtor.com, and therefore you will need to go into the individual sites to find most of that agent's inventory of listings.

As with all other types of advertising, web sites vary a great deal from broker to broker. Some sites are good, and others are not so good, but you will quickly learn which sites are easily accessible and which ones you will avoid. The following section will give you some ideas as to what information can be obtained from good, well-organized, and easy-to-use broker web sites.

Example Broker Sites

www.ThousandOaksProperty.com and www.simivalleyhomesearch.com

Broker Barbara Simmons has learned over her many years in the business, that the more information and service that you provide for people, the more listings and sales you will have and her multiple web sites (Figure 10.22) certainly reflect that philosophy. Loaded with content and pertinent information, each of her web offerings is extremely easy

FIGURE 10.22   An example of a successful broker web site in Ventura County, California. (Barbara Simmons.)

to navigate and provides exactly what you look for as an investor. That is probably the main reason that her sites are consistently some of the top sites for activity on the entire West Coast.

As you will see, most of the sites that you enter will have some type of navigation, either across the top or on the side, that will direct you to the information that you want. Primarily you will be looking at that broker's listings, the listings from the local MLS, and any other information about the area that is offered on the site (see Figure 10.22).

Some of the sites will require you to register before you can obtain the information (see Figure 10.23). It is up to you if you wish to register, but for the most part I choose not to do so until I am ready to make a contact with that broker. Most times I only will want to look at the inventory and not make contact with anyone until I am ready to start viewing properties. If I do register and a broker calls me, I am very direct and honest. I tell them what I am looking for, the kind of deals

FIGURE 10.23   Some broker web sites require that you register before they will provide information and listings. (Barbara Simmons.)

Site Map

WELCOME:
- Return to welcome/home page

FOR HOME BUYERS:
- Why homebuyers in the Thousand Oaks and Westlake Village area choose Barbara Simmons
- Get Barbara Simmons' latest Thousand Oaks and Westlake Village listings of homes for sale first!
- MLSTrac: an exciting new technology, not because of its MLS automating ability, but because of the opportunities MLS automation unlocks to you.
- Are you a first time homebuyer in Thousand Oaks and Westlake Village, CA? Barbara Simmons can guide your home buying search
- 15 Minute Loan: Pre-qualify for a mortgage or loan for your Thousand Oaks and Westlake Village house or other real estate or property
- Property Management Division: Realty World Equity Center Property Management Division successfully manages single family homes, apartments and condominiums, while focusing on achieving the highest level of income for the property owner.

THOUSAND OAKS AND WESTLAKE VILLAGE INFO:

FIGURE 10.24   Site maps on broker's web sites offer access to information on the areas they cover and often on the brokers themselves. (Barbara Simmons.)

I want, and *exactly* what they can do for me. If they are not interested, that's fine. However, good agents or brokers who want to make money, know what they are doing and understand the potential that I am offering them, will almost always start looking for the type of properties and sellers that I identify.

Some sites have a great deal of content and information about the areas they cover. That information can usually be accessed through the site map, as shown in Figure 10.24.

Also, you can usually find some information specifically about the broker and his or her experience. Look at that information. It could be important for your future relationship with this broker.

Both the Thousand Oaks and the Simi Valley sites offered by Barbara Simmons are good examples of easy-to-use, well-thought-out broker sites that can help you to locate information and properties that you may need.

www.startpackingidaho.com

Kevin Hughes from Boise, Idaho, is another broker who offers a great site with ease of operation and a huge amount of content (Figure 10.25). The site is easy to navigate and requires no sign-up to view all of Kevin's listings as well as the entire area MLS (Figure 10.26).

After you have searched a few broker Internet sites, you will know what you are looking for and where to find it, but you will probably find one or two sites for each area that will give you all of the information that you need.

Finding For-Sale-by-Owner Properties

You will find many for-sale-by-owner properties in the conventional ways—going through the newspapers and classified ads, driving through the neighborhoods and looking at bulletin boards, and searching other

FIGURE 10.25   The title page of the Boise, Idaho, web site of Kevin Hughes. (www.startpackingidaho.com.)

FIGURE 10.26   Example page of startpackingidaho.com web site. (www.startpackingidaho.com.)

places where listings can be posted. However, there are several sites on the Internet where information regarding for-sale-by-owner properties can be found in abundance.

For-Sale-by-Owner Sites

There are many for-sale-by-owner sites available on the Internet, but many of them are user-pay sites and often, after joining and paying the fee, a user may find that there are not many listings. There are several for-sale-by-owner sites that can be useful for your property searches and that we recommend:

www.ForSaleByOwner.com (Figure 10.27)
www.fsbo.com (Figure 10.28)
www.owners.com (Figure 10.29)

FIGURE 10.27   Home page of a for-sale-by-owner web site. (www.ForSaleByOwner.com.)

FIGURE 10.28   Another home page of a for-sale-by-owner web site. (www.fsbo.com.)

FIGURE 10.29   The owners.com home page for for-sale-by-owner properties. (www.owners.com.)

Information and Specialty Sites

www.realestateABC.com

The realestateABC.com site is an excellent resource for a great deal of information. It offers all of the different calculators for payments, qualification and much more. Also, there is a section showing the top Internet sites for hits in different real estate-related sites, across the country. There are literally hundreds of great information and broker sites.

www.bestplaces.net

Sterling's Best Places was discussed earlier in the book, but this site is so terrific that I have to list it again. Spend some time on this site. It has tremendous tools and is very interesting.

Foreclosures

There are many, many sites that list foreclosures on the web; however, many of them require payment to receive the actual property information. The following are a few sites that provide good, detailed information.

    www.forclosurestore.com
    www.foreclosure.net
    www.foreclosurefreesearch.com
    http://www.governmentauctions.org

Making the Web Your First Stop

Regardless of the topic, if you are seeking information, my suggestion is to *always* start with the World Wide Web on the Internet. There is no other comparable source for information availability and since your time is extremely valuable as an investor, you will want to maximize your efforts. The first and best way to do that is *use the Internet* every chance that you have to do so.

11

Successful Negotiation Techniques—How to Create Win-Win Transactions

Being a good negotiator can be the difference between being able to structure a fair deal or a terrific deal. Your own personal negotiation skills will be extremely important to your financial success in real estate investment.

Important Factors to Remember When Negotiating

Negotiating must become second nature. You must be able to move into a negotiation mode immediately when you come in contact with someone with whom you might eventually do business, whether you have prepared specifically for that negotiation or not. You must be knowledgeable and ready to do business at all times. In all negotiations, there are a few factors that you should understand:

1. You must establish trust and credibility with every person with whom you are negotiating. You must learn to establish that trust in a very short period of time.

2. As much as possible, you must quickly develop a rapport with every person with whom you are negotiating. You must seek to find a common ground whereby you and every other person with whom you're dealing is comfortable. That common ground may or may not be the real estate on which you are negotiating. Remember, fishermen like to talk about fishing, hunters like to talk about hunting, car buffs like to talk about cars, etc. Many times, what you say is not as important as how you say it.

3. You must take the time to discover the needs and the desires of the people with whom you're negotiating and then move to satisfy those needs and desires. Patience and thoroughness are key aspects of that process.

4. You must be careful not to display a great deal of self-interest. It is important in a win-win situation that all parties are willing to work to meet the needs of everyone involved in the transaction, and your demeanor and actions should lend themselves to that end.

5. You must keep in mind that the party with whom you are negotiating must have at least as much desire to complete the transaction as you have or you are probably wasting your time.

6. You must keep emotion out of your negotiations as much as possible. If you feel pressure or uneasiness starting to develop, it is better to back off and continue the negotiations at a later time.

7. Never make assumptions for which you have no basis in fact. Assuming that a seller will not be interested in assisting in the financing, accepting a low down payment, taking a lesser price for their property, etc., are common assumptions made by new investors. Those assumptions can kill a transaction that otherwise might have gone together with a little positive effort.

8. Be extremely careful saying things that are critical or negative about the property on which you are negotiating. The thinking

by some investors that a great deal of criticism of a particular property, when dealing with a seller, will result in a better deal on the property is definitely flawed thinking.

9. Keep your negotiations focused on the terms that matter most. Do not get sidetracked by superfluous items that may cloud the important issues. That said, there are times when you will use nonessential items to offset the more important terms and issues in a transaction.

10. Concentrate your efforts on identifying and solving the problems of the other parties to the transaction, while at the same time meeting your own needs and desires.

11. Most important of all—you must be *persistent*. Through all levels of your negotiations, make sure that you are unrelenting in your effort to get the deal *you* want.

The First Impression Is the Most Important

It is extremely important that your first meeting with a seller goes well if there are to be any potential future negotiations. It is always best if the first contact be very low-key and not necessarily get into the specifics of the transaction. Your goal in the first meeting will be to accomplish five things:

1. Collect as much information as possible about the property and the seller and identify any needs and problems that may exist with either the property or the seller. These needs and problem areas will help you to prepare an offer that will be suitable to you and the seller.

2. Establish a rapport and working relationship with the seller.

3. Set the stage for the next meeting when you will begin to discuss terms for the purchase of the property.

4. Establish a trust with the seller and tell him or her exactly how and when your next contact will occur.

5. Show special attention to the seller's needs, interests, and desires.

Usually, after the first meeting with a seller, you will know if there is a possibility that you may be able to put the transaction together. However, sometimes the first meeting will not provide you with enough information to allow you to make a decision as to how you want to structure an offer. If you feel that you will require more information, make sure that you leave the seller with the understanding that you will be contacting him or her for whatever information you require before you make your buying decision.

The most important aspect of the first contact, from your point of view as an investor, is to measure the seller's need and desire to liquidate the property. This aspect is most important for two reasons. You will base the terms of your offer partially on that need and desire, and you can measure the urgency with which you need to develop your offer. Obviously, if a seller is in foreclosure and there are only three days left in the redemption period, the seller is going to be highly motivated and want to see some resolution for the problem in a very short period of time.

Identifying the Most Important Topics of Negotiation

The most important topics of negotiation are fairly easy for you to identify as an investor:

1. Price

2. Financing terms: How the financing will occur, and the terms of financing

3. Terms of sale: Who gets what, for what, and within what time frame; include all conditions, contingencies, and exceptions

4. The what ifs: Everything that can, might, or will occur during the term of the transaction; cover all the bases

As easy as it is to identify the most important topics of negotiation for the investor, it may be equally as difficult to identify those important topics for a seller. That is why it is critically important to identify the problems, needs, and desires of the seller as early as possible in the negotiations.

Educate the Seller

You will be working to resolve all of the issues for the seller in a manner that will be acceptable to you as the investor. To be able to accomplish that, it will be necessary for you to educate the seller so as to avoid a negotiation environment that can quickly turn sour. The more the seller knows about the buying process, the easier it will be for you to structure your transaction.

As I said earlier in this chapter, in the section that identified the most important factors to remember when negotiating, *it is often not what you say, but how you say it that is most important.*

Probably the most difficult point of negotiation on most every sale will be *price.* Nearly every seller with whom you will deal will believe that his or her property is worth "top-dollar," and it is important that you have the proper support materials if you are going to soften this view on the potential sale price. Also, as you learned in an earlier chapter, many sellers are emotionally attached to their properties and through that emotion become rather jaded when it comes to pricing.

One problem that you will consistently run into with sellers is that they will quote to you listing prices as sale prices. It is very important for you to always have the proper comps and other sale data with regard to the actual sale prices so that you will not have to argue about the closing price on any comparable property. Many times the seller will rely on information that has been provided by neighbors with regard to the prices for which certain properties sold. Unfortunately, some sellers would have their neighbors believe that they received a great deal more for their property than they actually did. Again, if you are armed with the proper comparable sales report, printed out in black-and-white, from a reputable title or real estate company, there usually will not be much argument from the seller.

The 12 Rules for Proper Negotiation—Memorize Them

1. *Listen first—then talk.* Being a good listener is the *only* way you will ever become a good negotiator. You must learn to collect the pertinent data and information from the person with whom you are negotiating, analyze that data and information, and then provide a response. *The first dictum of negotiating: He who offers first, loses.*

We have had hundreds of thousands of investors, brokers, agents, mortgage lenders, and title and escrow people attend our programs in nearly every state and six countries around the world. It never ceases to amaze me that, as often as I have said it, written it, and proclaimed it, "Listen first—then talk," this is still the hardest rule for everyone to remember and follow. Therefore, I will share with you a short story that came from one of our long-time students that will help you to remember the importance of this rule. Dean wrote,

> I was negotiating a lease for a title company in a large complex in northern California. I had done my homework and found that most of the leases in the complex had been in place for approximately two years and they were priced at an average of about $0.75 to $0.80 per square foot.

When I met with the owner, I immediately indicated to him that we had done comps for comparable buildings in the area and had discovered that his building was priced approximately $0.05 to $0.10 per square foot higher than comparable properties.

I was looking for a good five-year lease at about $0.70 per square foot, but I really wanted the company to be located in that building. The owner seemed a little surprised and I took it to mean that he was uncomfortable with the $0.70 per square foot price that I had thrown out to him.

He stated, "Well, I suppose I could do that since you are willing to do a five-year term and the company is very strong and would be a good tenant for the building." As he was saying that, he had begun to take paperwork out of his briefcase and he immediately put it back and indicated to me that he would have to put the paperwork together at the new pricing.

A week later we signed the lease at $0.70 per square foot for 14,000 square feet, exactly what I asked for.

Within about three months the building was sold and when the new owner's representative was signing the papers with the escrow officer at our title company, he said, "You know we really appreciated your company coming into the building when you did—during our negotiations for the purchase. The sale was hanging on one condition: that the previous owner find one solid, anchor tenant that would accept a five-year lease at $0.60 per square foot, or more. We are sure glad that you showed up when you did."

When I heard that, it came back to me how the seller of the property had very quietly slid his paperwork back into his briefcase on the day that we had met. Obviously, he had prepared the paperwork at less than $0.70 per square foot and when I opened my big mouth, he graciously accepted my gift. Although, I felt that I had negotiated a good deal, if I had just waited to hear what he had to say, it would have been even better. One slip of your cardinal rule cost us about $84,000 over the five-year period.

Boy, did I learn that lesson well: He who offers first, usually loses.

2. *Always negotiate in person.* Eye to eye, toe to toe is the only way you will ever be able to get the feel for the seller's true desires, and it is the best way for you to build a rapport with that seller. Also, avoid written negotiations except in counteroffer situations, and never negotiate terms and intricate details over the telephone.

3. *Use all of the terms of the offer to achieve what is most important to you.* You must remember that there are six areas of negotiation that will be most important in almost every transaction. They are: price, down payment, interest rate, payments, dates, and terms. If keeping the payments low so you can have a cash flow from the property is most important, you can use a combination of price, down payment, interest rate, dates, and terms to facilitate your receiving the payments you are seeking. If you are looking for the best price possible, you could use down payment, interest rate, payments, dates, and terms to achieve that.

4. *Use nonrequisite terms during negotiations whenever possible.* As an example, if you are negotiating on a four-plex, you might ask the seller to resurface the entire parking area, knowing full well that some minor repairs to the surface would be adequate. If the seller knows that the complete resurfacing would be $5,000 to $7,000 and you are willing to compromise and save the seller a portion of that cost, in the mind of that seller you have made a concession and he or she may feel obligated to compromise on terms that are truly more important to you, such as price or down payment.

If you give up five or six nonrequisite items during a negotiation, the seller will have less problem conforming to your wishes with regard to one or more terms that truly have more importance to you.

5. *Be patient.* In any negotiations, it will usually take time for the other parties to understand and accept your point of view. Do not try to hurry, but instead allow the seller to express his or her needs, desires,

and point of view and adapt your presentation to the things that are most important to the seller. You may need to explain certain benefits of the transaction, again and again, before the seller will understand.

6. *Ask questions and paraphrase the answers back to the seller if you do not understand the seller's motivation.* The best way to build a seller's trust is to identify exactly what *makes that seller click,* what he or she is truly trying to achieve out of the sale. The following example is a few lines from a negotiation that I was involved in for a residential duplex:

Investor: "How much cash do you need to pay off the medical bills that are an immediate burden?"

Seller: "I need almost all of the equity to pay them off."

Investor: "I want to make sure that I can put together an offer that will meet your needs, so to be sure that I understand, you now have over $50,000 in medical bills that must be paid out of this escrow?"

Seller: "Well, no, not exactly. We have about $7,500 in current bills, some of them are already late, and the treatments could go as high as $50,000 over the next two years."

Investor: "I see. So your immediate concern is to cover the $7,500 and then to structure a way that you can be sure that the medical payments can be made in a timely manner, so as to keep your good credit intact?"

Seller: "Yes, that is exactly what I want."

As you can see, by asking the right questions in the proper manner, you can easily clarify the seller's concerns and needs and better understand how you need to structure an offer that will satisfy that seller's needs.

Many more examples of these types of question and answer scenarios are included in the chapter on dialogues.

7. *Always work from a maximum baseline.* In most cases, before you ever meet with a seller for the first time, you will have established a

maximum price and down payment that you are willing to pay for a property. The payments, interest rate, term, and other conditions and terms of the deal may be more flexible and negotiable. Once again, it is important that you do not become emotionally involved in the negotiations and inflate your offer below the maximum baseline that you have established for price and down payment and any other terms that are critically important to your investment. That is not to say that should you identify other factors about the property that might increase the value, you could not increase your baseline figures.

I once met a professional gambler in Las Vegas who had been extremely successful throughout his life, making a living playing poker and blackjack in Nevada casinos. When I asked him what one item he would identify as the most important to his success, he said it was the fact that he had baseline limits for winning and losing and that he had never deviated from the limits that he set each time that he sat down at a table. He presets his loss limits and his win limits and he leaves the table when he reaches either one. Having baseline limits and knowing when to walk away from a negotiation process is one of the most important rules of investing.

8. *Continually identify the value of the terms your offer.* Throughout all of your negotiations you must continually identify for the parties with whom you are negotiating all of the benefits they will be receiving by accepting your offer. In other words, if sellers are receiving the cash they need to handle any current financial issues they may have, monthly payments that will help with their ongoing economic dilemma, the relief of the pressure of owning a property, removing the obligation of the sellers to make repairs on the property, etc., the value of these items is their motivation. You need to mention those things at every opportunity during the negotiation.

Just as though you are distributing a product, you must make the parties with whom you are negotiating aware of all of the features and benefits associated with your offer, and you must do so over and over again until they see those features and benefits in the proper manner.

9. *KISS.* The old cliché, keep it simple stupid (KISS), is very appropriate when it comes to all levels of negotiation, especially with non-professional property owners. The more simply that your offers can be prepared, the easier the negotiations will be. That is not to say that you needn't be thorough with your paperwork and all other aspects of the transaction.

The following is a condition, that was written by a buyer into an offer and that was presented to a seller of a single-family home. The seller, who later came to one of our seminars, ultimately did not accept the offer that was presented, primarily because he or she could not understand what the buyer was trying to say in several sections of the contract. One segment read:

> Buyer to accept and govern tenure of property preceding escrow finality, only if total contractual imbursement for seller and other conventioned expenditures are acquired by escrow holder and seller is contented by the buyer's obligatory requirements associated with the covenants and conditions of the indenture.

If you said, "What in the heck does that mean?" you responded exactly the same way the seller did. Now, can you imagine an entire purchase agreement written in that manner? What the buyer was trying to say was:

> Buyer to take possession of the property prior to close of escrow only if all of their funds to close the sale have been deposited into an escrow account and the seller is satisfied that the buyer has met all of the requirements of the contract to close the escrow.

What the buyer actually wanted was to deposit all of his or her funds into the escrow account, satisfy all of the requirements of the contract and be able to begin working on the property before the close of escrow.

As much as possible, keep your negotiations, offers, counteroffers, contracts, and all other elements of your buying, selling, and investment procedures as simple as legally possible.

10. *Have alternatives in mind at all times.* Just as you will have baselines preestablished before you meet with a potential seller, you also should have in mind several alternative ways that you might be able to structure a transaction if you find the seller to be flexible and accommodating.

Many investors will prepare more than one offer when the negotiations have reached a point that it is time for the actual purchase contract to be put in place. I do not necessarily agree with that method of operation. Although it may be effective in certain situations, I find those tactics to be a little too suede-shoe for my liking.

Nearly all of the most effective negotiators that I have worked with over the past 25 years have used somewhat the same technique or formula that I use when it comes to reaching agreement on the terms and stipulations of a real estate transaction. Here is the most comfortable and effective scenario that I have found when it comes to negotiating:

1. I prepare a list of absolutes that I feel are absolutely necessary for me to be able to put the deal together. Those absolutes usually include price, down payment, and monthly payments, and may also include other stipulations with regard to the terms or the property itself.

2. I prepare a second list of preferred items that I would really prefer to have included in the transaction, but that are not as essential as the absolutes and can be used as needed during the negotiation process.

3. I prepare a list of nonrequisite items that are not essential and do not have much bearing on whether or not I will be able to structure a transaction with the seller or person with whom I am nego-

tiating. As mentioned earlier, these nonrequisite items can become very important when it comes down to who gets what and who gives up what.

Prior to the first meeting with a seller I will review my list of absolutes, preferred items and nonrequisites, and throughout the meeting I will be mentally organizing the ways that I may be able to utilize all three areas with regard to the seller's needs, desires, and interests.

Usually, by the time we have concluded the first meeting I have a good idea if there is potential for purchase and generally how I will structure a purchase contract. So that I will not forget anything when I begin to prepare a purchase agreement, I make it a habit, no later than a few minutes after the meeting, to write down everything that was discussed and identify the importance to the seller of any preferred items and nonrequisites so that I will be sure to use these items most effectively.

11. *Take time when it is needed.* Many times in the midst of negotiations you will reach, for lack of another term, a standoff situation and it is best to just take some time to let the state of affairs cool down a bit. As it is with all types of negotiations, there are times when nothing but a little space will do any good.

However, as I always say, "Time is only a test of trouble, not a remedy." After some time passes, it will be important for you to get, as Gene Autry sang, "back in the saddle again" and restart the negotiation process. In many cases, after a break or some time has elapsed in the negotiation process, you will need to start over at the beginning and again identify all of the essential aspects that are most important to the person with whom you are negotiating.

The following is an example of how a break in negotiations can positively impact a transaction: Greg was attempting to structure a low-down purchase transaction on a high-end beach property in Manhattan

Beach, California. Greg had rented the property from the seller for two years at a rental rate of $3,000 per month and was aware that the seller's payments on the first mortgage were approximately $1,200 per month. Greg was also aware that the seller, who resided full-time in Hawaii, did not want the responsibility for the property in California any longer.

When Greg advised the property owner that the residence was going to require a new roof, the owner indicated that he had several notes on which he had been collecting income for several years, and that they were all to be paid off within 30 days and he didn't feel comfortable spending the money to replace the roof. He further indicated that he felt that it might be a good time for him to sell the property and offered it to Greg for a sales price of $950,000.

Greg knew that the value of the property in peak condition would be approximately $1,100,000 and he indicated to the seller that he would be interested, but that he needed a day or so to put his thoughts together as to how he could structure an offer. He found out from the seller that the notes that the seller had mentioned, which had been providing income for the seller, totaled approximately $2,600 per month. He further determined that the seller was flexible with regard to down payment and monthly payments, but he was adamant about the fact that he wanted to carry a note on the property for no more than five years.

Greg owned several investment properties, but had continued to rent his personal residence because he could not purchase a property on the beach and have payments as low as $3,000 per month. As a young executive earning over $250,000 per year, he definitely needed write-offs and could pay more than the $3,000 per month if it made sense with regard to his tax situation.

The first offer that Greg structured for the seller had the following terms:

$0 Down

Wraparound mortgage for $920,000

Interest rate of 6 percent

Monthly payments of $4,600

All due and payable in five years

Buyer to accept property in as-is condition

With the terms of this offer, the seller was still responsible for the first mortgage payment of $1,200, which gave him a net income of approximately $3,400 per month. However, the seller had previously been receiving approximately $4,400 per month net from Greg's rent and the notes for which he had been receiving payments, and after he had made the first mortgage payment on the property.

When the seller received Greg's offer, he called Greg and he was quite agitated. He indicated that with Greg's offer he was losing $1,000 per month income, the price might be less than market value, the interest return was too low, and he would rather raise the rent, put on a new roof, and keep the property.

Greg recognized the agitation of the seller and deferred any further negotiation, simply stating that he would be happy to assist the seller in finding a roofer who could do the work on the property. Apparently, the seller was quite surprised that Greg did not argue his points or dispute the seller's point of view.

Greg collected seven quotes on the new roof as promised, and they ranged between $11,300 and $14,600. He provided the information to the seller within about 14 days after their telephone negotiation contact. Greg then waited approximately two weeks before contacting the seller and when he did so, he only verified that the seller had received the roofing information and indicated that he might be interested in presenting another offer to purchase the property. However, Greg said that he would prefer to come to Hawaii to present this offer because he felt that this would be the only opportunity for him and the seller to reach an agreement. The seller agreed.

Knowing that the time that had elapsed had allowed the final payments on the notes to the seller to be made and that the seller had probably stressed over the impending cost of the roof, as well as the decrease in his income, Greg felt that it was a good time to make another offer, closer to the baseline limits that he had established for the purchase. Three days later Greg arrived in Kona and within two hours of his arrival, he had purchased the beachfront property with the following terms:

$0 Down

Wraparound mortgage for:	$994,285
Interest rate of:	7 percent
Monthly payments, interest only, of:	$5,300
All due and payable in five years	
Buyer to accept property in as-is condition	
Seller to make payments on first deed of trust of:	$1,200
Seller to receive 10 percent of the increased	

    equity when the property was resold (seller would

    receive 10 percent of the sale price above $994,285).

Greg presented his offer in the following manner: The seller would receive $5,300 per month, out of which he would make the $1,200 first deed of trust payment, netting the seller $4,100 per month. The seller had been paying taxes on the property of approximately $500 per month out of the note and rental proceeds; therefore, since he would no longer be responsible for those taxes, he would have a net increase in his income of approximately $200 per month. The interest rate had been increased to 7 percent. The sale price had been increased by $74,285. The seller would not be responsible for the $11,000+ cost of the new roof.

The seller would have no out-of-pocket expenses for the sale of the property. Greg pointed out that the typical real estate commission in that area would have been over $65,000 and that the other normal seller closing costs would have exceeded $5,000. By allowing the seller to share in the future equity earned, above the sale price, when the property resold, the seller has the opportunity to continue to profit in the appreciation of the property.

Greg's accepted offer addressed all of the seller's stated complaints about the original purchase offer and allowed the seller to accept terms that he felt met his needs. From Greg's point of view, the additional interest write-off that he would receive from owning the personal residence more than paid the difference between his new mortgage payment and the original rental payment. His entire out-of-pocket expense to close the transaction was approximately $4,100 closing costs and the new roof cost approximately $12,000. He had purchased a $1,000,000+ property for about $16,000 out of pocket and little increase in his net after tax payments. Less than two years after Greg's purchase of the property it was appraised for $1,490,000.

Time often helps in negotiations so don't be afraid to back off when it appears that you are not making progress. Everything happens best, when the time is right.

12. *Give it a shot: what do you have to lose?* When you have analyzed a seller's needs and desires and you feel you are in tune with what the seller is trying to achieve, don't be afraid to make an offer that only comes close to giving the seller what he or she wants. You may be very surprised at how many times you will get a positive response. If nothing else, the shot-in-the-dark offer will at least give you an idea of how stringent the seller is going to be on his or her requirements.

As a real estate broker, I once presented an offer on a motel that was listed for over $600,000. The investor had insisted that we meet with the seller prior to his making an offer and that he wanted some time to examine the property in the seller's presence. I was quite surprised at the immediate rapport that the investor developed with the seller. They both had an extensive knowledge of construction and obviously enjoyed talking about the work that would be necessary to bring a motel up to an acceptable standard. The seller made clear to the buyer that he wanted to sell the property an as-is condition and I was again surprised when he blatantly stated, "I'll come off the price considerably if I can get an as-is offer that will give me a pretty good return on my investment. I paid $210,000 for the property two years ago."

I learned a very good lesson that day when I presented the buyer's offer for $325,000 and it was accepted with no counteroffer. The buyer put approximately $40,000 into the property over the next two-month period, relisted the property with me, and sold it for $585,000 six months from the day he had made his original offer to purchase.

Had I explored with the seller the opportunity to purchase the property instead of only taking the listing, I would have profited much greater than the two commissions that I earned. The original buyer netted over $200,000 for the six-month investment. My commissions totaled just over $26,000—quite a difference. Remember, "Give it a shot—you have nothing to lose."

Other Important Factors Pertaining to Negotiation

1. Be sure that all owners or parties to the negotiation are present at the time of negotiation.
2. Do not ask for too much at any one time. Get approval on each term or requirement as you move through the negotiation. Do not hit them with everything at once.
3. Do not try to use scare tactics. There is no need to use unethical methods to achieve what can be done legally and honestly.

4. Always present your offers back to front. Start with the many items that you are giving away and that benefit the seller and work up to the most important terms, which are usually price and down payment.

5. Always make your offer prices uneven numbers, such as $139,330, instead of $140,000. The seller will believe that you have structured the offer more exactly to meet his or her needs.

6. State interest-only payments in dollars and cents. In other words, do not say, "interest of 5 percent per annum." Instead, state the payment as, "$655 per month, interest-only payments."

7. If you run into a problem in the negotiations that could be a deal breaker, ask for time to consult with a third party such as an attorney or an accountant. Make the bad guy someone other than yourself.

8. Make sure that there is symmetry between your words and your actions. Body language can be a dead giveaway if you are feeling uncomfortable.

9. Never allow a seller more than 24 hours to accept your offer.

10. Always be cool. Never let your emotions show if you begin to feel uncomfortable. Keep your poker face on and maintain the approach that you will get a win-win deal for everyone or it does not bother you in the least to walk away.

Using a Negotiation Checklist

Before and after every negotiation of any kind, go over the negotiation checklist shown in Table 11.1 and give yourself a grade. When you start out, you may be getting 70 percent and 80 percent, but after you have made four or five presentations you should easily be above 90 percent. It is imperative that you learn good negotiation techniques if you are to ever prosper as an investor.

Table 11.1   Negotiation Checklist

1. Were all owners or decision makers present?
2. Did you make a good first impression?
3. Did you find a common ground with the other parties?
4. Did you establish trust and rapport with the other parties?
5. Did you negotiate in person?
6. Did you ask, listen, clarify and paraphrase, and then talk?
7. Were you patient?
8. Did you KISS?
9. Were you aware and careful of you body language?
10. Did you identify with the other party's motivation?
11. Did you address the needs of the seller numerous times?
12. Did you concentrate on solving the problems of the other parties?
13. Were you careful not to display to much self-interest?
14. Did you concentrate on the most important terms?
15. Did you have all the information that you needed?
16. Were you careful not to be to negative about the property?
17. Did you have alternatives in mind and use them when needed?
18. Did you have a terms list of absolutes, preferreds, and nonrequisites?
19. Did you use throw-away terms to help get the absolutes?
20. Did you maintain you maximum baseline limits?
21. Did you use third party diversion if negotiations stalled (lawyer, taxes, etc.)?
22. Did you continually identify the value of the terms of you offer?
23. Did you "Give it a shot," asking for great terms or an overall great deal?
24. Did you present your offer starting with the benifits for the other parties?
25. Did you base assumptions on fact and data only?
26. Were you careful not to ask for too much at one time?
27. Did you avoid using scare tactics?
28. Did you use a sale price that was not even 1000s?
29. Did you state interest payments in dollars and cents rather than percentage?
31. Did you address the what-ifs?
30. Did you take time—a break in negotiations—if necessary?
32. Did you allwow the other parties 24 hours or less for decisions?
33. Did you set the stage for future meetings, if necessary?
34. Did you stay cool?

Making the Offer—The Climax of the Negotiation Process

Of all of the areas of negotiation, the one that seems to frighten most people is the actual preparation and presentation of the offer. However, if you have done your job well in the negotiation process, you have already primed the seller for nearly everything that he or she will be seeing in the sales contract or the deposit receipt.

A contract is really nothing more than an agreement between two or more parties to do or not do certain things. Although some contracts can be verbal, all real estate contracts must be in writing. Whether you plan to use an attorney, a real estate licensee or you plan to prepare the purchase contract yourself, there are certain aspects of contract law that you need to understand and there are certain facets of the actual written contract that you need to comprehend.

The main focus of your purchase contract should be to record each and every stipulation on which the buyer and seller have agreed. When the purchase contract has been signed by all parties to the transaction, there is considered to be a "meeting of the minds" and that purchase contract can then be used by the attorney closer or the escrow officer to guide them in preparing their closing instructions.

There are many companies and entities that offer "boiler plate" purchase agreements and counteroffers, and many of these documents cover the basic sale stipulations. However, when you're structuring creative purchase agreements, it will be up to you to clarify the specific aspects of the contract. Many times on boiler plate agreements there will not be enough room for you to fill in all the items that have been agreed to by you and the other parties to the transaction. In those cases, it will be necessary for you to use a form known as an addendum to specify all the contract components. Usually, between a boiler plate purchase agreement and a one-page addendum, you will be able to complete a purchase offer.

You will find in the appendix a copy of a real estate purchase agreement (Appendix A), addendums (Appendix B), and a counteroffer (Appendix C). They are fairly simple to understand and it would be good for you to study the documents before you attempt to prepare an agreement or write an offer.

Throughout this book you will see many examples of actual transactions and the basic terms of those deals are explained. However, I believe that most investors who are new to real estate business are not always best served to try to write a purchase contract without the help of either an attorney or a real estate professional. If you feel uncomfortable in preparing the contract, do not hesitate to contact a transaction broker or a real estate lawyer and have them prepare the paperwork.

The Sections of the Purchase Agreement in Detail

The main sections of any of the documents known as a purchase agreement, deposit receipt, or purchase contract are pretty much the same. However, some contract forms will be one or two pages and others that are used by real estate licensees may be as many as 12 to 13 pages. You will need to decide with which forms you are comfortable and obtain those documents. Many companies and entities offer the forms on the Internet. Some of the sites you might check are:

www.urgentbusinessforms.com
www.uslegalforms.com
www.legalwhiz.com
www.buyincomeproperties.com

Most of the purchase agreements will contain the following sections:

1. The initial identifying basic contract information, such as:
   The date of the agreement
   The buyers' and sellers' names
   The amount of the deposit
   The sale price
   The property address or some type of property-identifying
      information
2. The body of the contract stating exact terms of the purchase, such as:

Financing, where all financing terms will be explained in detail

Existing loan information

Requests for notice of default

Tax service information

Insurance requirements

Any miscellaneous items or terms

3. The condition of the property, including;

Seller warranties

As-is clauses

4. Transfer disclosure statement, including seller's disclosure

5. Property disclosures, such as hazard zones, flood zones, fire responsibility areas, mello-roos, earthquake safety, smoke detectors, etc.

6. Government compliance

7. Fixtures: what stays and what doesn't

8. Personal property included in sale

9. Home warranties

10. Septic system

11. Pest control, inspections, and work to be completed and by whom

12. Any contingencies, such as buyer must sell property, seller must close another escrow, etc.

13. Contingency release clauses

14. Tax withholding

15. Other contingencies or covenants

16. Time frames of transaction progression, including inspections, approvals, etc.

17. Final walk-through, approval, and verifications

18. Court identification and administration of disputes

19. Broker information, if any involved

20. Liquidation damages clause

21. Attorney's fees

22. Multiple listing service information if any involved

23. Other terms and conditions

24. Time is of the essence, entire contract, and changes explanation

25. Broker agency confirmation, if any

26. Explanation of: This is the complete offer

27. Buyer's signature and buyer's broker's signature

28. Acceptance section

29. Broker identification, if any

30. Signatures of sellers and selling brokers, if any

Again, if you are uncomfortable writing your own contracts, use the services of a real estate lawyer or a transaction broker. You are better off spending a few hundred dollars for an attorney or a broker and putting the deal together properly, than stumbling through the process and possibly not getting the deal at all.

12

Viewing and Inspecting Properties

To become a successful investor, you must learn how to view homes thoroughly and methodically, keeping in mind the purpose for which you are buying the property. Usually your focus will be on one or two investment purposes: to buy and hold the property as a long-term investment or to buy the property to resell immediately and generate cash. Regardless of the purpose of the purchase, it is imperative that you properly inspect the properties, going over them with the proverbial "fine tooth comb."

With some properties, your only intent will be to buy them in an as-is condition for as low a price as possible. Even in those cases, it is critically important that you know exactly what work will be required to bring the property back up to standard and what time and financial outlay will be required to accomplish that goal.

Where Do You Start?

There are several important factors that you must think about when you are viewing properties that you are considering for investment:

1. Location
2. Overall condition of the property and structures
3. Age
4. Livability of the area (rental)
5. Income potential (rental)
6. Time and financial outlay required to bring property to marketable state

All of the issues above relate only to the property. Keep in mind that none of those issues will have any relevance if you are unable to make a deal with acceptable terms with the seller. You should never spend the time and effort to thoroughly inspect a property until you believe that the possibility exists that you will have the opportunity to make that deal. Note that I said that the "possibility exists." I am not saying that the deal has to be done, just that the opportunity exists. You will understand exactly to what I am referring after you have completed the following chapters on contacting and negotiating with potential sellers.

Let's Look at Location

Almost everyone has heard the statement that the three most important factors involving real estate are *location*, *location*, and *location*. And, I suppose if you are buying a property that you are going to occupy, that may be the case. However, when you begin looking at properties purely from an investment standpoint, some of the emphasis on location is reduced. It still may be very, very important but the significance of the location most often will relate directly to the purpose for which you are buying the property. Some of the highest returns that I have experienced have been on properties that were in poor locations. However, I was able to purchase the properties at such terrific prices or with such great terms that the location was really no detriment. *never* turn down an investment opportunity solely due to a less than perfect location. If you have taken the time to choose the neighborhoods and areas that you believe are acceptable for your investment purposes, and you concentrate your efforts only in those areas, most of the location issues should be resolved.

Overall Condition of the Property and Structures

As I said earlier, you will view investment properties differently than you will properties that you might occupy. However, it is often easier to segregate the investment standpoint and look only at the property from the position of an occupant/owner, and then go back and add in the investment prospective.

As you get your first look at a property, you will be looking for what we have always called the three Ds: dirt, discoloration and damage. If a property is just dirty, or even filthy, it can be cleaned and spruced up. But, you must keep in mind, that generally the cleanliness, or lack thereof, will give you a great deal of insight into the upkeep and care that the property has had in the past. Since you will be looking for comparable properties when you begin to establish a valuation, start by comparing your subject property to other properties in the area. Is it average, above average, or below average? How does it compare overall to other real estate in the area?

Discoloration is often the predecessor or product of a more significant problem. As an example, if a ceiling or wall has a great deal of discoloration, it is often the result of water damage beneath the surface. If the water has seeped into the ceiling or wall, there is a good chance that there may be other structural damage and you might be wise to open up the walls or ceiling and look further into the structure. Discoloration on tile or linoleum often means that there has been leakage either underneath the surface or from a continual source above the flooring. It is a good idea to ask the property owner specifically what has caused the discoloration for two reasons. First, most states have disclosure laws that require the seller to disclose any problems that they know exist in the property. Second, most property owners will have already looked into what repairs are needed and if you ask, will often either share the information with you or even offer to make the repair if you purchase the property.

Another common discoloration problem occurs from water runoff on structures that are not properly guttered. If the water runoff has been severe enough and lasted for a long enough period of time, the affected area, usually the exterior of the structure, might require extensive work to make proper repairs.

Damage is pretty much anything that is in need of repair. Many times you will purposely be purchasing property that has minor damage because you are looking to buy the property at less than market value, make cosmetic repairs, and rent or resell the property. In those cases, it is important that you identify exactly what repairs you are willing to make and what financial outlay will be required to make those repairs. Major structural damage can be very costly to repair and often can only be identified by a professional engineer or builder. If you are unsure about the magnitude of damages, make sure that you consult an expert *before* you buy a property. Most often, in those cases, you will make offers *conditioned upon* specific inspections and approvals.

Inspecting Potential Investment Properties

Viewing and inspecting properties should be done in a three-step process:

1. Do a cursory viewing of the entire property, inside and out, primarily to determine if the real estate has any possibility for the

purpose for which you are interested in buying the property. If after making this cursory viewing you would consider the property for purchase, go to step 2.

2. Do an investment inspection and view the property again, paying close attention to the details regarding the investment possibilities, rent, appreciation, and future benefits. If after this viewing you believe the property is a potential investment in which you are interested, make the third and most comprehensive inspection of the property

3. Using the property inspection form (Appendix D), again go through the property, this time taking detailed notes while you're inspecting every inch of the property inside and out. If the seller will allow you to do so, take pictures or use a video camera to capture every possible nuance of the property.

Remember, when it comes to investment property, you are looking for major potential. You are not necessarily looking for the perfect home to move into and live in the rest of your life, so don't be too critical of a property that has not been cared for to the standards that you set for your own properties. Be open-minded and remember you want to *make money* and *build your investment portfolio*.

Each Inspection Step in Detail

Because many investors begin their careers with little or no experience, I feel it is necessary to go through each inspection step in detail. I have found that this extra effort with new investors seems to give them much more confidence when they actually begin to look at properties.

Step 1—Cursory View

You begin your cursory view when you drive up to the property. "Curb appeal" is a term that is often used by real estate professionals and refers to how the property appears, literally from the street. Look at the property from several viewpoints. How do you feel about the property as an investor? How would you feel about the property if you were a renter looking to move into the property? What you would do to the property to make it more appealing either to another investor or owner/occupant? Curb appeal is nothing more than the first impression that most people would have of the property if they were to view the exterior from the street.

As you make your first view of the property, you will be looking for only the aspects that make this property potentially a good investment. If it is a single-family home or a small multiunit property, some of the considerations might relate to the livability of the property: things such as overall layout, number of bedrooms and bathrooms, kitchen amenities, traffic flow through the property, yards, and most importantly, the general feeling of the property.

Also, you will be looking for major damage or structural problems that might be too expensive for you to repair or overcome in the investment property: things such as cracked foundations, brick-mortar-rock structures cracked or broken, major portions of the roof damaged or missing, evidence of water damage, dry rot or termites, or any other major problem that might be very costly to correct.

If after you make your cursory view, you believe that the property does not have the potential you are seeking, don't waste any additional time. Simply go to the next property. If there is a possibility that the property might meet your needs, go to step 2.

Step 2—Investment Inspection

Go back through the property, doing an investment inspection, and look at the potential for the rental, appreciation, and ultimate trade or sale of the property somewhere in the future. Determine the overall investment potential of the property.

Step 3—Your Own Professional Inspection

Many years ago as a real estate broker, I required that my agents spend the time to learn how to professionally inspect properties. I felt that it was critically important that my agents were able to properly inspect and thereby be able to properly advise their sellers and buyers. As an investor, you may not always ask that repairs be made, but you will always want to be aware of *all* repairs for which you may become responsible if you are the owner of the property. Remember, every property you buy, you do so thinking of selling.

Always use the property inspection form (Appendix D) when you are making your last inspection of the property. Record as much of the information as possible that will help you to make a decision as to how you want to structure an offer on the property. Often, you will find many problem areas in the property that the seller is unaware of. You will use that information for your benefit when you begin negotiating to purchase the property. As I said previously, your inspection must be very systematic. I will try to guide you through a single-family inspection to give you the basics of using the property inspection form.

 TERRY'S TIP: Often, new investors have a difficult time spotting and recording problem areas when they are making their detailed inspections. The main problem seems to be that most people do not narrow their focus enough to see the specific problem areas. By that I mean that most people have a tendency to look at the overall, big picture, rather than narrowing down their viewpoint to the smallest details, which many times are the most important. There are two techniques that I have used for years to train both agents/brokers and investors:

1. Take a tip from the great directors like Spielberg and Howard and narrow your view to a "camera-like" observation. If you are really good, you can hold your hands up in the U shape, like you see the

directors do in the movies to get the feeling for a particular scene. However, getting the proper view is more difficult than it looks if you've never tried it. To make it easier, my suggestion is that you take a flat, blank piece of cardboard, approximately 8 inches by 10 inches, and cut a hole in the center about 4 inches wide and 3 inches high. When you view properties, hold this makeshift viewing card about a foot from your face (like the viewing screen of a movie camera). Look at every nook and cranny of the property. You will be quite amazed at the small details that will jump out at you when you are using a viewing card. If possible, have an assistant help you by taking notes while you identify all the details about the property.

2. Another way that you can identify every possible problem area and be able to record all the information necessary during your inspection is to use Post-it notes. Each time you discover a potential problem, make a note and put it on or near the problem area. Some rooms may end up looking like the bulletin board at your local grocery store, but this will give you the opportunity to go back and record all the information if you're working alone.

Getting Down to the Nitty-Gritty

Once you have made the decision that a property is a potential for investment, then it is time to really get down to the nitty-gritty and look over every inch of the property. You will still be looking for the three Ds: dirt, discoloration and damage, but now you're going to record on your home inspection form everything you see for future reference. The home inspection form is broken down for each segment of the house to guide you through the entire inspection process. Rather than trying to go room to room, you will find that this inspection method will provide the best results. You may be able to cover two or three sections on each pass through the house, such as floors and baseboards, ceilings and wall coverings, windows and window coverings, or walls and doors. However, when you put the sections together, make sure that it is comfortable for you to be able to cover every inch of the property. Always save the garage, exterior, and yard and landscaping for last, after you have inspected the interior of the property.

Keep in mind that time is critical and if while you are inspecting the interior of the property you find something that will preclude you from buying the property, stop your inspection and don't waste any more time.

Walls and Doors

Go through each room and inspect the walls and doors for cracks, spots, dirt, fingerprints, holes, and chipped or peeling paint. If any of the walls have wallpaper or some other covering, check the seams carefully.

Make sure that all doors operate smoothly, the doorknobs turn easily, the hinges are tight, there are no squeaks, all of the locks work, and the doors or door frames are not swollen and do not have cracks or missing pieces. Look to see that all sliding glass doors operate and lock smoothly. Look for any signs of leakage around the doors. Make sure all exterior doors are solid core. If there are any trap doors to attics or to the basement, make sure that all of the pulldowns, hinges, and stairs are in good order.

Floors and Baseboards

Go through every room, noting each spot, tear, scratch, loose or broken tile, discoloration, or imperfection in any floors or floor coverings. Be very critical and take detailed notes of any tattered carpet or chipped or broken tile. Record as much information as possible. Remember, the work that will be required to bring the property up to standard will be one of the main factors that you will use when you prepare your offer to the seller. After you have purchased the property, you can decide exactly what you will repair. If a property is furnished, you may need to have the furniture moved for your inspection. If a seller does not want to move the furnishings, you may be able to handle any potential problems with a seller disclosure form.

Make sure that you look closely for discoloration along the base-boards and on the floors and carpets. As I said earlier, most often this discoloration will be an indication of leaks and possible water damage. If possible, check underneath the rugs and carpets and see what kind of shape the flooring is in.

Windows

Windows can be expensive to replace so it is important that you carefully examine every window in the property. See that all windows operate smoothly and lock and unlock easily. See that all screens are in good shape and are securely in place. Make sure that all latches, handles, and cranks operate correctly.

If it is an older property and the windows slide up and down, with or without a rope/pulley attachment, see that all of this equipment is in good shape and operates correctly. Often these older windows will need to be replaced, and this can be an expensive venture. Also, look to see that there is no discoloration from water seepage through the windows, especially with the older style wooden frame windows.

If there are bars or security devices covering the windows, do they open properly from the *inside* for safety purposes? Make sure all of the locks on the bars and security devices work properly.

Window Coverings

In most cases, when you are buying an investment property, you will want to ask for all window coverings to be left in the property. That is, of course, if those window coverings are in good shape and can be used by the new occupant. See that drapes and curtains are in good repair. In most cases, you will have to have the drapes or curtains washed or dry-cleaned, which can be very expensive.

Make sure that all pull cords or opening and closing devices work well. See that all blinds and other coverings are in good shape and operate smoothly. Make sure that all curtain rods are straight and strong and attached to the wall properly. Look for any stains or discoloration on the inside of the drapes, drape linings, or blinds. Again, that discoloration often means that there is water seepage from the windows or the ceiling. Also, be sure that all of the window coverings fit the windows properly. With the advent and prevalence of mini-blinds, you will find many cases where the blinds are either too long, too short, too wide, or too narrow. Most of these mini-blinds can be replaced fairly inexpensively.

Ceilings

Inspecting the ceilings is very important because the cracking, chipping, discoloration, peeling paint, or blown acoustic tile can be indications of bigger problems. If the blown acoustic ceilings are discolored and the problem that caused the discoloration has been corrected, it is often less expensive to have the ceiling re-blown instead of trying to repair and paint.

Lighting and Electrical System

Remember, you are only doing the basic inspection. Don't try to become an electrician. Check all lighting fixtures that are installed throughout the property. This includes ceiling and wall lighting units. I make it a habit to have three or four light bulbs with me when I am inspecting properties, with different size bases, just in case a light fixture is inoperative and it appears that bulbs are burned out. Bulbs are cheap, but electrical repair can be very expensive and I want to know exactly what I'm getting into.

When you are checking light fixtures is a good time to check all wall outlets and switches to make sure they are in good working order. I make it a habit to carry a small light unit that can be plugged into the wall outlets to test them for operation. Remember, many outlets are connected to a wall switch and if a wall outlet is inoperative, look for a switch that may control the power to that outlet.

Because you will be buying the property, always thinking of using or selling, there are some things relating to livability about which you should be concerned. Are there an adequate number of outlets or lights in every room? Are all of the wall plates and covering devices in good shape? Are all outlets and switches attached properly and secure? Do all dimmer and specialty switches work properly? Are there any outlets that appear to be overused? (If you see six or seven plugs working off one outlet, that can be a problem, so check carefully around the plug.) Are there any black or burn marks around any of the outlets or switches? If there is any specialty lighting such as track lights, lighting over a pool table, or spotlights, does the wiring appear to have been done properly? Also, if there are any pull switches, often in the attic or basement, are they well connected and in good shape?

When you check the attic, basement, garage, or any other area where wiring might be exposed, be on the lookout for any problem areas such as exposed, burned, broken, or hanging wires, loose sockets, blackened faceplates, or generally shoddy wiring.

Going Through the Individual Rooms

As you go through the individual rooms, remember that you are looking for problem areas but you are also looking for livability issues. If you will be keeping the property as an investment, you want it to be easy to maintain and keep rented.

Kitchen

Since the kitchen is probably the most important room in most properties, that is probably the best place to start your room inspections. How are the cupboards and drawers? Are there enough of them? Are they the right height? Is there a pantry? Do all of the doors and drawers open or slide smoothly? Are all shelves secure and strong? Are all handles in good shape? Is there enough light in the kitchen? Are all of the electrical sockets working properly? Do all of the stove and ventilation fans work properly? Does the lighting on the stove or in the oven work properly? Do all built-in clocks work? Are the burners and drip pans in good shape? Are the exteriors of all appliances free of stains and damage? Are all stove racks in place and in good shape? Do the stove, microwave, and oven work properly? Are all stove and oven handles and buttons in good shape and working smoothly?

Are the sinks in good repair with no cracks, stains, scratches, or chips? Are all faucets and handles in place and in good shape? Check that both hot and cold water is available. Turn on the water in the sinks and look underneath to see if there are any leaks or problems. Do all the drains look and sound like they are working properly?

Do all the appliances, such as the dishwasher, garbage disposal, and trash compactor, work properly? If freestanding appliances such as stoves or refrigerators are to be included in the purchase of the property, make sure that they are in good operating condition. Always check the icemaker, if there is one, in the refrigerator.

Check to see that all of the countertops are in good shape. Take special care to be sure that the flooring near the sinks, dishwashers, and refrigerators is free of bubbles, swelling, or discoloration.

Living, Family, Bonus, and Play Rooms

A property may have both a living room and a family room. Use the home inspection checklist for each room in the property. Here's where a little objectivity goes a long way. Do the living and family rooms have a good "feel" to them? Once again, you're looking for the livability. Is there good traffic flow through the rooms and to the rest of the house? Are the rooms large enough? Will noise carry to or from these rooms? Are these rooms convenient to the bathroom? Is there good heating, cooling, and ventilation? Are all shelves, cabinets, and built-in furniture secure? If there are any handles, knobs, or other fixtures, are they all secure and in good shape?

If there is any kind of plumbing in these rooms, possibly for a wet bar or kitchenette area, use the bathroom inspection checklist when examining those areas. Also, if there is a bar, is it secure and in good shape? Are all upholstered items in good shape? Are all rails secure and undamaged? Is the specialty lighting all operative and in good shape?

Bathrooms

Bathrooms are important areas that need to be scrutinized carefully. Are the tubs in good shape with no cracks, discoloration, peeling, or chipping? Is the tile and caulking secure and not discolored? Do all drains work properly? Do all faucets work properly with no leaks or drips? Do all drawers and doors work correctly? Is there good water pressure? Are all of the plugs and stoppers in place and operating correctly?

Do all of the ventilation fans or special wall heating units work properly and quietly? Are all of the countertops in good shape with no chipping or loose edges? Are there any leaks under the sinks or around the tubs? Is the ceiling in good shape with no peeling, mold, chipping, or soft spots? Are all shelves in place and secure? Are all mirrors in good shape?

Are there any leaks or seepage around the toilets, showers, tubs, or sinks? Do the toilets flush and refill properly? Is there good water pressure and do both the hot and cold water taps work properly? Are all of the soap trays in place? Do all of the showerheads operate properly? Are the shower doors or curtains in good shape? If there are other devices such as hot tubs, bidets, or steam rooms, does everything operate properly?

Make sure that you look for stains that may be difficult or impossible to remove from tubs, sinks, and showers. Often in areas where the water is hard or has a high iron content, stains will result that cannot be removed.

Bedrooms

It is interesting that people spend 30 percent to 40 percent of their lives in their bedrooms and yet those rooms might be of little concern when they purchase or rent a property, but will become very much an irritant if they are not comfortable afterward. Are the bedrooms in the property that you are considering large enough to accommodate a reasonable quantity of furniture? Do the rooms have a reasonable shape? Is the lighting good? Are the windows acceptable?

Is the traffic flow comfortable? Are the bedrooms accessible to the bathrooms? Are these rooms situated in the home for convenience and privacy? Are the closets large and convenient enough? Are there any views? Is there acceptable ventilation, heating, and air-conditioning?

Closets

Adequate closet space always seems to be a problem in any property. Make sure that you check the amount of closet space that is available in the property. Are there enough closets both for hanging clothes and for shelf storage? Are all of the hanging rods in place, secure, and in good repair? Do any closets have a bad odor? Is there adequate lighting for the closets?

Laundry Areas

Laundry rooms and mud rooms are often overlooked, but they're very important in any property. If you're negotiating to keep the washer and dryer, make sure that they operate properly. One suggestion, which I explain later in the book, is to always ask for a home warranty with the purchase of most smaller investment properties. This will help you to be sure that you will not have major repairs soon after you buy the property. If any of the appliances are natural gas or propane, make sure that there are no leaks or any gas odor.

Check all connections for the appliances: gas, and electric, hot and cold water. Is there any floor or wall damage around the washer or dryer either from movement or water seepage? If there is a sink, does it drain properly and do all of the faucets work correctly? Are all of the countertops, shelves, and handles in place and in good shape?

Staircases

Are the staircases wide enough and are the steps the proper height? Is the incline proper and to code? Does the staircase make any sharp turns that will make it difficult to move furniture in to or out of the property? Are the stairs solid or do they give when they have weight on them? Do the stairs squeak, groan, or make other noises? Does sound reverberate through the house when someone goes up or down the stairs in a hurry? Are the handrails secure?

Is the covering or finish on the stairs in good shape? If the stairs are covered with carpet or some other floor covering, is the wood or other material underneath in good shape? Are there any nails or screws protruding from the stairs or railings?

Is there adequate lighting on the staircases? Is there is a pull-down staircase that goes either to the basement or attic? If so, is it in good shape? Do all parts on the pull-down work properly and can it be operated with little strength?

Fireplace, Inserts, and Wood Stoves

If you are looking at a property in the summer or winter, make sure that you take time to build a fire in the fireplaces, inserts, and wood stoves, to be sure that they operate properly.

Are there any cracks in the brick, rock, or other surface material of the fireplace or in the surrounding structure? Are there any cracks in the glass, frame, or the insert itself? Are there any excessive burn or soot areas around the fireplace pipes or the doors on the stove? Is there a wood grate in place and does it appear to be the right size for the unit? Is there an adequate screen, glass, or covering to prevent spark or cinders from escaping the unit? Do the screens, doors, or other entry to the unit operate smoothly?

Are the size, shape, and style of the wood stove, insert, fireplace, hearth, and mantle something that will be acceptable to an occupant? Also, is it a new enough style that it will be acceptable to a buyer several years in the future?

Is there a fan or forced-air unit and if so, does it operate effectively and quietly? If there is a gas starter or a gas unit, does it work properly? When the gas unit is turned off and the fireplace is not in use, is there any gas odor? Are there any signs of water leaks around the chimney or pipes where they exit the room into the ceiling or wall?

Shelves, Bookcases and Drawers

Examine all shelves, bookcases, and drawers not already covered in other sections. Are all handles in good shape? Do the doors and drawers move smoothly? Is the finish on the inside and outside in good shape? Do all hinges move smoothly? If there is any specialty lighting for these units, is it all operative and in good shape?

Heating and Cooling Units

It is advisable to have all heating and cooling units professionally inspected and serviced prior to purchasing a property. Have the units been serviced on an ongoing basis and have they been serviced recently? Do they operate properly? Is there a strong air flow? Do all of the vents open and close easily? Is there air flowing from every vent? Do the units operate quietly? Do the units adequately heat and cool the home?

If there are window units, are they secure and are the frames sealed tightly? Are all of the exposed portions of the units properly covered and safe? Is all exposed ducting secure and insulated properly? (This includes in the attic and basement as well.)

Do all thermostats work properly? Do all timing mechanisms on the units work properly? Do the pilot lights stay lit? Is there any gas smell around the gas furnace? If oil heating is used, are storage tanks easily accessible? If propane heating is used, is the tank accessible in all seasons?

Basements and Attics

Basements and attics are of most concern if they are to be used as linear storage spaces. Are there any leaks or is there any dampness in these areas? Are there stains or other evidence of prior water leakage? Is there enough headroom? Can the space be used adequately? Are there posts or dividers that break up the rooms or space uncomfortably? Are there appliances, such as a washer, dryer, heating unit, cooling unit, water softener, or water heater, that might make the areas less comfortable?

Are there adequate heating, cooling and ventilation? Is there adequate lighting? Are all the entryways and exits adequate? Are all staircases safe? Are all shelving units, cabinets, and storage areas secure, accessible, and in good shape? Do any of these areas appear to have any problems with bugs or rodents?

Soundproofing and Insulation

It is always good to inspect the property with another person who can help you determine if there is adequate soundproofing. Some homes are just noisy, and due to layout, that problem may never be able to be corrected. However, often the noise level can be reduced with insulation in the interior or exterior walls. If it is a two-story property, it is even more important to check out the noise level. For example, make sure that you turn on showers and tubs and move throughout the house while water is running.

Having someone walk through the upstairs in a property while you are inspecting downstairs will give you a feel for the quality of construction and soundproofing. Another suggestion is to have someone talk loudly in different parts of the house while you are inspecting other rooms.

Remember, if you're going to use a property as a long-term investment you want your renters to be comfortable. Soundproofing and insulation can often be a major problem in level 1 properties. You'll learn in the management section, later in the book, that there are a number of inexpensive methods, including soundproofing and insulation, that will help you make a property more livable.

Odor

Surprisingly, the number one complaint from buyers about properties that they are considering buying is smell. That's right, bad odors in a property can be a major problem. Once again, it is very important to make your property as appealing as possible when you put it on the rental or sale market. You'll be competing with other properties out there for sale or for rent, and you want to make sure that your property is the most marketable.

In a survey with thousands of people across the country, the odors that were most often mentioned as a major "turn off" for renters or buyers were cigarette smoke, animal odors, and mold. Unfortunately, in a home that has been inundated with a bad odor for a long period of time, it may be very difficult to get rid of that smell.

When you are looking at a property from the investment standpoint, it is critical that you ask yourself about the marketability of that property either for sale or for rent if it is to be a long-term investment.

Porches, Decks, Patios and Exterior Entryways

If properties have decks, porches, patios, or exterior entryways, make sure that you check them out for looks, accessibility, and usability. In some areas around the country, it will be critical that you have disabled access for certain properties, especially commercial-type buildings needing access for the public.

Are all stairs, guard rails, and handrails adequate and secure? Do the guard rails provide enough security? Are there any unsafe areas for children? Are the decks, porches, or patios large enough that they actually add value to the property? Are the surfaces of these areas finished properly and well cared for? Are all of the floors level? Does there appear to be any water damage, rotting, or other problems? If any of these areas are screened, make sure the day screens are in good shape—no rips, tears, or pulling away at the seams or edges. Replacing large areas of screening can become expensive if you are not capable of doing the labor yourself.

If any of the areas are glass, is the glass in good shape with no breakage or discoloration? Is the roofing or other overhead covering in good shape? Are the built-ins such as barbecues or bars in good shape, and are all the sinks and equipment operating properly? Are all locks, latches, doors and cabinets in good working order?

Garage

Garages are often overlooked when people are inspecting properties, but they can be very important when it comes to owning the property on a long-term basis. Is the garage large enough to meet the needs of the average user of that type of property? Is it well lighted when the doors are open and closed? Is the floor in good shape and not damaged, marred, stained, or discolored? How bad are the oil spots on the garage floor? Are the doors and windows secure, working properly, locking adequately, and operating smoothly? Are all cabinets or drawers operating correctly? Are all benches and work shelves secure? Are all fans or ventilation systems working properly? Does all overhead storage offer adequate access, and are the areas secure? Is there adequate space for garden or power tools?

Do all electrical outlets and switches work properly? Do the main garage doors open and close easily? Are all hinges, springs, and mechanical parts in good working condition? Is there an electric garage door opener, and does it work properly? If the laundry area is in the garage, is it accessible even when cars are parked inside? If the water heater, water softener, or other appliances are located in the garage, are they out of the way, secure and pose no hazard?

Pools and Spas

It is advisable always to have a professional check out the pools and spas before you make an offer on an investment property. Pumps, heating units, cleaners, skimmers, hoses, and drains can become very costly when they need repair or need to be replaced.

Has the pool or spa been professionally serviced or owner maintained? Is it clean with no discoloration, mildew, or mold? Is the water clear and clean? Does the water appear to have the proper chemical balance? Are there any bugs in the water? Are there any algae near the waterline or on the sides or bottom of the pool or spa? Is there any chipping or peeling of paint, stucco or fiberglass in and around pool areas?

Are all pumps, heating units, cleaners, skimmers, hoses, and drains working properly? Are all ladders, steps, slides, diving boards, nets, and ropes in good shape? Does the water spray on the water slides properly?

Is there safety equipment, will it stay with the property, and is it all accessible and in good working order? Are all gates, fences, and locks around the pool in good shape? Are all safety signs visible? Does all lighting work properly?

Is the pool or deck furniture that stays with the property in good shape? Is the decking in good shape with no cracking, chipping, or peeling? Are all walkways around and to and from the pool in good shape?

Saunas and Steam Rooms

Do all heating units work properly? Are the benches in good shape with no splinters or nails? Does the unit seal tightly? Does the timer work properly? Does the unit steam as it should?

Structure Exteriors

The exterior of all structures should be inspected as closely as the interior. Many problem areas will be visible, even to the untrained eye. Check the exterior walls for any cracks or holes in the stucco, wood, or other finish. Is the overall paint or finish in good shape? Any peeling, chipping, or major discoloration from the middle portion of the walls upward might indicate leaking. Is there any excessive water splash or discoloration near the ground?

Are all gutters and downspouts in good repair and cleaned out? Use a water hose to run the water into the gutters to check for proper drainage. Are any of the eaves peeling, chipping or molding? Are any of the corners of the building chipped or broken away? Are all of the window frames properly caulked and sealed?

Are there any cracks in the foundation? Is the foundation painted or sealed properly? Is there a crawl space under the house and if so, is it accessible? Is the crawl space access screened or closed? Are ventilation openings both under the eaves and beneath the house open and screened?

Are there any wooden structures attached to or leaning against the main structure of the property that might promote termites or other infestation? Are any bushes, hedges, trees, or plants situated so as to rub or push against the exterior of the structures? For security purposes, is all shrubbery trimmed back from the windows and doors? Are all exterior doors, including the garage door, painted or finished properly?

Roof

As an investor, in most cases, you will not get up on the roof to check that portion of the property. For the most part, if the roof is not safely accessible, have a professional roof inspection done if you think it is necessary. If the roof is pitched, not flat, you will be able to see most of it simply by standing back and using binoculars.

Are any tiles, shakes, or pieces missing or out of place? Are there any holes or worn places? Is all caulking in good shape at the edges of the tile or composition and around any pipes or fire places? Are there any trees, limbs, or bushes scraping against the roof?

Are there any major areas of stain or discoloration possibly left by standing water? Are there any low areas or sections that appear to be sagging? Are there any antennas or satellite dishes that appear to be causing damage to the roof? Are there any other wires connected to the eaves or roof that could create leakage or other damage?

Yards

Yards are another area that are often overlooked but should be very important to the investor because they often will be a major factor for a renter or buyer of your property.

Are the bushes, trees, and hedges all cared for and in good shape? If there is a sprinkler system, does it work properly? Make sure that you check every sprinkler. Are the sprinklers set low enough to allow easy upkeep of the lawn? Is the lawn healthy? Are all the plants and trees healthy? Do all the plants stay with the property?

Are the yards generally set up for easy upkeep? Are all fences in good repair, well painted and secure? Do all gates operate properly, and latches work well, and are all locks secure? Is there any chipping, peeling, or major discoloration on the fences? Are all driveways in good shape and free of major stains? Are all walkways in good repair? Are RV or special parking areas maintained and in good shape? Are all of the special play or animal areas in good shape?

Warranties and Guarantees

When you're inspecting a property, make sure that you ask the owner for all copies of any warranties or guarantees on any appliance, work, or repair that will remain in effect and pass with the sale of the property. An example would be a roof. Some roof guarantees are as long as 50 years.

What Repairs Must Be Made?

If an appraisal is completed either at the buyer's or lender's request, the appraiser may list certain repairs that must be made before the transaction can close. Also, the appraiser may request that certain professional inspections be made before a loan will be approved. Those inspections usually include roof and termite inspections, or even a complete home inspection.

For you as a professional investor, it is important that you recognize as many problem areas with the property as possible. All of those repairs or areas that will require work can be used as ammunition when you're preparing your offer on the property. It never hurts to ask the seller to make the repairs; however, many times you can make a much better deal on the property by identifying all of the problem areas and then offering to make the repairs or do the work yourself. Later in the book, we discuss the best ways to prepare your offers to purchase so as to create the most positive opportunity for you to obtain the property.

Sweat Equity

Many investors have the expertise and will want to make necessary repairs themselves. In those cases, even when a loan is being put in place, the investor will ask the seller to take a specific dollar allowance off of the property's sale price as an offset for the work that needs to be done. If there is a loan involved, usually the lender will allow the transaction to close and allow the buyers a certain period of time to complete the repair. After the work has been done, the lender will have the opportunity to inspect and approve the work.

As an example, if an appraiser called for a wall in a bathroom to be repaired, due to water damage, and an estimate for the work was given at $1,500, the investor or buyer could offer to do the work and ask the lender to allow a $1,500 deduction on the down payment for the property for the "sweat equity" work that was being done. Even with government loans such as FHA and VA, this type of sweat equity option may be available.

Understanding Seller Disclosure

As an investor it is important to understand the responsibility of sellers to disclose to potential buyers any defects about which the sellers are aware, prior to the sale of property. Since the mid-1980s, many states have made it mandatory for sellers to disclose to buyers any existing problems or defects. Prior to that time it was pretty much the buyers' responsibility to discover on their own any defects that might exist on a property. The Latin phrase caveat emptor (buyer beware) wasn't much more applicable than in real estate transactions. It should be understood that sellers can choose to sell a property in any condition as long as they disclose any and all problems or defects that would affect the value of a property.

As of January 1, 2003, sellers in 36 states are required to complete a seller disclosure form or statement at the close of a real estate transaction. These forms cover everything from appliances to roofs, plumbing, flooring, and other structural defects. In some cases, they may even require disclosure with regard to a seller's knowledge of potential zoning changes, or new bonds or assessments that might affect the cost of living in the property or in the area. Other areas of disclosure that have become critical are environmental hazards such as lead, asbestos, and radon. Certain states require special testing for these and other hazards.

In states where seller disclosure is voluntary, not necessarily mandated by the courts or laws, it is still recommended that every seller disclose all problem areas. Losing a potential buyer is always better than making the sale and ending up in court.

 TERRY'S TIP: With regard to seller disclosure, it is important to remember that sellers are not guaranteeing anything and they are not agreeing to fix a specified problem; they are merely disclosing the problem area. How the problem will be addressed will be up to the agreement between the buyer and seller.

If you have questions with regard to required seller disclosure in your particular area, a reputable real estate broker can explain what is required. However, it is always best to check with a lawyer if you have specific questions. If you do not have access to an attorney or broker in whom you feel confident, call your State Department of Real Estate and they will be able to direct you to the proper source.

The Seller Disclosure Statement

An example of a seller disclosure statement appears in Appendix E. When completing the form, the seller should be very specific about any defect or problem areas. As an example, if a seller indicates that there is water damage beneath the house, the seller should indicate exactly where the problem exists, how extensive it is, and what has caused the problem.

Seller disclosure is critical in real estate transactions. You are looking to develop a good, long-term working relationship with buyers, sellers, renters, brokers, and other investors in your area and it is important to your success that you maintain a good reputation. Proper seller disclosure when you are selling property will help you to maintain that reputation.

Proper Inspections Can Save You a Bundle

It is critically important that you learn to inspect properties in a professional and comprehensive fashion. Many times you will purchase an investment property without using the services of a professional inspector, and it is incumbent upon you to be sure that you have made a concerted effort to see and know all of the problems that could crop up during your ownership of the property or during a sale, if you should decide to liquidate the property.

Having said that, I will tell you that when you do have questions about damage or problems with a property, and if you feel you are not competent to make a proper decision, *without question*, spend the time and the money to get a professional opinion. It could save you thousands of dollars.

13

Four Favorite Creative Low-Down or No-Down Investment Techniques for Any Market

Learning to Think Creatively

For many years in my seminars I have taught buyers and sellers creative methods that they can use to buy and sell properties. There has always been a certain amount of reticence and uncertainty to believe that low-down or no-down techniques can be used legally and ethically and provide win-win transactions for all parties involved. A few of the transactions that I have detailed previously in the book should give you some conception as to how these type of transactions can be structured, but every deal is different and you must learn to think and act creatively at all times. Remember, your primary objective is to solve the problems that the other parties to the transaction are facing, and, while doing so, put together a transaction that will work for you as an investor.

Many times, what seems ingenious to one person will seem like common sense to another. Let's face it—we all think differently. The old right-brain, left-brain dilemma is always in play, and no one person will ever have all the answers. However, it is important that you always try to "think outside the box," when you're trying to structure a creative real estate transaction.

Many real estate professionals, licensed brokers and agents, become mired in their thinking about how transactions should be structured. They get in the habit of expecting that every buyer must go get a new loan to cash out the equity for every seller in the market. That type of thinking is certainly flawed and prevents many, many transactions from being consummated. Creativity is simply finding as many acceptable ways to solve existing problems as possible.

After you have worked in the investment field for a period of time and you begin to creatively structure more and more transactions, you'll be amazed how many times you will hear someone say: "That's a great idea; I never thought of that." Granted, it takes time and practice to hone your skills, but you will be surprised at the countless number of methods that you will find to solve problems when the creative juices start flowing and you have successfully structured a few transactions.

Keep in mind what I said previously: Every transaction is different. That should mean to you that although bits and pieces of transactions may be the same, every ultimate solution will also be a little, or a lot, different. Therefore, you must never stop looking for new and creative ways to solve the problems that you will face every day as an investor.

Misunderstandings and Fallacies about No-Down or Low-Down Investing

1. *Creative financing and investing techniques are all illegal and unethical.* This is by far the most common and most flagrant misunderstanding

about all types of creative investing. What most people do not understand is that most multimillion-dollar transactions are done with some type of creative financing techniques. But, for the most part, buyers and sellers of smaller properties have become very stagnant in their thinking about the way that transactions can be structured.

Unfortunately, in the early and mid-1980s, many illegitimate and unethical methods were used to close transactions and they were called "creative financing," which in turn gave *all* creative techniques a bad name. You must always strive to keep your transactions on the up and up because one bad deal can cost you more than 10 good ones.

You will put together your own team of professionals with whom you will work on an ongoing basis. That group may include one or more attorneys, licensed real estate professionals, accountants, escrow officers, title people, appraisers, or any other individuals who will be able to assist you in building your own real estate portfolio. This group will also help you to keep your transactions ethical, principled, and legal.

2. *In a creative transaction, the seller never can cash out or receive any cash.* As you have seen with examples discussed previously in this book, this is simply not true. If a seller agrees to carry a note out of the sale of property, that does not necessarily mean that the seller will not receive any cash. Later in this chapter, you will learn that there are many ways to create cash for the seller that will still allow the buyer to purchase the property with no money out of pocket.

3. *The property must be distressed.* There are times when a property that needs cosmetic work will be a good investment opportunity. Sellers often allow properties to deteriorate for any number of reasons and many times do not want to take the time or make the effort to bring the property back up to standard. However, as often as you as an investor will have the opportunity to purchase a distressed property,

you will have the same number of opportunities to purchase properties that are in great condition.

This is not to say that the highest returns will not occur with distressed properties. They probably will. But, if you are an investor who does not have the expertise or does not want to spend the time working on properties, there will still be many opportunities for you to find successful investments.

4. Sellers must be penniless and destitute to accept a creative transaction. We have talked a great deal about solving problems for sellers who face foreclosures, have financial problems, or are involved in unusual situations. Some of the sellers with whom you will structure transactions will be down and out. However, many of the sellers who will be interested in carrying paper or in some other type of creative transaction will be very well off and simply will not need to cash out of the property immediately.

5. Creative techniques will not work with sellers who are inflexible or who need cash out of their property. This absolutely is not correct. Many times a seller will actually receive his or her equity out of the property when the transaction is closed. Again, that does not necessarily mean that the investor will have to put out-of-pocket cash into the transaction.

The Most Important Rule in Creative Investment! Learn it! Never Break It!

When you have completed this book, you will have been shown many techniques that you can use to buy and sell creatively. How you apply those techniques will be up to your own discretion. Many times, you will be able to buy with little or no money down. However, it is my sincere hope that you will always follow one rule that I personally *never* break, and that I encourage my students to *never* break, when buying investment property: *You must have equity in every property that you buy, of at least 5 to 10 percent or more, the day that you close the escrow and you must never encumber that property above 90 to 95 percent of its value.*

Most no-down or low-down gurus who have heard me say that over the past 25 years have scoffed at my rather conservative concept. They say that if a property supports itself, providing a positive or small negative cash flow and you can obtain the property for no cash out of pocket, why not buy it and hope that the appreciation will catch up and build equity?

My answer to that argument is simple: I have seen too many people get into properties way over their heads, not be unable to make the payments if a vacancy occurred and couldn't be filled immediately, not be able to sell the property because it was overencumbered (they owed more than the property was worth), and ultimately end up in foreclosure or even bankruptcy.

Appreciation has occurred on real estate, on a long-term basis, without fail. But, if the early 1980s taught us anything, it is this: *A great market can turn into a terrible, devastating market practically overnight. If that occurs and you have not bought wisely, maintained equity positions in every property that you own, and cannot support the properties for a reasonable vacancy period, you may lose it all.*

This is not said to frighten you or to take anything away from real estate and the tremendous advantages that it offers as an investment. But you must be aware of the increased risk that you incur when you purchase a property and it is overencumbered or you have no equity position. *If you always buy right, even with little or no money down or cash out of pocket, you will have equity from day one that you own the property.*

Four Favorite Low-Down, No-Down Techniques

Throughout the years I have found that the easiest way for new investors to understand methods by which you can buy and sell property creatively is to have the opportunity to see and clearly understand actual transactions that have occurred. Many of the following methods are those that we have used for several years and some are those that have been shared by our students, escrow officers, and other creative investors with whom we work.

Favorite No. 1: The Quick Fix: to Rent, Own, or Sell

Distressed properties are always a prime focus of investors. This type of property offers an opportunity for quick financial returns and in many cases provides investors the ability to generate ongoing income, as well as long-term wealth building. However, there will be times when you will purchase a property with the full intention of making the necessary repairs and ultimately, when the work is completed, decide to keep the property for rental income and appreciation growth.

It is almost always our recommendation, if possible, that you hang onto properties that you purchase and refurbish as long as you can, up to the point of diminishing returns. If a property does not stay rented or requires a great deal of time or effort, that is usually the time to liquidate the property.

The following is a good example of the quick fix technique. Mike, a former bank employee, had pooled all of his resources to be able to purchase the controlling share of a small plywood mill in southern Oregon. Mike was able to put together a deal that would mean that he would have to run the mill successfully for one to two years before he could sell the business and recover the nearly $350,000 that he had invested in the purchase. The upside was that he would nearly quadruple his money if all went as planned.

A student in our seminars for many years, Mike said that this was the biggest risk that he had ever taken in that he had really "put all of his eggs in one basket." He later told us that it was probably not the smartest decision that he had ever made, but he really needed a change in his life and this certainly met that condition.

Because Mike had invested all of his money into the business, he had no cash to use for a down payment for a home to live in while he would be running the business. He was also taking only a small salary out of the business and could not qualify for a standard bank loan. However, after about three months, he was very tired of the $700 per month apartment that he had rented and he began to search for property, specifically a distressed property, in which he could live and make repairs in his spare time.

After looking at about 30 properties, Mike found one that needed a considerable amount of cosmetic work, but that was structurally sound and was owned by a seller who appeared to be quite flexible with regard to terms. However, the seller did not want to do any work before she sold the property. The home, a two-bedroom, two-bath located on 5.5 acres was free and clear. The seller was asking $80,000 for the property, and she indicated that she wanted a minimum of $7,000 down to pay commissions and closing costs. She wanted a minimum of 6 percent interest on her note. She stated that she wanted a higher rate but didn't think that the market would support it. She also wanted a monthly income in payments from the property of at least $650, what she had been receiving in rent for the property.

When Mike presented his offer, he explained very carefully his intentions with regard to making all repairs and refurbishing the structures and the property, and that he would have the work done in no more than 12 months, at which time he could refinance or sell the property and provide a cash payment to the seller. It was important for the seller to understand Mike's intentions because he wanted her to fully comprehend that she would have very good security for her note on the property, since the improvements would increase the value. He included a short document he called a "statement of intended work to be completed," showing not only the intended work, but also the time frame within which each improvement would be made. He also pointed out that he was willing to give the seller the income that she wanted, and a higher interest rate than she expected, and allow her to share in the profit when the property resold.

The offer that the seller ultimately accepted had the following terms:

Sale price:	$70,500
Down payment:	$0
Interest rate:	8 percent
Monthly payments:	$650

Note all due and payable in 36 months or less

Buyer to pay all closing costs (seller would
   not have any closing costs)

Buyer also to receive an additional $5,000 when
   property was sold at no later than 7 years
   from date of original sale.

Mike then made a deal with a coworker who was looking to buy a property but could not do it on his own. Since the coworker could do carpentry work, Mike offered him a deal to share in 40 percent of the profit that would be realized from the property if he would move in, share the property with Mike, help do the refurbishing, and pay $500 per month in rent. He had the coworker pay first and last month's rent ($1,000), as security.

The closing costs on the sale were approximately $1,600, so Mike's out-of-pocket expenses were $600 to close the transaction and his monthly outlay for rent (mortgage payment) was reduced by $550 from what he had been paying. Over the next 12 months this is what transpired:

The house was painted inside and out:	$ 550
Wood floors were installed in two rooms: (Wood was acquired very cheap from a house that was raized.)	$ 650
New carpets were installed in two bedrooms: (Carpet acquired at a remnant sale.)	$ 400
New windows throughout house:	$1,300
Kitchen cabinets refinished:	$ 300
Two new exterior doors:	$ 500
Two small horse covers:	$1,200
One small hay barn:	$ 900
Fencing:	$ 400
Round pen for horse training:	$1,100
Total spent on improvements:	$7,300

Mike's saving for the year in rent was $6,600. Consequently, improvements were a total of $708 out of pocket. With closing costs and improvements, his total investment was only $1,308 above his normal rental expenses, or about $110 per month extra.

The property was placed on the market as a completely refurbished, ranchette horse property, sold for $113,500, and closed in less than a month. The following is a breakdown of payments to all parties:

Paid in payments to original seller:	$ 8,450
Pay off to original seller ($68,250 + $5,000 kicker from original contract):	$73,250
Total	$81,700
Mike's partner received ($113,500 sale price) − $73,250 (loan payoff) − $4,700 (closing costs) × 40%):	$14,220
Mike received ($113,500 − $73,250 − $4700 − 14,220):	$21,330

Mike's rate of return on his investment of $1,308 was a whopping 1,600 percent, which is not bad for a little part-time investment.

There are literally hundreds of ways to make quick fix methods work for you, but they do require that you are able to either make the improvements yourself or allow enough potential equity to be able to get the work done. The quick fix is not for everyone, but for those who are so inclined it is a great way to generate ongoing cash flow; if you can manage to hang onto a few of the properties, it can be a tremendous long-term wealth-building technique.

Favorite No. 2: Buying Properties with Multiple Parcels

Many potential new investors who attend our classes do not understand the concept of multiple parcels. Actually, it is a rather misunderstood topic area even for many real estate licensees. However, when an investor understands multiple parcel buying techniques, he or she can often buy property with no money down or even purchase property for no money down and receive cash back.

Every property in the United States, and in many other countries, has an assessor's parcel number. This number identifies each property for tax purposes. When you search properties through county records or through title companies, often you will find a property that appears to be one parcel that may actually be two or three separate parcels, being utilized as an undivided property. It is not uncommon in rural areas to find a home on one parcel and discover that the owner also owns three adjoining parcels.

When you find a property of interest that possibly includes additional parcels, there is often great potential to tie up those properties with a purchase contract, have an opportunity to find a buyer for one of the additional parcels, and use that buyer's money for the purchase of the primary property in which you are interested.

Let me give you an example. David found a property through a real estate broker that had been listed for quite some time. It was a newly constructed home that had not been finished due to the contractor going over budget and being unable to complete the project. The contractor had deeded the property back to the bank that was doing the construction financing, in lieu of foreclosure. The bank had loaned the contractor over $200,000 for the construction of the steel frame, three-bedroom, two-bath, 2,100 square-foot custom home and the home had sat unfinished for over a year.

Remember, when you are working with foreclosures or other properties that have been taken back by the bank; banks do not want to own property—they want to loan money, collect the interest, and get their money back. Consequently, many times they will liquidate a property for much less than they have invested, especially if they have had the property on the books for a long period of time.

When David ran the property profile, he found that the home had been built on one five-acre parcel and that the adjoining five-acre parcel had been owned by the same contractor and was included in the deed in lieu of foreclosure, deeding both properties back to the bank. David determined that the home and five acres, when completed, would be worth approximately $195,000 and the additional five-acre parcel was worth approximately $40,000.

When David viewed the property, he found that it was nearly completed and that the only work left on the property was to install the carpets, kitchen and bathroom flooring, a wood stove, and the gutters on the exterior of the house. When he presented his offer to the bank, he asked that those items be completed if he were to purchase the property and that he be deeded both five-acre parcels in the sale. His first offer was as follows:

Sale price:	$139,000
Down payment:	$ 25,000
Bank to carry first deed of trust for:	$114,000
Interest at going rate:	9 percent

Deed of trust securing the property to be placed
against only the five-acre parcel that included the
home. The other parcel was to be free and clear.

The bank's REO (which stands for real estate owned) officer returned
a counteroffer with the following terms that David accepted:

Sale price:	$169,000
Down payment:	$ 25,000
Bank to carry first deed of trust for:	$144,000
Interest:	9 percent

Bank to complete work on house, excluding the
wood stove installation.

Deed of trust only on individual five-acre parcel
that included the home, as requested.

David's closing costs would be approximately $3,500, and including
the down payment he needed approximately $28,500 to complete the
escrow that was slated to close in 60 days or less.

Armed with his accepted offer from the bank, David began to contact contractors in the area to see if he could find one who would be
interested in buying the additional five-acre parcel that was included
in his purchase. The third construction company that he contacted
indicated that they would be willing to purchase the 5 acre parcel for no
more than $30,000, but they would be willing to pay all closing costs.

David's escrow closed as follows:

The construction company buying the additional five-acre parcel
deposited $31,600 into the escrow. $1,600 of that amount was

for closing costs for that five-acre lot. The remaining $30,000 was credited to David.

Out of that $30,000, $28,500 was used for David's down payment ($25,000) and $3,500 for closing costs.

David received $1,500 at the close of escrow, out of which he used $900 to have the wood stove installed that the bank had declined to include in the work that they had done on the property.

By selling the additional five-acre parcel out of the original escrow (sometimes called a double escrow), David was able to close the transaction, own a nice country property, and put $600 in his pocket. Less than a year after the purchase of the property, the home and five acres were appraised at just over $270,000.

There are investors who concentrate on nothing but multiple-parcel properties. If you are fortunate enough to reside in or near a rural area where property divisions are, or have been, commonplace, there is a great deal of opportunity for you to find terrific deals with a little effort by searching the county records.

Favorite No. 3: Subject-to Transactions or Assumptions— In and Out in a Hurry

Primarily due to the many foreclosures and excessive losses in the mid-1980s and into the 1990s, banks and savings and loans began to include and/or enforce preclusions of buyers from automatic assumptions for mortgages and deeds of trust. Triggering devices such as due on sale clauses became commonplace and, for the first time, forced sales were beginning to be imposed on buyers who did not go through the process to properly assume a mortgage or deed of trust. In other words, even if a seller agreed to allow a buyer to assume, or take subject to, their deed of trust or mortgage, the bank could refuse the new buyer and force the loan to be paid off or a foreclosure could occur.

TERRY'S TIP: The difference between an assumption and a subject-to transaction is this: An assumption means that the buyer has fully assumed the responsibility for the payment and obligation of the deed of trust or mortgage and the original seller has no further obligation, whereas, in a subject-to transaction, the original buyer remains on the note and deed of trust and will, in a sense, remain obligated to the lender for the payment of the deed of trust or mortgage should the new buyer falter on that obligation.

Around the turn of the century and into the current market, banks and lending institutions have become less stringent with regard to the qualifications for real estate buyers. Also, assumptions and subject-to transactions have become more and more prevalent, even though almost all mortgages and deeds of trusts do include a due on sale clause.

Buyers and sellers need to be aware that although the use of assumptions and subject-to transactions has again become very prevalent, there is often no guarantee that a bank will not enforce a due on sale clause when a transfer of ownership occurs and the documentation is recorded. Some of the banks and lending institutions actually send out verification forms to the original buyer/borrowers each year, asking those buyer/borrowers to verify not only that they still own the property, but in some cases, that they still occupy the property as their primary residence. A buyer/borrower should *never* mislead a lender if he or she is asked to provide that type of verification.

Having said all that, and almost in the same breath, I will tell you that many, many great deals can be made by using existing financing, based on the information about lenders that I provided in the last example. Remember what I said: Lenders do not want to own property. They want to make loans, collect the interest, and eventually get their money back.

If you as a buyer make the payments and keep a loan current, there is a good chance that most lenders will not contact you, or the original borrower, for months, years, or ever. But, if lenders become aware that a transfer has occurred, they may ask that the new buyer qualify for a full assumption, pay the fees to obtain a new loan, and possibly adjust the interest rate to the current level. There is also the possibility that the new buyer may not qualify if he or she has had any credit problems.

If you are buying a property with the intent to turn it over quickly and during the short time of your ownership you keep the loan current, you may in fact never have contact with the lender until it comes time to pay the lender off out of your final sale of the property. But keep in mind that it is a risk that you and the seller take should the lender decide to call the note.

An example of how a subject-to transaction is as follows.

Karen had been renting a two-bedroom apartment in a four-plex located in Las Vegas, Nevada, and paying $1,000 per month rent. She was thinking of moving because the property had not been well maintained. After she attended one of our seminars, Karen decided that she would take a shot in the dark and contacted the owner of the property, asking if he would be interested in selling the property. The owner indicated that he hadn't really thought about selling because he had a positive cash flow of about $1,000 per month, but he knew he needed to do some work on the property and that he would consider an offer. He indicated to Karen that he thought the property was worth about $400,000 and that he owed approximately $250,000 on the first deed of trust. The payments on the property, including taxes and insurance, were $2,170 per month, including 7.25 percent interest, a very good rate for a rental property.

Karen knew all of the tenants and with their permission made a complete inspection of all of the units and determined that paint and a few minor repairs would correct most of the deferred maintenance that was needed in the seven-year-old property. She found out from the tenants that two of the units were rented for $750 and $800 per month and one unit was rented for the same as she paid, $1,000 per month. Two of the tenants had lived in the property since it was new. The total income from the rents was $3,550 and the vacancy rate had been nearly 0 percent for the past four years.

After running the comps, Karen determined that the property, in excellent condition and with rent increases for the two units that were quite below market, would be worth approximately $395,000 to $405,000, and if put on the market, would probably sell fairly quickly. Karen structured an offer to the seller that was accepted with the following terms:

Sale price:	$380,000
Down payment:	$ 5,000
Buyer to take existing loan in a subject-to transaction, accepting all responsibility for the obligation.	$241,600 remaining balance
Buyer to execute second deed of trust to seller for:	$133,400
Interest on second deed of trust:	8 percent
Second deed of trust all due and payable in three years or less	
Monthly payments on second deed of trust:	$ 1,300
Monthly payments total:	$ 3,470

The benefits of this transaction to the seller were:

Karen had been an excellent renter, always on time with rent, so the seller was comfortable that she would be timely on the payments and that she would handle the obligation for the existing deed of trust with the current lender, even if the lender called the note.

The seller was able to increase his income from $1,100 to $1,300 per month, so he was not concerned about the small down payment.

The seller did not have to worry about increasing the rents for the renters that were below market.

Most importantly, the seller was also relieved of the obligation for the maintenance and repairs that he knew would have to be done on the property within a short period of time.

The benefits to Karen were:

She was able to buy her first property for no money out of pocket. She took a cash advance on a low-interest (6.3 percent) credit card and paid all of the closing costs, down payment and cost of repairs ($10,900—minimum monthly payment of $112). Her total payments were $3,582 and her income was $3,000, reducing her monthly expenditures, because of the reduction from the rental rate that she was paying, by over $400.

Karen completed all of the work on the property in 30 days for less than $4,500, and she raised the rents on the two below-market units to $1,000, making all of the rents consistent with, but still slightly below ($10 to $15 per unit) the comparable rentals in the area.

After owning the property for eight months, Karen refinanced the first and second mortgages, obtaining a new loan for $375,000, 6.6 percent interest, and payments of $3,008 for principal, interest, taxes, and insurance. The rents from the three other units paid the entire payment and Karen had $0 rent and mortgage payment.

Due to the allowable write-off, Karen had a tremendous reduction in her tax liability, creating a sizable tax return (instead of the near break-even that she had in the past), which she used to buy another rental property.

If a seller accepts an offer whereby the buyer asks that they can take a note in a subject-to transaction, it is imperative that the seller remain aware of the status of the loan, since the primary responsibility for the payment of that loan is still in the name of the original seller. Therefore, it is suggested that the seller require that the buyer provide the seller with a copy of each canceled monthly payment check, showing that the payments on the note are current.

Buying property using existing financing on a property is commonplace, especially for short-term situations where the buyer will either refinance or sell a property in a short period of time and can be a very lucrative method for low-down or no-down opportunities.

Favorite No. 4: Broker/Agent Participation

You may recall in an earlier chapter, I told you of the lady in Albuquerque, New Mexico, who allowed a real estate broker to participate in a transaction and fund the substantial repairs that were required on a property before it could be resold. You also may remember that the way the transaction was structured, the buyer was able to create some cash for herself out of that financial participation from the broker. That type of joint venture/partner participation can, of course, occur with anyone with whom you might feel comfortable working for a period of time and with whom you are willing to share some of the profits from the venture.

However, because real estate and mortgage brokers are very much in tune with the industry, it is often easier to get them to participate in a deal that you might put together. If a person has not previously been involved in real estate transactions, he or she may be reticent to take part in a venture.

After you have completed a few transactions in your own area, it will be very easy for you to utilize your track record to attract other investor/partners for at least the short-term, quick-return opportunities. However, when starting out, the potential investor/partners will be more interested in the deal, and how solid it looks to them, rather than you personally. Make sure that any time you approach a potential investor/partner that you have all the information that person will need to make an intelligent decision. An example of a typical broker participation deal follows.

In October, while working on his sailboat at the marina on Lake Huron, Alec, a young accountant, was told by one of his dock neighbors that they were selling their boat and moving to Florida in about 30 days. They indicated that they both had new jobs starting in about five weeks.

After the typical conversation about the benefits of the warmer climates, Alec asked if they were going to keep their home in Michigan. They advised him that they were planning on selling, but that they didn't think it was the best time of year and that they needed to do quite bit of sprucing up before it could go on the market. They thought that they would try to rent the property and come back several weekends in the spring, get the work done, and put the home on the market.

Alec proposed that he might be interested in buying the property, as is, and asked if they would consider a no-down payment offer. They emphatically said no. Alec said that he might still be interested and set a time to see the property. As Alec explained it,

> This was the most disgustingly filthy house I have ever seen. The family had several cats, all living in the house and with only one massive litter box that hadn't been cleaned for days, so the odor was horrid.
>
> Most of the rooms were so jam-packed with old furniture and stacks of dolls (they were collectors) that there was practically no way to walk through the house. The wife had been trying to get an Internet sales business going, so she had hundreds of empty boxes (supposedly for shipping of potential sales) stacked in every corner of

every room, and the cobwebs throughout the home gave the feeling that you were in a Halloween haunted house. Also, the two-car garage was so full, floor to ceiling, with the same type of clutter that filled the home, that the front garage door would only open halfway.

I wanted to run out of there but I stayed cool, trying to remember the financial potential that might exist. The sellers just kept saying things like, "we will probably throw away half of what is in this house, we are just so far behind on getting things done. We don't have any idea how to haul all of this stuff off. We might be better off to just leave it and let someone else clean up the property, and we have no idea how we are going to get this place rented and get out of here in three weeks."

As bad as the filth was, I clearly could see that the basic house was in good shape and a professional cleaning, paint, and massive yard work would produce a great rental or resale property.

Most importantly, Alec realized that these people had a *major* problem—they needed to be in Florida in five weeks and the way they were going, they were looking at six months of cleanup and garbage disposal on their property and were starting to reach a significant level of panic. Alec put the comps together and found that the home should sell for a price around $84,000. He was amazed to discover that the property was free and clear, with no loans of any kind. The sellers were adamant that they *must* cash out so they would have money to buy in Florida.

Alec first called a garbage company and determined what it would cost to place a large dumpster at the property. He then called every necessary trade worker that it would take to fumigate, paint, and clean the property. He determined that with no major glitches, the work could be done in a week or two with the occupants out of the way. Alec also called a commercial general cleanup, remodeling and repair firm that did all of that type of work in Detroit and got an estimate to have all of the necessary work completed. They quoted just over $18,000.

His offer, term as follows, solved a lot of problems for the sellers:

Sale price: $60,100 as is, all cash

Close of escrow: 15 days

Buyer to pay all closing costs $ 1,700 (approximate)

Sellers may occupy property for 30 additional days with no rent

Dumpster(s) to be delivered immediately to property at buyer's expense

Anything remaining in property would be disposed of by buyer

Buyer to advertise and refer calls for seller's boat to the seller at no cost to seller, for a maximum of 60 days or until the boat sold

In the presentation, the buyer pointed out the following positive aspects of his offer:

1. The sellers would receive all cash and would not have to carry paper.
2. The escrow would close in a short period of time and the sellers could stay in the property with no rent until they left for Florida.
3. The buyer would provide the availability of dumpsters for the sellers to be able to clean out their property.
4. Anything that the sellers did not want to move could be left for the buyer to dispose of.
5. The sellers were looking at repairs and cleanup costs of as high as $18,000.
6. If the sellers were to market and sell their property through a full-service real estate broker, it would cost them approximately $5,000 for commission.
7. The seller's normal closing costs would have been approximately $1,400.
8. Assuming the sellers could bring the property up to standard and sell at market value for $84,000, after deducting the repair and

cleanup, commission, and closing costs, they would be left with only approximately $61,000.

9. This buyer's offer netted the seller nearly the same amount plus the sellers could get to Florida in a timely fashion, not have to worry about doing all of the work, and they would have assistance in getting their boat sold.

The sellers accepted Alec's offer. Alec then went to a local mortgage broker who had done the financing on Alec's own residence and offered that broker a partnership on the property if the broker could arrange for quick financing to pay off the sellers. The mortgage broker arranged for the money to cash out the sellers equity and make the required repairs and cleanup necessary to put the property back on the market.

Ninety-four days from the original close of escrow, the property was resold and closed the second escrow at a sale price of $83,000. The cleanup and refurbishing of the property ended up costing approximately $6,400 and Alec indicated that he himself had put approximately 25 hours of work into the effort. The sales fees and closing costs on the resale of the property were approximately $4,200. After all fees and expenses Alec, and his broker/partner netted just over $12,800 out of which Alec received 60 percent, just over $7,600. His partner received $5,120.

Alec's only investment was the original $500 deposit, so his return on investment was astronomical. The broker/partner had borrowed the $70,000 for four months at 7 percent interest, putting up none of his own money except the payments each month for four months ($1,633 total), and his net return was $3,490, over 100 percent return on investment. The broker estimated that his total time investment was less than three hours for the entire transaction.

This win-win transaction benefited all parties and provided a small chunk of income for both the buyer and the broker. As an aside, Alec did find a buyer for the original seller's boat and the seller sent Alec an additional $300 finder's fee.

Second Nature Creativity

Each of the transactions detailed above illustrates a certain amount of creativity. However, what is not immediately obvious is the second-nature actions and responses that each of these investors exhibited during the negotiations and throughout the transactions.

I have said for many years that practice does not make perfect—instead, perfect practice makes perfect. You must learn the negotiation process and then you must practice, again and again, to become good at it. You will make mistakes. When you do, learn from them and move on. What ever you do, do not dwell on the deals that you don't get. If you only close 2 to 3 percent of the dozens of potentials that you find, you most probably will be far wealthier than you ever imagined possible.

14

Six More Creative, Seller Participation Low-Down or No-Down Investment Techniques

Every Day Is Different—But Every Deal Is the Same

The more transactions you close, the more you will discover that although every one of those transactions is different, in a sense, every one is the same. Each individual transaction involves you as the investor, the seller (for whom you are probably solving some kind of problem), and possibly other parties who are going to help provide financing and all of the other necessities such as escrow and title. It is pretty much that simple, and nearly every transaction will have that list of players.

Surprisingly, it is in the negotiation process where the transactions actually become more complex. That is why it is critically important for you to be able to quickly analyze the problems as they exist, put together several feasible ways that the problems can be solved, and help sellers to understand that, one way or the other, you will be able to help them overcome whatever difficulty that they face by selling their property to you, on your terms.

At the very beginning of the book, I spoke about how critical it is to establish an immediate, good relationship with sellers and to put in place a trust level that will carry you through the transaction. Now, as you have begun to see the actual ways that you can structure transactions, you are probably starting to comprehend why that trust and those relationships are so important. In many cases, you are asking sellers to sell their property in a way that they never imagined and certainly has never been presented to them. Remember, for most people, anything out of the ordinary is a little scary.

Favorite No. 5: Short-Term Seller Desiring High, Above-Market Interest

In some cases, sellers have a near obsession for high interest rates, even when those rates are only earned for a short period of time. In many situations, a lower price offer will be accepted if sellers are offered a high rate of interest on the financing that they provide. For a buyer in a planned short-term purchase and resale transaction, high interest is not necessarily a bad situation, as evidenced by the following example.

Johl was interested in purchasing a four-unit office building in an area that was consistent with that type of property. All four units in the building were rented on a month-to-month basis; however, three of the units, occupied by the same tenant, were going to be vacated within 30 days. Originally, Johl had contacted the owner looking for an office to rent. After a short discussion, the owner made it clear that he was exceedingly tired of managing the property, doing the yard work, and collecting rents. Johl indicated that he might be interested in purchasing the property.

Prior to the inspection Johl had run the comparable sales, determined what the comparable rents were in the area, and calculated the approximate value of the property, using the income analysis approach.

Johl found that the rents in the area were approximately $0.25 to $0.40 per square foot higher than the property he was looking to purchase. The calculations on the 3,000-square-foot building showed that the property should generate $750 to $1,200 more per month than the $4,200 that it was producing at the current time.

During the inspection, Johl found the property to be in only fair shape and while he and the current owner were going through the offices, the renters that were moving out at the end of the month were detailing all of the things that needed to be fixed before a new tenant could occupy the property. Although most of the complaints were cosmetic repairs, the seller, a 64-year-old retired teacher, was obviously becoming more and more distressed at the thought of the work that was going to be required. He also was not pleased at the prospect of having to rerent the three units. To top it all off, the renter in the fourth unit advised the seller, in Johl's presence, that they, too, were going to be leaving the building within a couple of months. Johl was wise enough to see that the seller had gone from being somewhat motivated to sell, to *extremely* motivated to sell.

When they finished the inspection, Johl went over each item of repair with the seller and together they established a cost that they both agreed was reasonable to get the work done. Johl never indicated that he himself might do the work and save a great deal of the cost if they were able to put a transaction together. All of the refurbishing costs were calculated at the standard rates charged by painters and contract people in the area, and the total was approximately $17,000.

The seller indicated that he had an existing loan on the property of approximately $188,300, with interest a little over 8 percent and payments around $1,500 per month. He further stated that he was netting approximately $2,000 per month out of the property and that he needed that income to supplement his retirement. He also indicated that he felt the property was worth at least $400,000.

Johl asked the seller what kind of an allowance he was willing to make if a buyer would take the property as is and would take the responsibility for getting all four units rerented. The seller responded, "No more than $20,000."

Johl's first offer contained the following terms:

Sale price:	$350,270
Down payment:	$ 4,000
Buyer and seller to pay normal closing costs (approximately $1,000 each)	
Buyer to assume or take in a subject-to transaction the existing first deed of trust in the amount of:	$180,250
Seller to carry a second deed of trust in the amount of:	$166,020
Including interest of:	9 percent
With monthly payments of:	$ 2,000
All due and payable in five years or less	

Johl fully expected the seller to counter his offer and raise the price, but to his surprise the only change that the seller wanted was a higher interest rate on the note that he was carrying. As outlandish as it sounded, the seller asked for 16 percent interest, which would mean that, with the payments remaining at $2,000 per month, the loan balance would be increasing by over $200 per month. Johl calculated that if he were to keep this note in place for two years the remaining balance would increase to approximately $172,015. However, Johl's intention was to make repairs on the property as quickly as possible, fill the vacancies in the building at the higher rental rates, and resell the unit, so he accepted the seller's rather unreasonable request for 16 percent interest on the note that the seller would carry.

Approximately six months after the sale, after the repairs were made and all of the units were rented at approximately $1.75 per square foot, a total of $5,200 per month, Johl received an offer on the property from another investor for $475,000, which he accepted. The final balance sheet on the deal was as follows:

Sale price:	$475,000
First loan payoff:	$178,300
Second loan payoff:	$167,345
Sale commission and closing costs for sale:	$ 16,255
Johl's credit line payoff (detail below):	$ 22,350
Total:	$384,250

$475,000 (sale price) − $384,250 (All Costs) =
   $90,750 profit to Johl

Cash Outlay from Credit Line

Down payment:	$ 4,000
Repairs:	$ 9,300
Payment (property vacant):	$ 7,400
Closing costs (first closing):	$ 1,100
Credit line interest:	$ 550
Total:	$22,350

As you can see, the investor did very well and once again, took no money out of his pocket due to the availability of his credit line. Even if the $22,350 had come out of his pocket, Johl's return would still have been over 300 percent for a six-month investment and about 60 hours work.

Favorite No. 6: Seller-Carry Note Sold for Cash

Sometimes you will find sellers who want cash out of their property, but they are willing to carry a note for a short period of time until the note can be liquidated and they can receive the cash they require. In other situations, if sellers must have the cash when the transaction closes, it will be incumbent upon you to find a buyer for the note (mortgage or deed of trust), and the purchase of the note will occur out of the original escrow.

Notes for either primary or secondary financing, secured by a mortgage or deed of trust, are often easy to sell to investors. If the property is good security and the loan-to-value ratio is not unreasonable, many investors are looking to buy those notes. However, most investors will want to discount the amount that they will pay for a note anywhere from 5 to 50 percent, depending on the terms of the note. If it is a long-term note with a low interest rate, the discount will be much higher. Conversely, if it is a short-term note with higher interest and still secured by a good property, the discount will be much lower.

This type of transaction can be used when a seller needs some or all of his or her cash out of the sale of their property. This method can also be used to reduce the price of a property if a seller is caught up with receiving a certain sale price, but is willing to sell the note that he or she carries at a discount. The following example better explains why a seller would be thinking in those terms.

Dan received a call on one of his buyer ads in the local newspaper. The caller indicated that he had a residential six-plex that he was interested in selling, but he made it clear that he needed to cash out quickly. He indicated that the property was in good shape, and fully rented and that the only deferred maintenance that might be somewhat expensive was a roof that needed to be replaced on the detached, six-car carport. He further indicated that he was not interested in carrying any paper on the sale and that he did not want a low-ball offer.

Dan met the owner, inspected the property, completed his seller interview and determined the following:

1. The seller had a pending IRS bill for back taxes for $65,000 that needed to be handled immediately and a second mortgage on the

property that was two months late on the balloon payment pay-off of $47,600.

2. The seller needed about $113,000, but he had approximately $173,000 in equity in the property.

3. The seller owned two other similar properties in the same area, and he did not want a low sale price on this property that would push comparables down and possibly adversely affect the value of his other rentals, both of which he planned to sell or trade within that year.

4. As indicated by the seller, the roof on the carport not only needed to be replaced, but was nearly nonexistent and had been tagged by the county building inspector. The repair cost was estimated to be $5,500.

5. The rest of the property was in good shape and did not need much, if any, repair work.

6. All of the units were rented on a month-to-month basis and the rents appeared to be within about 10 percent of the market.

7. The seller was extremely motivated and needed to see an offer and a close as quickly as possible. He did not have time to make the repairs, and list and sell the property—he needed to move quickly to prevent his problems from getting worse than they already were.

Using the income analysis and the comparable sales methods, Dan calculated the value of the property to be in the range of $390,000 to $400,000, and he felt that there was only a little room for rent increases, about $30 per unit maximum. Total rent and income from property was $4,150 per month. Expenses, insurance, and taxes were approximately $760 per month.

The existing notes on the property were a first mortgage for $177,100 at 7.5 percent interest payable at $1,309 per month, a second mortgage that was to be paid off out of the sale of the property, and a third mortgage for $44,600 at 6 percent with payments of $213 per month. After three counteroffers, the following are the terms that seller accepted:

Sale price:	$395,000
Down payment:	$ 2,000
Buyer to take first mortgage in a subject-to transaction:	$177,100
Seller to carry back second mortgage (payments of $1,153 per month at 8 percent interest, due in 5 years):	$173,000
Buyer to assume third mortgage:	$ 42,600
Seller to pay all closing costs:	$ 2,200

Buyer to purchase or in some way cash out the second mortgage at close of escrow, at a 30 percent discount ($51,900) for $121,100

Seller to rebate to buyer $2,000 at close of note liquidation

Buyer to take property as is and take responsibility for roof repair

The buyer sold the second mortgage out of the escrow, which means that he found a buyer for the note at a 25 percent discount, which left 5 percent of the discount agreed to by the seller, to go to the buyer ($8,650). Because the original second mortgage was paid off, the third would have normally moved to second position in the order of title recording and priority of payment. However, because Dan needed someone to purchase the new second that was being created out of the sale, he negotiated with the holder of the third to subordinate to the second and remain in third position. For that accommodation, Dan agreed to pay the third note holder $2,000. Had Dan left the new second to fall third in priority of payment, the discount would have had to be 50 percent or more to be able to liquidate the note.

Are you feeling just a little confused? Well, don't be. A quick and simple overview of the whole deal should make things clearer.

The seller got what he wanted: The property sold for near market value, creating and maintaining the comparable value for his other two buildings, which were sold within a few months for prices above the sale price of the first sale, and he received a little more cash out of the sale than he needed—even after rebating $2,000 to Dan out of the sale of the note, solving the immediate financial problems that he was facing ($121,100 − $2,000 to Dan − $2,200 closing costs = $116,900 net to seller).

Now think about that for a minute: If you add the first and third mortgages that were assumed by the buyer, the net cash that was received by the seller, and the normal closing costs that the seller paid, it totals $338,800. If the market value of the property was $390,000, the seller actually discounted the sale price by *only* about 13.13 percent. To achieve a quick sale, closing in only 12 days, that's not too bad!

The person who purchased the note out of the escrow paid $129,750 for a note worth $173,000. With a 25 percent discount, the rate of return on the investment was over 10.7 percent per annum, about twice what the money would have earned in a savings account.

What about the investor, Dan? He had three mortgages to pay, a roof to put on, and only five years before a big balloon payment came due on the second mortgage, right? Wasn't that a bad deal for him? To the contrary, he really made a nice deal for himself. Out of the sale of the note (remember, he got to keep 5 percent of the discount), Dan pocketed $8,650. After the seller rebated his down payment to him of $2,000, he had a total of $10,650. He paid for the roof on the carport and a few other minor repairs and ended up with $4,000 in his pocket.

He raised each of the rents $20, increasing the income on the property to $4,270. The payments, taxes, and expenses on the property were a total of $3,435 per month, leaving Dan with a positive cash flow of $835 per month. When the balloon payment on the second mortgage comes due, Dan can either refinance the property or sell it. If appreciation is only 5 percent per year for the five-year period, the property will be worth approximately $510,000.

What Made This Deal Work?

1. The seller had several problems but was flexible as to how they might be solved. However, he needed a quick sale and some cash to resolve his immediate problems.
2. The seller had two other comparable properties; he needed to protect the value of those properties and could not just reduce the price and quickly sell the property that Dan wanted.
3. The buyer was creative, acted quickly, and found the buyer for the second mortgage that provided all of the cash that was needed to close the transaction and make the repairs on the property.

Remember, win-win for all parties is the key to successful investing. This transaction was obviously good for all parties, but the key is finding that seller who has even a little problem that you can help solve.

Favorite No. 7: Low Price, High Appraisal, and Refinance

This technique is very simple. You must find a seller who is willing to sell at a price that is at least 20 to 25 percent below the going market rate on comparable properties. Don't say to yourself, "It just won't happen in today's market," because it happens every day, many times across the country. Like the old cliché says, "You will never get, if you do not ask." Too many investors, new to the business, are simply afraid to make low-ball offers and take a shot at getting a super deal on a piece of property.

The following example details a property that was purchased with this technique and in a terrific seller's market where you would never imagine that a deal like this could be made.

One Saturday afternoon I stopped at a yard sale at a property located in a tract of very consistent, three- and four-bedroom, 20- to 25-year-old homes. I actually had seen, on one of the tables, an old Victrola record player and thought it might be worth something as an antique. The lady who was holding the open house immediately told me that she had been asked to move by the property owner because the owner was going to refurbish the house and sell it. I told the lady that I bought properties and asked if it would be possible to take a look at the house. The lady was very gracious, letting me view the entire home and backyard.

The property was in rather poor condition, but almost all of the work was cosmetic. Nearly every wall in the home had been wallpapered at one time or another, and the wallpaper was peeling off in every room. The acoustic blown ceilings were nearly all covered with dirt and grime, refrigerator and freestanding range both appeared to be about 20 years old and on their last legs, as did the water heater in the garage. The garage door opener was inoperative, and several windows in the home were cracked. There were no screens on any of the windows. The linoleum in the kitchen and one bathroom needed to be replaced, but the only apparent structural damage appeared to be the subfloor underneath a claw-foot bathtub in the master bathroom.

The renter advised me that she had been paying only $650 rent for five and a half years, with no increase. She said that she hated to move because almost all of the rents in the area were upwards of $850 per month. She also gave me the owner's name, address, and telephone number.

After purchasing the Victrola, I cruised around the neighborhood and decided that it appeared that there were a fairly high number of rentals in the area; however, there were only two properties listed for sale in about an eight-block surrounding area, one for $139,500, listed for two weeks, and one for $149,000 that had been on the market for over 6 months. I called a couple of real estate brokers and asked what they thought the rents were running in that area. Both brokers advised me that the rents for a standard three-bedroom two-bath home should be around $1,000 to $1,100 per month for a property in good condition.

I ran the comparable sales and determined that the property, in good condition, would be worth approximately $130,000 to $135,000. However, there were two recent comps (90 days) that were in the range of $90,000. Ownership information showed that those two properties had been purchased by the same buyer and when I drove by those properties, it was obvious that they had just been completely refurbished.

When I contacted the owner by telephone, I was able to find out that the lady was interested in selling the property because she wanted to do some traveling, she had some physical problems, she did not want to carry paper, she felt that the property needed a lot of work, and the existing financing on the property was an old FHA loan with a balance of about $22,100 at 8½ percent, payable at about $515 per month, principal, interest, taxes and insurance.

Armed with the property inspection form detailing every specific item of work required on the property, the cost analysis of property reconditioning (Appendix F), and the printout of the two comps at $90,000, I met with the seller. After a few minutes I had discovered that the seller was a retired real estate broker, in poor physical condition, quite distraught at the thought of having to get all of the work done on the rental property, and absolutely ready to make a deal.

Normally, I would have only gathered information at the first meeting; however, there are times when you must act quickly if you find a deal that is ready to be made. I was ready, willing, and able to offer the seller $90,000 for the property, but instead I handed the seller the comp sheet and the cost analysis and said, "You've been in the business, you know the time and money that it is going to take to refurbish this property. What do you think would be a good price for both of us?"

She obviously had thought about it because she didn't hesitate and said, "I want to get $65,000 net out of the property and not a penny less. You figure out the sale price that will do that and we have a deal."

After a few calculations, I wrote, and the buyer accepted, an offer for $88,000, property as is, buyer to assume responsibility for the first mortgage, buyer and seller to pay normal closing costs, and seller to net a minimum of $65,000. That was one of the easiest negotiations that I have ever had. The seller wanted out from under the responsibility of the property ownership, and she was reasonable about what she wanted to net out of the sale.

I used a credit line to cash the seller out and pay for the reconditioning of the property that ended up costing a little over $20,000. I then obtained a new appraisal for $136,000, using the upper-end comparables for the value basis; obtained an 80 percent loan-to-value, non-owner-occupied conventional loan for $108,800, 6 percent interest, and payments of $701 per month; and paid off the existing FHA first mortgage. The taxes, insurance, and expenses on the property were approximately $150 per month.

The property was rerented immediately after the reconditioning was completed for $1,050 per month and the positive cash flow on the property was approximately $200 per month. The most positive aspect of this transaction was that after the new loan was in place, I had *no cash out of pocket* and over $17,000 in equity.

What Made This Deal Work?

1. I found the property *before* it was reconditioned and put on the market for sale.

2. I was able to see the property, and determine what work needed to be done and the cost to do the work before I spoke with the owner.

3. The seller, after seeing and understanding all of the work required, could not or did not want to do the reconditioning of the property.

4. The seller was reasonable in her expectations as to what she wanted to achieve out of the sale of the property.

5. The resources were available to me to be able to close the original sale transaction, have the work done on the property, and put a new loan on the property with terms that were good enough to allow for a breakeven or positive cash flow situation. (If I had not been financially able to handle this transaction by myself, I would have found a partner who could do so.)

6. After refurbishing the property, the value of the property was high enough to obtain a refinance loan that would allow me to take out all of the cash that I had invested.

Favorite No. 8: Equity Participation with Seller

Almost everyone who has ever owned a parcel of real estate understands the concept of appreciation. If you look at the simple economics of what has happened over the last 30 years, it is pretty simple to comprehend that when you purchase real property, there is a good chance that the value of that property will increase over time. At what rate that appreciation will occur, and over what period of time, is almost anyone's guess. However, if you stay aware of all of the economic nuances and conditions of a particular market, you should be able to make fairly accurate estimates of future appreciation growth.

One of the most successful techniques that I have used in real estate investing and that many of my students have indicated to be extremely effective over the years has been sharing a portion of future appreciation with a seller. Often, the reason that a seller is reticent to sell property for even a small percentage below market value is a concern that the property will have a big surge of appreciation immediately after the sale. Almost every seller has a story that ends with, "...and if I had just hung on to that property, it is worth $$$$ in today's market." Well, the old adage, "Hindsight is always 20–20," really applies to those situations.

If you want to take advantage of a seller's desire to never again miss out on appreciation growth, use a shared equity appreciation offer and watch that seller's eyes light up. The following is an example.

After selling her home, Helen was renting half of a large duplex in an upscale neighborhood. The primary reason that she had chosen to rent a property, rather than buying another home, was that she did not want the responsibility of the yard care and upkeep of a single-family residence, but she also did not want to live in a condominium or apartment complex. She did own four single-family residences that were rentals where the renters had the responsibility for yard care.

The duplex in which she was living was only connected by the garages and, for all intents and purposes, each half of the duplex was a single-family home. When the owner, an Air Force officer who occupied the other half of the duplex, mentioned to Helen that he was being transferred, she asked if he would be interested in selling. He said that he owned two other single-family houses in other areas where he had been stationed and always hated to sell because he wanted the equity appreciation on the properties to eventually supplement his retirement income in about 10 years, when he planned to retire. However, he added that he was a little concerned because this property was a duplex, a little more upscale than his other homes, and it might require a little more management to keep both units occupied.

Because there were no comparable sales in the area for similar duplex or triplex properties, Helen used the income analysis method and comparable home sales to determine that the duplex had a current market value of approximately $340,000 to $350,000. She also recognized that it might be difficult finding a renter who was willing to pay the duplex rental rate, for which a renter could actually rent a single-family home in the area. Helen had been paying $1,450 per month and she knew that she was about 15 percent under the average rent for a home of her duplex's size and quality.

The existing mortgage on the property was a conventional loan with a remaining balance of $269,250, interest of 7.25 percent and monthly payments of $1,837. The property was in excellent condition and had no deferred maintenance to speak of.

Knowing that the seller's hot buttons were not losing the future appreciation on the property and fear of the management of the property, Helen prepared the following offer:

Sale price:	$341,200
Down payment:	$ 0
Buyer to assume or take subject-to first mortgage:	$269,250
Seller to carry back second mortgage with interest of 6 percent, payments of $360 monthly, and all due in 10 years:	$ 71,950

Buyer and seller to pay normal closing costs

Seller to share in the appreciation (30 percent) when the property sold or receive appreciation in a lump sum, value established by an appraisal, at the end of 10 years

Helen explained that she had established the price by taking the estimated market value and deducting a small amount for sales costs. She also included the following appreciation table to show the seller his continued appreciation at the end of one, three, five, seven, and ten years:

Sellers Equity

Appreciation Rate	Year				
	1	3	5	7	10
5%	$ 5,118	$16,135	$28,280	$41,671	$ 56,434
7%	$ 7,165	$23,036	$41,200	$62,035	$ 85,825
10%	$10,236	$33,881	$62,492	$97,111	$139,999

The formula that was used to calculate the appreciation was:

(Current value or sale price) × (appreciation rate) =
(appreciation increase) × (percentage of appreciation that
the seller is receiving) = (seller's portion of the appreciation)

From the table, for the first year at 5 percent appreciation, the seller's portion is:

$$\$341,200 \times 5\% = \$17,060 \times 30\% = \$5,118.$$

Over a 10-year period, the seller would receive in

payments:	$ 43,200
The remaining balance on the note would be:	$ 71,950
And the additional equity kicker at only 5 percent would be:	$ 56,434
Total	$171,584
And if appreciation averaged 7 percent:	$200,975

If it was such a good deal for the seller, how did the buyer fare? Helen leased the other side of the duplex to a retired couple for two years at a rental rate of $1,675 per month, but gave the renter/lessor $100 per month allowance off of the rent for yard work and upkeep on the property. The net rent collected was $1,575 per month. Helen's payments and expenses were as follows:

First mortgage:	$1,837
Second Mortgage:	$ 360
Taxes:	$ 350
Expenses:	$ 50
	$2,597 total monthly outlay
Rental Income	$1,575
Negative cash flow:	$1,022
Savings from rent she was paying:	$428 per month

After taxes, Helen was saving over $10,000 per year *and* the appreciation that she received was over two times as much as the seller was receiving. At only 5 percent appreciation per year, Helen had an equity position of over $94,000 after 5 years and over $214,000 after 10. Not bad considering Helen's only cash out of pocket was the $1,850 closing costs when she bought the property, all of which she recovered when the new renter moved in and paid first and last month's rent, a total of $3,250. Most importantly, she had over $855 *additional* monthly to spend.

What Made This Deal Work?

1. The seller wanted a long-term return.
2. The seller did not expect or need cash out of the sale.
3. The seller was able to add to his current income and still share in the continuing equity increases.
4. The interest rates were low enough that the buyer could easily afford the payments on both first and second mortgages.
5. The rent from the other half of the duplex was adequate to cover a substantial portion of the payments and expenses on the property.

Favorite No. 9: The Wraparound—Seller Receives Interest on Bank's Money

Recently I was speaking with an escrow officer and she said it was amazing how many of the old financing techniques she was starting to see in today's market. She mentioned the wraparound specifically and said that a broker who had brought her a wraparound deal thought that he had a transaction that would really confuse her. She said that she had to laugh because when she had started in the business in the early 1980s, "wraps" were a part of nearly half of the transactions that she was doing. She said that it is just like the song, "Everything old . . . is new again."

It appears that the escrow officer's observation is quite correct. Wraparounds have become quite common again, not so much for residential, single-family homes, but for multiunit residential and commercial properties.

 TERRY'S TIP: As I have mentioned earlier in this book, there still are risks involved when using any type of subject-to transaction. Remember, when a bank or other lending institution has a due on sale clause included in their note with the original buyer, that bank or lending institution can call the note due if a sale occurs and the new buyer has not been approved by the lender and gone through the full assumption process. However, that is not to say that the lenders will call every note that is taken in a subject-to transaction. I have been aware of, and a party to, dozens of transactions that involved subject-to transactions, and I have only known of *one* situation where a buyer was forced to go through the full assumption process and pay the fees to obtain a new loan.

If a seller is what I call "interest-oriented" he or she may be a prime prospect for a wraparound transaction like the following example.

Carl lived in the suburbs of a metropolitan area, had a good job, commuted by train into the city each day, and had a few stocks and bonds, but had never been able to save what he thought was enough money to be able to buy real estate. He rented a large, four-bedroom, 4,100-square-foot home for $1,700 per month that, if he were to purchase the property, would have cost at least $500,000. Carl needed the space because he had a secondary, in-home business—tee-shirts and specialty clothing—that required warehousing a substantial amount of merchandise and took up about two bedrooms and half of the garage. However, Carl's tax situation was killing him financially. With a gross income of over $72,000, he was still filing the short form, 1040A, and he had practically no write-offs. Consequently, his goal was to buy a home that would give him the deductions that he desperately needed and that was at least as large as the property he currently rented.

After attending one of our seminars, Carl began to search the newspapers for seller ads and to contact owners, looking for a seller that might be open to a low-down purchase offer. However, because the market interest rates were very low, buyers were everywhere and most of the sellers seemed to be adamant about cashing out on most homes that he viewed.

One morning, on the way to work, Carl noticed a three-story commercial building that was located about six blocks from his office in a mixed neighborhood of older residential homes, some of which were being converted to commercial uses. Carl noticed that railroad tracks, an old spur line that was no longer used, ran next to the property and there was a loading dock on the side by the tracks as well as two large gravel parking lots, one on the side and one in the back, that could accommodate at least 20 to 25 cars.

Carl remembered that at one time there had been a binding company on the ground floor level. He had passed that property hundreds of times, never really looked at it, and could not even remember when the binder had vacated. The exterior of the brick building and the windows and doors all appeared to be in good shape and, from what he could see, the roof was in excellent condition. There were several broker sale signs on three sides of the property. One had a line that read "9,400 Square Feet," and another read "Freight Elevator."

TERRY'S TIP: When you see several broker's signs on a property, that probably means that there is either no actual listing on the property, but the seller has allowed the brokers to put signs up for advertising, or the seller has agreed to an open listing, which means that any broker that brings a buyer to that seller can earn a commission. When you see a property with several broker signs, you have the choice to contact one of the brokers or go directly to the owner. My suggestion is, unless you feel that you need representation, go to the owner directly.

Carl obtained the ownership information from his local title company and found that the building was owned by a family trust. Running the name on the trust through several Internet white pages, Carl was able to obtain a telephone number and contacted the administrator for the trust who, after he was satisfied that Carl was not a broker looking for a listing, was very happy to provide all of the information on the property.

The trust administrator and his brother had owned a binding company that at one time was quite successful. With the surge of the computer industry and the many neighborhood printing stores, the business had slowly deteriorated. After his brother died, he had decided to sell the business. However, after two years of trying to sell the company, he had finally given up, closed the business, and decided to sell the real estate.

Unfortunately, some problems had occurred with his brother's ex-wife, and the probate on the property had gone on for over three years. Since the business was closed, the probate court had allowed him to refinance the property to be able to put on a new roof and to continue making the payments, cover expenses, and do the upkeep, but had balked at his initiating any long-term leases with companies that had shown interest in the property and wanted him to allow only month-to-month renters. He had a list of nine companies that had contacted him and were interested in leasing the building. Much to his chagrin, four of the nine were copy/printing companies.

The owner said that the probate had just been settled a few days prior to Carl's call and he just hadn't gotten around to listing the property. He said that he thought that it would be better for selling if the property was rented and he could now find a long-term lessor for at least the lower level of the building. However, he stated that, at 71 years old, he would rather just sell the property and let the new owner take care of placing and managing the renters in the building.

Through the interview process, Carl was able to obtain all the information that he needed to recognize that there were definitely possibilities for the property. The existing financing was a conventional loan with a balance of $330,400, interest of 6.1 percent and payments of $2,150 per month. The seller indicated that he would consider helping with the financing, but he stated several times that unless he got a substantial down payment, he wanted much higher interest than the current low rates. The seller thought that the property should sell for no less than $850,000. Carl made an appointment to view the property that afternoon.

Although it had been vacant almost a year, the building was in excellent condition. It had 3,200 square feet on the first and second floors and 2,800 square feet on the third floor. The freight elevator at the rear of the building operated smoothly and serviced all floors. Each floor had numerous windows and all the rooms were bright, wide open, and spacious. There were two bathrooms on the ground floor and one each on the second and third floors. After viewing the property, Carl told the owner that he needed to do some additional research, but that he definitely wanted to make an offer and he made an appointment to meet again with the owner in three days. He told the owner that if they were unable to make a deal, he would still take the time to help the owner get the building rented at no cost to the owner. The owner provided Carl with the names and contact information for everyone that had shown interest in the property. At Carl's urging, the owner agreed that he would wait to talk to anyone else about the property until Carl presented his offer.

Carl took the next three days off from his job and really went to work. The first day he contacted the city and found that he could get a variance for the commercial zoning on the property that would allow residential usage for the upper two floors. He also confirmed that the railroad line beside the building was completely abandoned and that it could no longer be used. He then began to drive that area of the city and made a list of every business that he thought might want to rent the lower level. He contacted three paving companies and got bids on the cost to pave and stripe the two parking areas beside and behind the building. Their bids were all around $14,000.

The second day Carl spent contacting companies that might rent the property. After only 20 calls he had six interested parties. He quoted a rental rate of $1.90 per square foot, the rate that seemed to be prevalent in that area for commercial storefronts. Knowing that he was going to have to rent the property, even if he didn't get the deal, he made two appointments for the next week to show the property.

Carl did his homework well, covered all of the bases, and this is how the creative young man was able to buy his first piece of real estate: He offered the seller the price that the seller had thrown out in their first meeting, $850,000, less 5 percent, or $42,500, the average commission that was charged by real estate brokers in the area and that the seller probably would have paid if he sold the property through a broker. Carl had determined through comparable pricing, that the actual value was closer to $950,000. (Remember, whoever mentions price first usually loses.) More importantly, Carl offered the seller a wraparound second mortgage that required the seller to continue to make the payments on the first mortgage, but allowed the seller to collect interest from Carl for the bank's money. The terms were as follows:

Sale price: $807,500

Down payment: $ 5,000

Wraparound second mortgage $802,500

(Interest rate 8.5 percent,

monthly payments of $5,685, all due in 10 years)

Seller to pay all closing costs, approximately: $ 4,450

Carl presented the wraparound to the seller as follows: The seller would receive 8.5 percent annual interest on the entire loan:

$$\$802,500 \times 8.5\% = \$68,213$$

The seller would pay 6.1 percent annual interest on the first mortgage

$$\$330,400 \times 6.1\% = \$20,154$$

This left a net interest to the seller of $48,059 for the first year. (Because the first mortgage was fully amortized over 25 years, the principal reduction would be a little more each year and the exact rate of return would change slightly.) Calculating the actual interest rate of return for the first year was done by subtracting the amount of the first mortgage from the amount of the wraparound second mortgage and dividing net interest by the actual loan amount provided by the seller:

$$\$802,500 - \$330,400 = \$472,100$$

$$\$48,059 \div \$472,100 = 10.18\% \text{ rate of return}$$

The seller receives a higher rate of return than the interest rate paid by the buyer because the seller is being paid 2.4 percent interest on the bank's money. Had the seller carried a straight second mortgage for his equity of $472,100, he would have received only an 8.5 percent rate of return. The seller very much appreciated the fact that he was being paid interest on the bank's money.

Once the property was in escrow, Carl nailed down a long-term tenant for the ground floor and half of the second floor for storage. The lessor turned out to be one of the copy/printing companies that had contacted the owner. The lease terms were:

$1.90 per foot for the ground level:	$6,080
$1.00 per foot for the second floor:	$1,600
Total monthly rental income:	$7,680

To be able to pay for the paving on the parking areas, Carl made the following deal with the company renting the property: Instead of asking the company to pay $1.35 per foot for the second floor, he would reduce the rent to $1.00 per foot, saving the company $33,600 over the term of the lease, if they would pay $23,600 additional, at the signing of the lease, for the paving to be done. They agreed, indicating that they would rather have the reduced monthly rent and include the up-front costs in their tenant improvements, allowing them to write off those improvements over the five years.

How did the deal work out for Carl? As you probably have figured out by now, he moved his residence into the third floor, creating a stunning loft-style flat, used half of the second floor that was not rented for his clothing business (he had a total of 4,400 square feet), cut two hours a day out of his commute and virtually eliminated his tax obligation. He bought the property for *no cash out of pocket*. The $23,600 that the renter paid up front paid for the paving ($14,000), the down payment ($5,000), and the improvements that Carl made to be able to convert the upstairs to a residence ($4,600). The figures broke down as follows:

Income from building:	$7,680
Less payment on wraparound mortgage:	$5,685
Less expenses, taxes, and insurance:	$1,730
Positive monthly cash flow:	$ 265

In addition to the $3,180 per year positive cash flow, Carl saved over $1,800 annually ($150 per month average) on commuting expenses and over $15,000 per year on his taxes, plus the savings of $1,700 per month for rent ($20,600 per year), for a total of $40,580 annual increase in spend cash.

What Made This Deal Work?

1. Carl being creative and open-minded in his approach to what type of property he would buy. Also, Carl's ability to structure a transaction that was creative.

2. Great timing! Carl found the seller at the perfect time—just after the probate ended and before he had been able to list the property. There is a lot to be said for being at the right place, at the right time, but I do not believe that it is just luck. If an investor is always looking, he or she will find a lot more properties and make a lot more deals than the person who puts little time and effort into finding the bargains.

3. A seller who was flexible and did not want to cash out. He wanted income and a high interest return. He received both.

4. Carl's speed in getting the property leased and the income in place.

5. Carl's approach to the seller helped the seller to achieve what that seller wanted. The seller later told Carl that he felt that Carl's offer to help him rent the property, whether they had a deal or not, was sincere and made him really want to put the transaction together.

Favorite No. 10: Generating Ongoing Income and Long-Term Wealth

As do investors, properties come in all styles, shapes, and sizes and you need to make some decisions as to the type of properties with which you want to work. Remember, we said, "Successful people are successful because they do the things they like most." Let me give you another example of a great investment technique used by one of our students.

After completing one of our training programs and looking at numerous types of properties, John, a delivery truck driver, decided that he wanted to work only with vacant lots and open land. Although he knew that it might be more challenging and possibly slower getting started working with vacant land rather than single-family homes or small multiunit properties, he felt much more comfortable working with lots and he was quite convinced that he could make it work.

John's personal action and goal plans were structured to generate a monthly income of $6,000 to $7,000, about twice his normal income, after the first six months of his investment work. The specifics of John's plan involved purchasing small rural foothill properties, 3 to 10 acres in size, that had no improvements. His plan was to make some improvements on the properties and put them immediately back onto the market for sale. In the beginning, the improvements would only include three actions:

1. Some clearing of the property
2. Cutting access driveways
3. Basic pads where a home could later be located

John's expertise as an equipment operator would allow him to be able to rent the equipment that would be necessary to complete the work, and he would not have to pay operators that normally receive a substantial hourly rate. The one stumbling block was that John had less than $200 to get started.

After making nine offers in only 12 days, John opened escrow on his first purchase. It was a five-acre, fairly steep parcel with a great view from the backside of the property. Comparable properties in the area, with no improvements, were selling for between $40,000 and $55,000. The terms of John's purchase were:

Sale price:	$26,000
Deposit:	$ 100
Down payment:	$ 0
Monthly Payments:	$ 0
Interest rate:	15 percent

Balloon payment, all due and payable in 6 months

All closing costs, approximately $754, were to be paid
   by the buyer

Improvements that were approved by the seller could
   begin immediately and did not have to wait until
   after close of escrow

After John had the deal in escrow he went to several real estate agents, explained his plan, and asked to borrow $2,500 to close the escrow and complete the work. He explained that he was willing to list the property for sale with the agent immediately after his purchase escrow closed. He also agreed to pay the agent 10 percent of the profit that was realized from the subsequent sale of the property. The fourth agent that John approached agreed to the deal, with the stipulation that he, the agent, would also have his name on the deed as an additional owner. Because John had anticipated this request and had included the extension of "et al" on the purchaser line of his original offer to the seller, he accepted the agent's request. John deposited the $700 necessary to close the deal with the title/escrow company. John now had $1,800 remaining.

John then went to the owner of a local equipment rental store and explained his needs. He offered to pay twice the normal rental rate for the equipment that he needed if the company would be willing to wait for payment and put a demand into escrow when he had made the improvements and had sold and closed escrow on the property. Fortunately, the store owner understood the value of local real estate and did not have a problem waiting for the payment. However, his only stipulation was that John would have to use the equipment on the days when it had not been reserved by another customer. The owner indicated that he was willing to work the same deal for any property that John acquired in the area.

In the next four days John found, made, and had offers accepted and opened escrow on two more properties that were both similar parcels, with similar terms, and were all within five miles of each other.

Nine days after John had made his first offer, he had three parcels in escrow and picked up the equipment he needed to complete the work on the properties. Because he was paying an increased rate for the equipment, he had decided to do the work on all three parcels, if possible, in one day. As he explained it, "It was a 14-hour marathon, but when the sun went down, the backhoe and tractor work was done." He spent an additional three days mowing, cleaning out some scrub trees, and generally sprucing up the properties.

John's first purchase escrow closed 12 days after it was opened and as agreed, the property with the new improvements, went back on the market, listed by his real estate agent/partner, at a list price of $49,500. John's partner was quite surprised when John gave him the two additional listings, one at $51,000 and the other at $55,000.

John now owned three properties, but he again had no working capital, so he spent the next couple of weeks finding potential purchase properties that he could move on as soon as he had some idea of when he would have revenues from the closing of his first property sale.

John was fortunate. The first property received a cash offer for $45,000 within two weeks and within four weeks of being placed on the market, the escrow closed and John received his check. The expenses were as follows: $4,500 for sales commission, $1,200 closing costs, $400 for equipment rental (one-third of the total amount charged for the equipment used on all three properties), $1,357 to the real estate agent/partner for his participation, and the payoff to the seller for the original purchase $26,000. John received his first escrow check for $12,008.

Since John had done his prospecting while waiting for his first escrow to close, he was able to buy and develop five more similar properties within the next six weeks. By the end of the year, in his first seven months as a professional investor, buying and selling the same type of properties, John earned $69,000 net income before taxes and still had two properties on the market for sale that ultimately brought in an additional $33,000 in income.

Having developed some stability and working capital, John went on to larger properties, splitting them into salable parcels, and within a couple of years began to complete the lots with wells and septic systems, which increased his expenses, but also dramatically improved his profits. Starting with $200, John's net worth grew to over $350,000 in less than three years and he continues to work successfully with open land sales.

Working the Properties and Types of Deals That Suit You

Each of the techniques discussed in this chapter has involved a certain level of creativity, but for the most part each one is simple to understand once you grasp the concepts. As the first section title says, "Every Day Is Different, but Every Deal Is the Same." You need a flexible, accommodating seller, a decent property that can be priced well, and you need to be able to figure out how to make it a win-win transaction for all parties.

15

Closing the Transaction

You Have the Deal—Now Get It Closed

The process of closing the transaction actually begins the day that you obtain the seller's signature on the purchase agreement. Whether the procedure is called an "escrow" or a "closing," the outcome hopefully will be the same. The overview below is the course of action that occurs in the escrow process.

The buyer goes to a title or escrow company and opens an escrow order. The buyer should have the purchase agreement signed by the seller and from that agreement the details of the escrow instructions are prepared. The escrow officers must be given the specifics and they are not allowed to advise any party to the transaction about any of the terms or details of the transaction, except to explain the escrow-related processes. In some areas, the escrow-opening documents must be signed by both the buyer and seller; in other areas, the escrow can be opened as simply as making a telephone call, and signatures are not obtained until the escrow has been completed and is ready to close. If a deposit is to be paid by the buyer, that deposit might also be provided to the escrow holder, depending on the conditions of the purchase agreement.

Whether the closing is handled by an escrow or closing officer, the function of that closing agent is to act as a neutral third party to gather all documents including the deed or deeds, prepare for recordation any documentation that requires that process, follow the instructions of any lenders that might be a party to the transaction, and make all transfers as indicated by the parties to the transaction.

After the escrow has been opened, the escrow officer orders a preliminary title report, often referred to as a "prelim," on the subject property. This report will show all liens and encumbrances and any other information that has been recorded regarding that property. A copy of that report will be sent to both the buyer and seller. Prior to the closing, it will be the responsibility of the buyer to review the title report and in many cases the buyer will have to sign off that he or she accepts the title to be transferred in the condition that it is shown on the report. If inconsistencies are recognized, the buyer should not close the transaction until those problem areas have been corrected. Some of the areas of concern are not only the liens and encumbrances, but also easements that are included on the deed.

When all necessary documents have been supplied to the escrow holder, a signing/closing meeting will be scheduled with the escrow officer and both the seller and buyer, or the escrow officer with the buyer and seller individually. At that time the seller will provide the deed for the property to the escrow agent, as well as any other necessary documentation, and the buyer will provide any funds or other documentation that will be needed to close the transaction.

If you are working through real estate brokers, they should, for the most part, set up and help you handle the closing process. However, typically, escrow officers and title companies that are handling the closing process will handle every detail, as they are directed by the escrow instructions. Don't be nervous about the process. You will have a lot of help if you work through a reputable escrow or closing officer.

Once all parties have signed all the documentation and approved all the actions of the escrow agent, the recordation process will occur, transferring the property from the seller to the buyer. At that time either the buyer or the escrow/title company will arrange for the deeds, deeds of trust, and mortgages to be recorded by the county or parish recorder's offices.

Some Considerations During the Closing Process

There will be many considerations during the closing process. It will be easier to track everything that needs to be done if you use the escrow closing checklist in Table 15.1. Some of the most important items on the checklist are:

1. *Choosing the closing date.* Many times buyers and sellers will be anxious to close a transaction. However, when you choose the closing date, make sure that you allow enough time for the escrow agent to be able to do his or her job. Another consideration with regard to choosing a closing date is the time necessary to obtain financing. If an appraisal must be completed, it may take longer to close the transaction. Sometimes, when the title companies are very busy, it can take as much as two to three weeks just to receive the prelim. Other times, they will have the title report in a day or two. Try to stay abreast of your own local market so when you do write a purchase agreement, you will have a pretty good idea as to how long it will take to close your transaction.

2. *Choosing an escrow or closing agent.* As with every type of service industry, closers and escrow agents may be good or not so good. After you have closed a few transactions, you will have a pretty good idea as to who you like to work with and who you don't. Until you have a few deals under your belt, you may want to ask some local real estate agents and brokers who they prefer as closers and escrow agents. Make sure that you also ask why they prefer that particular escrow officer or closer.

3. *Examining the title report.* Once again, until you are fully capable of examining and understanding a title report, you are better off asking the title or escrow officer to assist you when you review that report.

Table 15.1 The Escrow/Closing Checklist

The following list is to confirm all the dates necessary to achieve a smooth closing. Please verify the dates with your clients and return a copy to me with your signature.

For Property at: _____

	Goal Date	Actual Date
1. Contract acceptance with all decision makers present	_____	_____
2. Property inspection by buyer	_____	_____
3. Promissory note inspection and approval	_____	_____
4. Listing disclosure signed	_____	_____
5. Agency representation document signed	_____	_____
6. Service contract approval	_____	_____
7. Income/expense approval	_____	_____
8. Permit approval	_____	_____
9. Inventory approval	_____	_____
10. Escrow instructions prepared	_____	_____
11. Escrow instructions signed	_____	_____
12. Deposit submitted	_____	_____
13. Deposit clears the bank	_____	_____
14. Professional property inspection	_____	_____
15. Inspection accepted	_____	_____
16. Estoppel certificates approval	_____	_____
17. Termite inspection	_____	_____
18. Earthquake and flood zones	_____	_____
19. Deposit increase to escrow	_____	_____
20. Preliminary title report approval	_____	_____
21. City approvals obtained	_____	_____
22. Loan submitted complete to lender	_____	_____
23. Appraisal made	_____	_____
24. Appraisal done	_____	_____
25. Termite work finished	_____	_____
26. Obtain insurance	_____	_____
27. Reappraisal done	_____	_____
28. Other work finished	_____	_____
29. PMI approval	_____	_____
30. FIRPTA signed	_____	_____
31. Other contingencies cleared	_____	_____
A._____	_____	_____
B._____	_____	_____
C._____	_____	_____
32. Formal written loan approval	_____	_____
33. Loan documents signed	_____	_____
34. Cleared funds submitted for down payment	_____	_____
35. Buyer's occupancy	_____	_____

Buyer's Agent_____ Date _____

Seller's Agent_____ Date _____

Missing or not understanding a critical item on a title report could cost you a great deal of money.

4. *Ordering title insurance.* In most instances, when you purchase real property, you will obtain title insurance, guaranteeing that the title is free and clear of any liens and encumbrances *except those of record*, and that all considerations with regard to the capability of the seller to transfer the title have been met. Title insurance is risk limitation insurance, unlike most casualty and life policies, which are risk assumption coverages. For obvious reasons, a buyer should always obtain a title insurance policy and not allow a property to be transferred without the title coverage. Another consideration is that if there is a gap in the title insurance throughout a chain of title, it could cause a problem for future transfers. In some areas, title insurance is called "title guarantee," or "title warranty."

5. *Existing title defects.* Inconsistencies on a title report are called "title defects." Those defects might include undisclosed liens, encumbrances, easements, etc. If title defects are uncovered, the seller must be notified and it will be his or her responsible to clear those defects before the transaction can close. The existence of title defects is not uncommon so don't panic if a title comes back with several items that you didn't expect. Most of the defects can be handled by the seller and the escrow agent.

6. *Rejecting the title.* In most cases, you will be able to receive a marketable title out of the escrow. If, during the escrow/closing period, you discover that there are defects in the title that cannot be corrected, do not close the transaction. Notify the seller as quickly as possible of the defects that need to be corrected and by what specified date or you will not close the transaction.

7. *The final walk-through.* Prior to making your offer, you probably conducted a complete inspection of the property. However, before the final closing, you should do one final walk-through inspection, once

again checking to see that all heating and cooling systems, electrical, plumbing, and all other details about the property and the structures are the same as they were when you made your offer.

8. *Existing leases and rental agreements.* Once again, prior to making your offer on the property, you should have examined all existing leases and rental agreements that are in effect and that will transfer with the property. When you are ready to close, reinspect all these documents to be sure that there have been no new agreements or leases added and that none of the documents have had material changes.

9. *Ownership of personal property that transfers with sale.* If valuable personal property, such as furniture or appliances, is to be transferred with the sale, a bill of sale should be included in the escrow/closing documents. Also, the seller should be asked to provide a notarized affidavit stating that there are no liens or encumbrances against the personal property and that they are owned free and clear by the seller and can be legally transferred.

10. *Ordering casualty and liability insurance.* When a transaction closes, the buyer should always be sure that a liability and casualty policy is in effect on the property. If the buyer is planning to continue an existing policy, he or she must notify the insurance company before closing and a binder for the coverage should be included in the escrow/closing papers prior to the recordation of any documents.

Final Closing/Escrow Considerations

Transfer of Funds

The escrow/closing companies may require that all funds deposited to close a transaction be provided in the form of a direct wire transfer or by certified funds. These companies must be able to verify what is referred to as "good funds," meaning that the transfer of the monies has been completed and cannot be reversed after the deeds and other documents are recorded. If funds are provided to the escrow holder that cannot be verified, the closing process may be delayed.

Closing Costs

Closing costs will need to be paid into the escrow/closing account before the transaction can be closed and recorded.

Real Estate Settlement Procedures Act

As an investor you need to understand the Real Estate Settlement Procedures Act (RESPA) that became effective in the United States in 1975. The primary focus of the act was to eliminate kickbacks and certain fees for services during a closing process involving a mortgage loan, if one is included in a transaction.

After the Closing

After the closing has occurred and all documents have been recorded, some additional things must be done:

1. Changing all utilities into the buyer's name and removing the seller from the responsibility for those utilities.
2. Seller should verify that all insurance coverages are adequate.
3. Notification should be made to all tenants regarding the change of ownership and any change regarding payments of rents.
4. Contact your tax preparer or accountant and provide him or her with all the documentation from the transaction so all the write-offs to which you will be entitled from the transaction and ownership of the property will be incorporated in your tax records.

Closing Is An Art—Become a Proficient Artist

Earlier in the book we discussed the team of experts that you will assemble to be able to assist you in your wealth-building process. Title companies and escrow officers are two of the entities that I indicated could be a tremendous help to you in achieving your goals. Be sure that you spend some time learning the escrow/closing process and if possible, take the time to spend a few minutes with an escrow/closing agent or officer and learn as much as possible from these professionals. They will be very important to your success.

As with any of the other professionals and service people involved in your transactions, be sure to reward the people at the escrow, closing, and title companies who help you to close your transactions. A bouquet of flowers or a box of candy goes a long way to see that you are not forgotten the next time that you need their services.

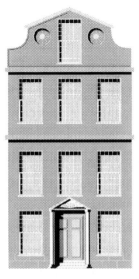

16

Property Management —The Simple Approach

Keep It Plain and Simple

When you begin your investment business, you not only will make choices about how and what properties you will purchase, but you also will have to make choices with regard to how you will handle those properties. Will they be a quick turnover, will they be held for a longer period of time and then sold, or will they be properties that you will keep to build your portfolio?

If you have set your goals properly, you should have a good basic plan to work from, but what usually happens is that you might be looking for properties to sell quickly and you will have the opportunity to purchase a property, with little or no money down, that will give you a positive cash flow and is more of a mid- or long-term investment. You must learn to be flexible and to be ready to move in either direction when the opportunities are presented to you.

Of course, the entire concept of wealth building is based around the generation of revenues. However, more importantly, you must also be

311

concerned with the long-term value of the estate that you are building. For that reason, good property management is almost as important as the actual transactions that you will put together. After you have been involved in the investment process for a period of time, you may own 2, 5, or 20 rentals and almost everyone, up to a certain point, will manage all of their own investments. Sometimes, the management expense will be the difference between properties having a positive or negative cash flow.

However, there will come a time when you will find that you have reached a point of diminishing returns with regard to the time that it takes for you to manage your own rentals. Since everyone has a different personality and a different tolerance level for the challenges they face, it will be a very subjective choice as to when you will transfer the responsibility of the management of the properties to a professional management company.

In any case, it is important for an investor to know and understand the management business even if they have a professional management company handling their properties. It will be much easier for you to understand if you are, or are not, receiving good management services if at one time you have done the job yourself and know what it takes to make it work properly. Remember, once you hire a management company, you will not be able to never think about the properties again. Instead, you will need to "manage the managers" and trust me on this one, most of them *do* require management.

Most likely, until you reach the point at which it is financially feasible to transfer the management to an outside company, you will handle those responsibilities yourself and it is important that you understand and utilize some basic concepts of good real estate management. For the most part, if you keep it simple and direct, the seven-part process is fairly straightforward:

1. Find the potential renters or lessors
2. Check the credit and references for potential renters or lessors
3. Prepare and execute the proper rental or lease agreements
4. Collect the rent or lease payments
5. Do the required maintenance on the property
6. Maintain an awareness of what is happening at the property
7. Maintain accurate records

In addition to the seven areas listed above, there may be times that you will be forced to evict a tenant, but if you have followed a good management plan, those times will be few and far between. The eviction process is discussed later in this chapter, but you may never need to use the material.

Finding Renters or Lessors

In most cases, if you have a clean, well-kept property and the rent is reasonable for the area, you will be able to attract renters or lessors and keep the property rented without too much difficulty. Two exceptions to that rule might be if a local area economy is struggling or if there is an oversaturation of good rentals in the price range of your property, creating a glut on the market.

Renters find the properties in which they are interested in many of the same ways that buyers find the properties that they are interested in buying. The National Property Management Institute indicates that renters located their properties in the following manner:

Classified advertising: 46%
Signs on properties: 24%
Property management companies: 14%

Other types of written or media advertising: 9%

Internet: 4%

Other: 3%

Depending upon several factors that will be more or less relevant to your specific area, most of your renters and lessors will come from classified newspaper advertising and for rent signs that you will put on the properties when you have a vacancy. You must remember that classified advertising can be expensive; however, it is even more expensive to have a property sitting vacant for a long period of time.

Often, after you have rented a property, you will continue to receive numerous inquiries. Make sure when that occurs that you ask the callers if they would like to be included on a list of potential renters for the property and notified should a vacancy occur at a later date. Most of the people will say yes, and eventually you will have a good list to call before you have to spend the money to advertise a vacancy.

More and more management companies and private individuals are utilizing the Internet, by way of personal web sites, to advertise rental properties. Also, many cities and counties are allowing property owners to list their rental properties on their governmental web sites. Even Realtor.com now has a section for rentals, and there are numerous listings for many areas across the country. When you have a vacancy, use every possible source to fill that vacancy as quickly as possible.

Working with Credit Reporting Agencies

Credit bureaus exist in nearly every local area across North America. With the advent of computerized credit screening and the Internet, a credit bureau in your locale has nearly instant access to credit information on an individual from anywhere in the country. As an investor and property owner, you may need to join a credit agency to obtain the credit information that you will need to make decisions about renters and lessors. Be sure that you run the reports on *all* adults who will occupy the property. The information that will be required for you to obtain a complete credit report is as follows:

Applicant's Information

Name

Present address—how long?

Own or rent—payment amount?

Previous address (If less than two years)

Telephone number

Social Security number

Date of birth

Nearest relative not living with applicant

Number of dependants (living with or not living with applicant)

Automobile

Applicant's Employment and Income Sources

Name of employer

Address and telephone number

Human Resources (HR) contact if large company

Previous employer (if less than three years)

If self employed—name of company

Sources of other income

Banking Information

Name of bank(s)

Account types and numbers (savings, checking)

Age of accounts and banking relationship (years)

Current creditors

Credit balances

If you have questions regarding the information that will be obtained on the credit report, most of the agencies that provide the information are willing to go through a report and help you to understand the layout and information that is provided. As a property owner much of the information in the credit report will be of significance in assessing your prospective renter:

1. Job stability
2. Residential stability
3. Credit balances
4. Excessive credit in general
5. Timeliness of payments
6. Judgments or liens
7. Collections

Preparing Rental Agreements and Leases

The first decision that you will have to make regarding the rental properties that you purchased is whether you will rent the properties month to month or utilize leases for terms that may vary from three months to two years. If the rental market will support using leases rather than month-to-month agreements, do so as often as possible. Vacancies cost you money and even if you are able to immediately rerent a unit that has come vacant, there may be a day or two between tenants and there will almost always be small cleanup and repair items that you will need to take care of before the new tenant moves in. Do everything that you can to keep your tenants as long as possible.

If you decide to use leases, try to get the tenants to take a lease longer than one year. Eighteen months to two years is a good lease for most properties. For prime properties in some of the major cities, leases are written for as long as five years, and options to extend the lease even longer are usually included. In those cases, rent increases are usually built into the lease.

What Should Be Covered in the Rental or Lease Agreement?

These are some of the specific provisions that should be included in all rental and lease agreements:

1. Rent payment incentive
2. Rent payment penalty
3. Specification of exactly how and when payments are due
4. Specific explanation of the security deposit
5. Specific explanation of the eviction process and applicable penalties
6. Specific explanation of move-in and move-out policies
7. Specific explanation of insurance coverages on rental

The 10 Commandments of Property Management

1. *Rents all due on the same day of the month.* One rule that you should always follow is that rents are due on the same day of the month. If you do not follow this rule, you will become a professional rent collector and will waste a great deal of time. Many years ago, when I was in college, I took over 152 units as a resident manager in a small college town in northern California. The previous manager had rents due nearly every day of the month. After two months of spending an hour to three hours writing receipts, collecting 5 to 15 rents every day, including, Saturdays, Sundays,s and holidays, I prorated all of the rents and had them come due on the first of each month. I could not believe what a squawk the tenants put up about change. From that date forward, for every property that I have owned or managed, the rental

agreement or lease has been set up in the beginning for the rent to come due on the first day of the month and be delinquent five days later.

2. *Have an incentive program.* Nearly all property owners have a delinquency charge built into their rental agreements. The wording on their agreements will usually say something to the effect that the rent of a certain amount is due on a certain day, and after that a late charge of an indicated amount will be collected. I have learned over the years that the success you will achieve in all types of negotiation and contract procedures will often have less to do with what you say and more to do with how you say it.

With regard to rental agreements and leases, I always suggest that the agreements be written at a rate 5 to 10 percent higher than the actual rental rate, with an incentive of the same 5 to 10 percent for payments made by a certain date. For example: *The rental rate shall be $1,000 per month, due and payable on or before the fifth day of each month. If rent is received on or before 5pm, the third day of each month, a good payment incentive shall apply and rent shall be reduced to $900 for that month.*

There may be special cases where you will need to bend the rules to obtain or maintain a good tenant. For example, if a tenant is paid on the 5th and 25th of each month and wanted to receive the incentive, you might allow that tenant to pay the reduced rental rate on the 5th rather than the 3rd. In the rental business, you must always remember that most people live paycheck to paycheck and that a small concession might help to keep a great tenant.

3. *Always collect more than the first month's rent as security.* As a property owner you must know and understand that 30 percent or more of the tenants that you will have for a two-year occupancy period or longer will, during those two years, have some kind of a financial crisis. They may quit, lose, or change their job, get a divorce, split up with their

roommate, overencumber themselves with debt, have a health problem, or encounter any number of other problems. Although you will have in place a rental agreement that specifies the term of occupancy, you must be prepared for situations that will require tenants to vacate the property before their agreement specifies. For that reason, it is important that you collect at least one month's additional rent at the beginning of the occupancy period. If the tenant does have to terminate the lease, at least you will have received the rent owing if a crisis occurs and the tenant cannot or will not pay the rent.

As far as collecting prepaid rent *and* a security deposit, many renters will have a hard time coming up with the first and last month's rent, as well as a security deposit. I usually require tenants to pay the first month's rent and the security deposit *before* moving into the property. If they cannot pay the last month's rent at the beginning of the lease, I will allow them to pay the last month's rent in up to four increments, during the first four months of their occupancy. Do I ever extend that? Of course, there are exceptions to every rule, but I try not to vary from the standard procedures any more than is absolutely necessary.

4. *Always collect and segregate security deposits.* It is imperative that you collect security deposits and explicitly specify the difference between those deposits and prepaid rent that is collected. I always suggest that security deposits be a different amount than the monthly rental rate. The reason for that is that invariably, if tenants pay a security deposit that is exactly the same amount as the monthly rental rate, they assume that deposit can be used for rent at the end of the occupancy period, even if they have also paid a last month's rent. To help solve the problem, in my rental agreements I make sure that there is bold print stating: *Security deposit CANNOT ever be used for rent at any time during the period of this lease agreement.*

5. *Always specify any non-refundable deposits.* Invariably, 90 percent of the time that you rent a property to a tenant for more than two months, there will be some cleaning or minor repair that will be necessary before the property can be rerented. For the most part, that cleaning and those minor repairs will be considered normal wear and tear. However, as a landlord you can specify that some of the security deposit can be retained if certain tasks are not handled by the vacating tenant. For example, you may choose to retain a specified amount of the deposit if the carpet has not been professionally cleaned. In other words, if a tenant wanted his or her entire security deposit returned, he or she would need to have the carpet cleaned when vacating the rental or the carpet cleaning allowance would be retained by the landlord.

Again, there are exceptions to every rule. I have had tenants move out of a property, after two years occupancy, and the unit looked as though no one ever lived in it. In those cases, it is only fair to return the entire security deposit.

I have my managers take photographs of every unit before a tenant moves in and at the time they vacate the property. Those photos are maintained in that property's file for at least two years after the occupancy. That way, we have evidence in case a former tenant ever decides to take us to small claims court over a security deposit. However, because we always strive to be fair with the tenants, I have never had an occasion where it was necessary to defend our actions regarding deposits.

6. *Develop and maintain a tenant appreciation program.* Good tenants are money in your pocket and the longer they stay in your properties, the better it is for you as the investor/owner. Long-term tenants and low vacancy rates help to make properties very appealing when you sell them. Also, when you and/or your managers maintain good relationships with the tenants, there is a lot less stress for everyone involved.

Each time a new tenant moves into a property, reward them. Although it may be something as simple as a plant for their new home, a full-service carwash, or a gift certificate from the local grocery store, the tenant not only will be surprised, but also very appreciative of the thought and effort. A $20 or $30 housewarming gift is a small token for a rental that may bring in $6,000 to $20,000 a year or more.

Throughout the year, sending the tenants Christmas or other cards is a nice touch, and sometimes a letter of appreciation helps as well. Also, since you will have the birth dates of the tenants on their original applications, send them birthday cards. They will certainly be pleasantly surprised by those actions. Over the years, I have developed good friendships with many tenants, a large number of whom I have helped to buy their first home; some of them to go on to be investors themselves. One young man who rented his first apartment from me over 20 years ago has directed numerous deals to me and now owns over 30 properties himself. A positive relationship with your tenants, directly through you or through your managers, will have many positive, long-term effects on your wealth-building efforts.

7. *Inform tenants their personal property is not covered by your insurance.* This is a real stickler and needs to be covered in every rental agreement and lease. If a tenant is burglarized or a fire or other damage occurs, the tenant must understand that the property owner's insurance probably will not cover that tenant's personal losses. The tenant should obtain a renter's policy that will cover those personal losses should they occur. If you own commercial property, such as office or retail space, a requirement should be made that the renter/lessor also maintains a liability policy, in case an accident should occur in that particular unit.

8. *Handle problem tenants immediately.* One problem tenant can create enormous overall difficulties for an entire complex. Do not allow a problem tenant to remain in your property any longer than absolutely

necessary. Use every legal means to get rid of the problem as quickly as possible. I have found that it is better to offer a tenant their unused rent back and an extra $100 or $200 to move by a certain date. This is a good method to get rid of them in a timely manner. Never jeopardize your relationship with the other good tenants in a complex by allowing unacceptable behavior from one bad apple.

9. *Keep precise records on every unit.* Include in those records all of the improvements and maintenance that is done before, during, and after occupancy. The photographs that I mentioned earlier will help you to be able to identify any changes that might be made to a unit by a renter/lessor.

Many years ago I learned that lesson the hard way when I rented an apartment to a white collar executive who, from her credit report and our first meeting, I thought was going to be an excellent renter. Throughout the six months that she occupied the property, I had continual problems getting her to pay her rent on time and when she moved out, I discovered that she had painted every wall in every room, except for the bathroom, black. The bathroom was painted dark maroon. Her security deposit did not come close to paying the extensive cost of the painting necessary to cover all of the dark walls. When I threatened to take action to recover my costs, she responded that the apartment had been that way when she rented it. I had no proof otherwise so I just let it go, but that was the one and only time that I allowed that to happen. After that, I kept precise records and always took the before and after photographs.

10. *Join the apartment associations.* The National Apartment Association is a tremendous asset for any property owner in that it offers its members many services including insurances, ongoing and updated information about changing laws, listings of properties that are for sale, precedent case filings that affect property owners and renters, and

much more. There are over 160 local affiliate associations across the country. The cost to belong to the association is minimal by comparison to the benefits that can be derived by a member. Contact the National Apartment Association (NAA) on their web site at: www.naahq.org or at: 201 North Union Street, Suite 200, Alexandria, VA 22314 (telephone:703-518-6141).

Management Is Simple and Easy If You Stay On Top of It

No matter whether you have 500 units or one single-family rental, the basic aspects of property management are pretty simple: You must qualify and screen the renters, stay abreast of and handle the problems quickly and efficiently, reward your good tenants, and keep good records. If you do those things throughout your investment career, you will never have to go through what I call a "managectomy," which means that you virtually have to rip out all of your bad habits and start over with the right techniques.

Samples of a rental agreement and a lease agreement are included in the Appendix. You may utilize what ever form or format that you choose, but it will be important for you to be sure that the stipulations discussed above are in all of your agreements.

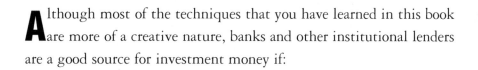

17

Institutional Lending—General Information

Although most of the techniques that you have learned in this book are more of a creative nature, banks and other institutional lenders are a good source for investment money if:

1. The borrower has acceptable credit.
2. The borrower can, in some way, produce an equity position of at least 10 to 20 percent (usually they like to see the borrower put some money down).
3. The property meets the requirements of the lending institution, usually including a required appraisal.

In most cases, the criteria for lending on investment properties will be somewhat the same as the requirements for owner-occupied property.

However, the lending criteria may be somewhat more stringent on a non-owner-occupied, investment property.

Typically, most institutional lenders want to see a buyer/borrower put at least 10 percent down on an investment property that will not be occupied by the borrower. Nonetheless, if a buyer/borrower can structure a transaction whereby the lender will be in the first mortgage position and the buyer or borrower has a substantial equity position although he or she actually put the lenders into the transaction, the lenders sometimes will still make the loan. Later in this chapter, you will see an example of that type of transaction.

What Lenders Are Looking For in a Borrower

Lenders use a process to approve loans that is referred to as "underwriting." This process includes examination and approval of both the buyer or borrower and the property. With regard to the borrower, the lender is concerned with two aspects: the borrower's ability to repay the loan, often referred to as the borrower's "repay capacity," and the borrower's credit score.

In very simple terms, institutional lenders are looking for investment borrowers who have established an adequate credit history that includes paying their obligations on time and who can demonstrate that they have the ability to repay a loan, even if vacancies should occur. They are also concerned that the properties that are used for the security for their loans have high enough values that they could be sold to pay the full obligation should the buyers fail to pay as agreed.

Roger Smith, Vice-President and Regional Manager for Action Mortgage Company, a subsidiary of Sterling Savings Bank, explained his view of institutional lending for the typical small investor:

Many homeowners continue to enjoy the benefits of homeownership for themselves in the forms of appreciation, tax benefits, pride of ownership, and knowing that they are putting their hard-earned money to work for their future. But, many stop there and never realize that they could put those same three benefits to work for them in non-owner-occupied or investment properties.

Typically, the loan applications on investment properties that we see are for one- or two-unit rentals that have a track record of rental income, or a property that is vacated by an owner-occupant and is being converted by the investor to an income-producing property. These properties are usually in existing neighborhoods that may or may not have other rental properties in the area.

In today's market, lending institutions offer a variety of fixed- or adjustable-rate mortgage (ARM) loan programs that can be obtained with as little as 10 to 15 percent down. These minimal equity requirements, coupled with the rates and fees that are usually only slightly more than the owner-occupied loans, make investment property a very attractive opportunity for the small or beginning investor.

As an institutional lender, I am always interested in looking at every transaction, whether it is for a first-time buyer or an experienced investor. We try to be there to help the borrowers in any way we can.

Figure 17.1 details the loan process as it occurs in most cases when a buyer or borrower is using an institutional lender. As an investor, you may find the process a bit cumbersome, especially if you are used to more creative types of financing. However, in some cases, it may be necessary to obtain a loan from an institutional lender.

Fixed-Rate versus Adjustable-Rate Mortgages

Many buyers and investors, as well as many real estate salespeople, believe that fixed-rate mortgages are always the best loans, regardless of the circumstances of the purchase or the financial position of the buyer. However, ARMs often outperformed fixed-rate mortgages over the terms of the loans. Investors must have the ability to calculate the

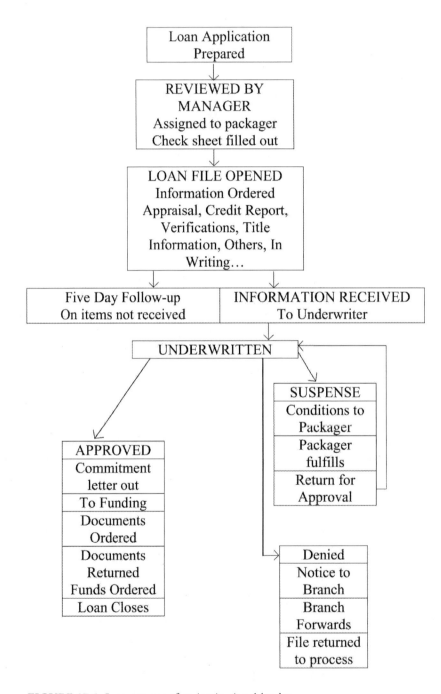

FIGURE 17.1 Loan process of an institutional lender.

cost of a loan over the term of the loan to be able to determine which type of loan may be the best for each prospective investment.

The main advantage of a fixed rate loan is the terms of the loan remain the same throughout the life of the loan. The disadvantages of a fixed-rate loan are:

1. The loan may be more expensive to obtain.
2. The rate and terms of the loan will never change even if the market pushes interest rates down.
3. The loan may have more stringent qualification requirements than an ARM.

Although interest rates can increase during the life of an ARM, the advantages of ARMs are numerous. Some of those advantages are:

1. Lower beginning or starting interest rates mean lower payments at the beginning of the loan and more borrowers and properties can qualify.
2. Because the interest rates and payments are lower, borrowers often can qualify for a larger loan amount and a more expensive property.
3. The cost to obtain an ARM is often less than a fixed-rate mortgage.
4. Because ARMs often have less stringent qualification requirements, it is often easier for borrowers to qualify.
5. If market rates go down, the interest rate and payments on an ARM also may reduce automatically, without rewriting the note or refinancing.

The main disadvantage of an ARM is that the interest rate and payments may increase during the term of the loan.

Table 17.1 Lender Comparison Chart

	Lender 1	Lender 2	Lender 3	Lender 4
Loan amount	$125,000	$125,000	$125,000	$125,000
Annual interest rate	5.0%	6.0%	6.5%	7.0%
Loan fees	1%	1%	$395	0
Points	2	1	1	0
Term	20	25	25	30
Monthly payments	$1,158.77	$805.38	$844.01	$831.63
Cost to obtain loan	$3,750.00	$2,500.00	$1,645.00	0
Total cost of the loan for the first 5 years (including interest, points and loan fees)	$52,594.78	$38,237.91	$44,488.24	$42,562.18

An investor should look at all of the advantages and disadvantages, as well as the overall cost, of the fixed-rate mortgage and ARM before deciding which loan to use for a particular investment. The lender comparison chart (Table 17.1) is a simple tool that will help you to compare the actual short-term and long-term cost of intuitional loans for any period of time.

Bonus Chapter

Letters and Dialogues for Successful Contacts

Contact Letters

Contacting potential sellers by mail can be effective if you are willing to follow up every letter with a telephone call. Otherwise, the letters, for the most part, will be a waste of time and money. However, letters or other mail contacts are good icebreakers and they can ease the tension a bit when you do contact the seller either in person or on the telephone. Also, if you can obtain e-mail addresses, these letters can be used for those contacts as well. Remember, the key to mail contacts is *keep it simple!*

The following series of letters contain the recommended dialogues that can be used for mail contacts. The first letter is complete and the following letters contain only the body portion of the letter. You will need to complete the headings, greetings, and salutations.

General Contact Letter

Mr. Tom Taylor
1218 Fourth Street
Anywhere, VT 00123

Dear Mr. Taylor,

My name is Terry Eilers and I am NOT a real estate agent trying to get a listing. I may be interested in buying your duplex located at 1417 Sawyer Lane.

Please contact me as soon as possible if you are interested in selling. My numbers are: Daytime: 845-3396 Evenings: 845-2271

or e-mail: TerryEilers@speednet.com.

Thank you,

Terry Eilers

Foreclosure Letters

Letter 1

Dear Mr. and Mrs. Harkin,

My name is Terry Eilers and I buy real estate. In most cases, I can close a transaction in a matter of just a few days. I am aware that a Notice of Default has been filed on your property at 1213 Anderson Way and if you are thinking of selling to cure the default, please contact me immediately. Defaults are a fairly common occurrence and are often not difficult to deal with, if you act quickly to handle the situation.

Please call if I can be of assistance.

Letter 2

Dear Ms. Chambers,

My name is Terry Eilers and I am a local real estate investor. I am interested in buying your property at 1717 Carlisle Court. I am aware that the property is in foreclosure and I would like to talk with you about how you might be able to get some cash out of the property very quickly.

If you are interested, please call me as soon as possible.

Letter 3

Dear Mr. Hoblet,

My name is Terry Eilers and I buy local real estate. As I am sure that you are aware, a Notice of Default has been filed on your property at 1111 Ostrom Lane. I do not know the complete status of your loan, but I would like to speak with you and determine if there may be some way that I can purchase your property and allow you to avoid the foreclosure process.

Please call me if you are interested.

Distressed Property Letters

Letter 1

Dear Mr. Calhoun,

My name is Terry Eilers and I am writing to inquire about the property that you own at 1244 Township Road. I prefer to buy properties that may need some maintenance or repair. If your property fits that description and you are interested in selling, please call me as soon as possible so that we might discuss structuring a transaction that would be good for all parties.

Letter 2

Dear Ms. Cooper,

My name is Terry Eilers, I am a real estate investor and I want to acquire one or more properties in the neighborhood of your property located at 239 Franklin Road. If you are interested in selling the property as is, please contact me as soon as possible.

Letter 3

Dear Mrs. Anderson,

My name is Terry Eilers and I need your assistance. I am interested in buying any multiunit properties in the area of the duplex that you own at 7654 Meridian Circle. If you know of any owner in the area that might be interested in selling, please have them contact me as soon as possible. I am not an agent. I am a buyer and I buy properties in AS-IS condition.

Collecting Information from the Seller—Use a Checklist

Many new investors find it easier to talk to potential sellers on the telephone rather than to see them in person. The problem with most telephone calls is that the caller is not organized and does not obtain all of the information that is necessary to properly qualify the seller and the property. If you will always follow an information checklist when making calls, you will be able to start to establish a working relationship with the seller and obtain the information that you are seeking.

The checklist below will guide you through nearly every contact that you will make to gather information about a property. Keep the form with you for reference when you meet with sellers in person and follow it closely when calling potential sellers on the telephone. Ask only the questions for which you do not already have the answers. If you have previous knowledge of the property or the owner, fill in the answers on your sheet before making the call to avoid duplicating your efforts.

TERRY'S TIP: Some of the questions in the checklist, particularly the section about the current loan status, may seem invasive to the seller. Explain, *before* you ask the questions, that you are an investor and it is imperative that you obtain all of the information about the property, including loan information.

The form is designed for collecting single-family home data. You may alter the questions when using it for multiunit or other commercial properties. Some prompts have been provided for other types of properties.

Seller Dialog Checklist—Phone or in Person

Identify yourself, be polite and nice, and remember: build a relationship!

1. Hello, my name is _____ and I am calling about the property at _____

Clarify ownership.

2. Are you the owner of the property?
3. Are there other owners or partners on the property?

Acquire property information (if a multiunit, obtain details for each unit).

4. Does the home have one or two stories?
5. How many total rooms in the property?
6. Do you know the approximate square footage?
7. How many bedrooms?
8. How many bathrooms? Are they full or half baths?
9. Is there a garage or carport? How many cars?
10. Are there appliances that will be included with the home?
11. What are the best features of the home?
12. Do you know the lot size?
13. Is the property fenced? Front and rear? Type of fencing?
14. Is there a pool or spa?
15. Are there other special features about the yard or surroundings?
16. What type of properties adjoin your property?
17. How long has the property been on the market?
18. Why are you selling?
19. Would you buy another home in the area?

Ask about the area.

20. Do you know if there are many rentals in the area?
21. What do you like most about the area? Least?
22. Do you happen to know what the rents are in the area?

Obtain pricing information.

23. What is the price that you are asking for your property?
24. How did you determine that asking price?

25. Are there similar homes for sale in the area? Do you know offhand what prices are listed?

Obtain information about existing financing

26. What type of financing is currently on the property? FHA, VA, conventional?

27. What is the approximate loan balance of the first loan?

28. What are the terms of the first loan? Interest rate, term, ARM, or fixed?

29. What are the loan balances and the other terms on any other financing on the property? Second mortgage? Third mortgage?

30. Who are the lenders on your loans?

31. Do you know if the loans are assumable?

32. If you don't mind me asking, are all of the payments current?

Determine if the seller is flexible. (The following questions you may or may not ask on the telephone—many times, these questions will be asked when you meet with the seller.)

33. Would you consider carrying some paper?

34. If you could be paid more money at a later date, do you need cash at the closing? If so, how much?

35. Has anyone ever explained to you how you might be able to be paid on equity earned *after* you sell your property?

It Is a Numbers Game

Regardless how you make your initial contacts, you must remember that the more people you contact, the more deals that you will close. The more "No's" that you hear, the closer you move to "Yes." That slim percentage (2 to 3 percent) of flexible, accommodating sellers are out there and you may hit pay dirt on your first, thirtieth, or hundredth call, but if you are persistent, it will happen.

Part III

Creating Your Own Plan for Success

18

Structuring a Personal Strategy

When you began this book, you may have had some preconceived notions about investment in general. We find that many people believe that it takes a great deal of money to become a successful investor and build a large real estate portfolio; others believe that it is virtually impossible to purchase quality real estate with no cash out of pocket. Many other people think that you must have great credit to be able to obtain loans and buy investment property. As you have seen, none of those misconceptions are correct.

Hopefully, we have been able to provide enough information to help you to understand that virtually *anyone* can become a successful real estate investor. However, from today forward, the onus is on you to set goals, create your own action plan, and go out and make it work. The practice is over. It is time to play the game, so what do you plan to do tomorrow to get started?

The following checklist is a suggested first-month strategy to help you to get started quickly and properly. You can alter it to fit with your own ideas and plans, but you must get started *now*, or you may *never* do it.

Week 1

1. Set your own goals and complete your own Action plan for three months, six months, one year, and five years.

2. *Every week*, review your goals and action plan *daily*. Track your results.

3. Set up your workspace in your home or office, including a telephone, and prepare to do business. If you can afford it, order business cards and put your property search binder together. Print the forms from this book that you will be using on an ongoing basis.

4. *Every week*, review the glossary terms and the buying techniques that you have learned in this book, and test yourself.

5. *Every week*, gain access to a computer and the Internet and begin perusing properties in your area on www.realtor.com, as well as the other sites that we have recommended in this book. Also, check out some of the local broker's web sites in your own area.

6. *Every week*, begin studying the real estate section and classified ads of your local newspaper. Study the market so you know what is selling and at what prices. Learn the real estate broker's names and check out who is doing most of the business. One or two of those people will probably be on your success team within a month or two.

7. *Every week*, when you see potentially interesting properties either on the Internet or in the newspaper, go check them out. Start looking for distressed properties or distressed sellers.

8. *Every week*, go through the local newspaper each day and find the notices of default (NODs). Make contact with the trustee or person who is in default and see if they are interested in selling the property before it goes to foreclosure sale. If they show interest, contact the lender who has filed the NOD and find out what it will take to cure the default. Many times, they will simply want a more responsible person to take over the note. If that is the case, go to the trustor/property owner and put a deal in place for as little cash out of pocket as possi-

ble. If this person is losing the property, even a little cash may look good. Once you have the deal, find the money and close it. Remember: It doesn't take money to make money—it takes a deal to make money.

9. Contact two local title companies. Go to see them. Explain that you are going to start investing in the area and you will need some help obtaining property and ownership information. Make a friend, and build a relationship. Find out if the companies offer the property profile information online.

Week 2

1. *Every week*, identify and become familiar with the areas and neighborhoods where you believe that you will begin working. Drive the neighborhoods every two or three days and watch for new listings, for-sale-by-owner properties, distressed properties or vacant properties, foreclosure notices on doors or windows, garage sales, etc. Start to talk to people in the areas and learn as much as you can about the residents. Try to find some bird-dogs. Get to know not only the sales prices but also the rental rates and ratio of rentals to owner-occupied properties.

2. Talk to at least three real estate brokers or agents and begin to build relationships with professionals who want to work with you and who either understand creative buying or are willing to learn the concepts. You may have to see 5 or 10 brokers or agents before you find one or two with whom you feel comfortable.

3. Run your own credit report. You can do it on the Internet and whether it is good or bad, you need to know where you stand. If you have questions about the report, each agency that produces the reports will give you help.

4. Go to your local bank and meet the manager. If you can do so, set up a credit line that you can use for investment purposes. Even if you're broke and have bad credit, you will not always be in that state, so begin building the bridges with a banking institution. They will

certainly want to bank your real estate earnings, so at least get a free checking account.

5. Continue to do all of the *every week* items from week 1.

Week 3

1. *Every week*, using your call dialogue checklist, telephone at least six potential sellers and set up appointments to see their properties. Call sellers *every day*. Be sure to obtain enough information so that you are fairly certain that each property that you view is potentially a property that you may want to purchase. Remember, your time is valuable.

2. Go to your local courthouse. Visit the recorder's office. Look up the ownership of at least three properties. If you have established a relationship with a title company, you may never need to use this county office but it is good to know the process just in case you run into a problem. Talk to the people in the recorder's office. Find out what time of day they record transfers of real estate. Find out if they offer special recordings and what the cost is for that service. There may come a time when you will need to record a transfer after the regular recording time and it is good to know what the additional fees will be. See if you can obtain a copy of all of the recording fees. They can vary a great deal from state to state and county to county. Also, visit the tax assessor's office and find out what the procedure is to determine the taxes in your area. Again, the formulas vary from state to state.

3. Identify at least one property on which you will make an offer. Even if it is going to be a low-ball offer that you don't expect the seller to take, it will at least give you the opportunity to begin gaining experience with the offer process. Put the offer together and get it presented.

Week 4

1. *Every week*, make at least five offers on properties. After three weeks of searching for potentials, you should have identified at least 10

or more properties that you would like to purchase. Keep in mind, it is a numbers game and you must look at a lot of properties and ultimately make many offers.

2. Find an investment club or organization. Join the group and begin to share ideas and information.

3. Begin to establish relationships with the other people who you would like to become a part of your investment team: an attorney, an accountant, a tax adviser, and any other person who may be able to help you with your investment business.

4. Start to expand the areas where you are working. Continue to widen the base of neighborhoods and areas in which you are interested in investing.

5. *Stay with the plan and do not give up!*

Two Examples of Successful Personal Action Plans

As we have discussed throughout this book, every investor will have a personalized plan to fit the goals that he or she is trying to achieve. The two personal action plans below are examples of different goal directions, but both investors are achieving success with their efforts. Your own goals will dictate how you will build *your* business.

More Income—Longer-Term Wealth Building

In the spring of 1999, Mark made a commitment to begin building a real estate investment income and wealth-building portfolio. Prior to that time, Mark's income had been derived primarily from a seasonal job at a ski resort near Lake Tahoe and whatever construction work that he could get in the summertime. Mark rented a small country property where he lived with his menagerie of three horses, two dogs, and several cats. Mark was 39 years old and had never owned a home or any real estate. He also had no savings or money to invest.

After attending one of our training programs, Mark spent a great deal of time pondering his future and realizing that his income and net worth had been, at best, static for nearly 10 years. He said that for the first time in his life he had started to realize that he had no real prospects for his life to improve. After he structured his goal sheets and personal action plan and it appeared that he had a solid direction.

Mark's daily action goals followed nearly exactly what is recommended on the first-month strategy outline above except that his efforts were tripled because he lived on the state border and he was working in two states and three counties.

Mark's short-term achievement goals were:

1. Develop an average investment income of $5,000 to $6,000 per month.
2. Buy at least four distressed properties per year, make the repairs, and sell them.
3. Buy at least two properties, distressed or not, to keep as rentals—these properties must have at least $100 per month positive cash flow.
4. Pay off all existing personal debt in 12 months or less, about $11,000 total.
5. Quit his existing jobs and become a full-time investor.

Mark's long-term success goals were:

1. After two years, have an ongoing annual investment income of $100,000 or more.
2. Buy at least six properties per year, of which three would become rentals and three would be repaired and sold.
3. Specialize in foreclosure and bank repossession properties.
4. Within three years, move his entire operation back to Arizona, where he could care for his aging parents.

So, how has Mark fared on his goals? After four years, Mark built a very good "buy it, fix it, and sell it" business. His annual income averages well over the $100,000 that was his original goal. He has built a very nice home on 12 acres, with a separate apartment for his parents, but he still lives in the same area in the northern Sierras. He said that once he got his business moving, it was just not in the cards to start over in a new location.

Mark owns seven long-term rentals that provide about $2,400 per month positive cash flow. He has said that if there is any area where he needs to work on his goals, it is the long-term wealth building. He indicated that he found himself caught up in the "buying and selling quick money" and he has not retained as many properties as he would like.

Mark's most recent project has been a 40-acre parcel that he is dividing into eight 5-acre parcels. Although his original goals had been to concentrate on foreclosures and bank repossessions, at this writing, Mark had not purchased one of either of those types of properties. He indicated that it was much easier to find other distressed properties or owners that had problems that he could help solve. Also, Mark said that he has never used more than $4,000 cash out of pocket, for any of the properties that he has purchased.

Mark said, "If I choose to, I am on track to retire at age 50. Not bad for a guy who had virtually nothing at 39."

Quick Wealth Building—I Don't Need the Income

Nancy had been a homemaker for 24 years. Her last job, outside of the home, had been a teller position in a bank when she was just out of high school. When she and her husband divorced, Nancy asked for and received a substantial monthly income, over $5,000 per month for five years, and the family home with a monthly payment of only $750 per month and equity of over $150,000. However, her husband was allowed to keep his entire retirement income and three rentals that the couple owned. Nancy recognized that she had five years to build an income and a retirement as quickly as possible.

Nancy attended one of our programs in Illinois one January. She said that her biggest frustration was that she was fired up and ready to get started the day she walked out of the seminar. She said that she would never forget her disappointment when she walked out into the parking lot, through two feet of snow and temperatures hovering around 10 degrees. She said that she remembered thinking to herself, how in the world can I get started in the real estate investment business when you can't even see the real estate. But, she said that she also persuaded herself that she was not going to wait until spring. All she had to do was get through a short vacation that she had previously planned to visit her daughter on the Gulf Coast in Florida the next weekend.

During the next few days she put together her goal sheets and personal action plan, studied the materials that she had received in the training program, and began looking through the newspapers, acquainting herself with the real estate market in her area. She also set up a credit line at her bank, utilizing the equity that she had in her home, that gave her over $50,000 to work with. Nancy's original short-term achievement goals were:

1. Buy at least three properties, possibly distressed, in the first year, that could be repaired and would be good rentals that had some positive cash flow.
2. Purchase a pickup truck that she could use in her investment and repair business.

Nancy's long-term success goals were:

1. Buy at least five properties per year that would become long-term rentals, a total of 25 in the first five years.

2. Have an income of no less than $6,000 per month after five years of investment.
3. Develop equity of at least $1,000,000 in real estate investment in the first five-year period.
4. Move to Florida in five years.

She said that when she boarded the plane to go to Florida she felt a certain disappointment because she was so excited about getting started with her investment business.

Upon her arrival in Florida, Nancy picked up a message on her cell phone, from her daughter, stating that she and her husband had a problem with their car and would be at least one hour late meeting Nancy. Nancy explained that almost unconsciously and because she had been doing it all week in Illinois, she picked up a newspaper and began to browse through the real estate section and the classifieds. She said that she was shocked at the number of properties that were available and the prevalence of low prices by comparison to the Chicago area. She said that she couldn't contain herself and began calling some of the for-sale-by-owners that she found in the paper. By the time her kids arrived, she had two appointments for the next day to view properties. As the old cliché goes, "...and the rest is history."

There is not much mystery as to what happened during Nancy's stay in Florida. She purchased three properties in just over 10 days, all with little down and all with at least breakeven cash flow. Nancy's son-in-law agreed to do the repairs that were needed on the properties and to manage the duplex and two single-family homes that she had purchased.

Less than 60 days after the escrows closed, the original three properties that Nancy had purchased were repaired and rented. In the next six months Nancy returned to Florida four times, purchasing at least one property during each trip. At the end of one year she owned nine properties, all with positive cash flows and she had spent only $17,000 out of her credit line. Her equity in the nine properties was over $134,000, and she had made her daughter and son-in-law partners on two of the properties.

At the end of the first year, Nancy sold her home in Illinois and moved to Florida. After three years, she and her family had joined forces and owned over 30 properties with equities over $1,500,000 and annual income of over $90,000. Nancy indicated that she has doubled her original goals.

Planning Your Future Success

I end each of my live seminars by saying, "Well, now you know what you have to do—the rest is up to you." The real estate investment business is like many other processes that you go through in your life—you have to learn a little, then go out and do it, learn a little more, go out and do it some more, and so on, until you become very good at what you do. There will always be trial and error, so don't expect to get everything right the first time—it just won't happen that way.

I was always told that "practice makes perfect," and I have learned that is not always the case. What is true is that "*perfect* practice makes perfect." Do not keep doing what has not worked in the past. Learn, adapt, and move on to all the success that you could ever desire. The time is "perfect" for you to begin to create your own *real estate millions in any market.*

Appendix

Appendix A Real Estate Purchase Agreement

REAL ESTATE PURCHASE AGREEMENT (RESIDENTIAL)
STATE OF _____
COUNTY OF _____
1. PARTIES:

_____

(Seller) agrees to sell and convey to

_____

_____ (Purchaser), and Purchaser agrees to buy from Seller the
Property described below.
2. PROPERTY: (a) Land: Address:

_____ [insert full
address] or more specifically described as:

_____

_____

_____

_____

_____, or as described in the attached exhibit. (b) Improvements: The
house, garage and all other fixtures and improvements attached to the above-described
real property, including without limitation, the following permanently installed and built-
in items, if any: all equipment and appliances, valances, screens, shutters, awnings, wall-
to-wall carpeting, mirrors, ceiling fans, attic fans, mail boxes, television antennas and
satellite dish system and equipment, heating and air-conditioning units, security and fire
detection equipment, wiring, plumbing and lighting fixtures, chandeliers, water softener
system, kitchen equipment, garage door openers, cleaning equipment, shrubbery,
landscaping, outdoor cooking equipment, and all other property owned by Seller and
attached to the above described real property. (c) Accessories: The following described
related accessories, if any: window air conditioning units, stove, fireplace screens,
curtains and rods, blinds, window shades, draperies and rods, controls for satellite dish
system, controls for garage door openers, entry gate controls, door keys, mailbox keys,
above ground pool, swimming pool equipment and maintenance accessories, and
artificial fireplace logs. (d) Exclusions: The following improvements and accessories will
be retained by Seller and excluded:

_____

_____

_____

_____

The land, improvements and accessories are collectively referred to as the "Property".
3. PURCHASE PRICE: The Total Price shall be $_____ payable as
follows:
        Earnest money: (Receipt of which is hereby acknowledged)
$_____
        Cash or certified funds due at closing: $_____
4. FINANCING: The portion of Sales Price not payable in cash will be paid as follows:
[Check applicable items below.]
_____ (a) Third Party Financing: One or more third party mortgage loans in the total
amount of $_____. If the Property does not satisfy the lenders'

underwriting requirements for the loan(s), this contract will terminate and the earnest money will be refunded to Purchaser. [Check one item only:]

_____ (1) This contract is subject to Purchaser being approved for the financing described in the attached Third Party Financing Condition Addendum.

_____ (2) This contract is not subject to Purchaser being approved for financing and does not involve FHA or VA financing.

_____ (b) Assumption: The assumption of the unpaid principal balance of one or more promissory notes described in the attached Loan Assumption Addendum.

_____ (c) Seller Financing: A promissory note from Purchaser to Seller of $_____ bearing _____% interest per annum, secured by [choose the appropriate instrument authorized within the state:] _____ mortgage, or _____ vendor's and deed of trust liens, and containing the terms and conditions described in the attached Seller Financing Addendum. If an owner policy of title insurance is furnished, Purchaser shall furnish Seller with a mortgagee policy of title insurance.

5. TITLE INSURANCE: Seller agrees to furnish to Purchaser a standard form title insurance commitment, issued by a company qualified to insure titles in _____ [state], in the amount of the purchase price, insuring the mortgagee against loss on account of any defect or encumbrance in the title, unless herein excepted; otherwise, the earnest money shall be refunded. Said property is sold and is to be conveyed subject to any mineral and mining rights not owned by the undersigned Seller and subject to present zoning classification.

6. PRORATIONS & HAZARD INSURANCE: The taxes, as determined on the date of closing, are to be prorated between Seller and Purchaser as of the date of delivery of the deed. Seller shall keep in force sufficient hazard insurance on the property to protect all interests until this sale is closed and the deed delivered. If the property is destroyed or materially damaged between the date hereof and the closing and Seller is unable or unwilling to restore it to its previous condition prior to closing, Purchaser shall have the option of canceling the contract and receiving back the earnest money, or accepting the property in its damaged condition, any insurance proceeds otherwise payable to Seller by reason of such damage shall be applied to the balance of the purchase price or otherwise be payable to Purchaser.

7. CLOSING COSTS & DATE: The sale shall be closed and the deed delivered within sixty (60) days from the execution of this Agreement by all parties, except Seller shall have a reasonable length of time within which to perfect title or cure defects in the title to the said property. The Seller agrees to pay the cost of deed preparation and a mortgagee's title insurance policy, all other closing costs shall be paid by Purchaser. Purchaser agrees to allow Seller to remain in possession of said property subject to separate terms of a month to month lease agreement to be executed at closing for a lease period not to extend beyond _____ [insert month/day/year].

8. CONVEYANCE: Seller agrees to convey a good merchantable title and General Warranty Deed of said property insuring that property is free of all encumbrances, except as hereinabove set out and Seller and Purchaser agree that any encumbrances shall be paid in full at the time of closing from sales proceeds.

9. CONDITION OF PROPERTY: (a) General Provisions and Obligations of Parties: Seller agrees to deliver the heating, cooling, plumbing and electrical systems and any built-in appliances in operable condition at the time of closing. It shall be the

responsibility of Purchaser, at Purchaser's expense, to satisfy himself/herself that all conditions of this contract are satisfied before closing. Said sale is contingent upon a satisfactory inspection of the property to be completed and reported to Seller prior to or on _____, 20____. Said contract shall only be renegotiable upon a major defect with an individual repair cost in excess of $500.00. After closing, all conditions of the property, as well as any aforementioned items and systems, are the responsibility of Purchaser and shall be deemed purchased AS-IS. (b) Lender Required Repairs and Treatments: Unless otherwise agreed in writing, neither party is obligated to pay for lender required repairs, which includes treatment for wood destroying insects. If the parties do not agree to pay for the lender required repairs or treatments, this contract will terminate and the earnest money will be refunded to Purchaser. If the cost of lender required repairs and treatments exceeds 5% of the Sales Price, Purchaser may terminate this contract and the earnest money will be refunded to Purchaser. (c) Completion of Repairs and Treatments: Unless otherwise agreed in writing, Seller shall complete all agreed repairs and treatments prior to the Closing Date. All required permits must be obtained, and repairs and treatments must be performed by persons who are licensed or otherwise authorized by law to provide such repairs or treatments. At Purchaser's election, any transferable warranties received by Seller with respect to the repairs and treatments will be transferred to Purchaser at Purchaser's expense. If Seller fails to complete any agreed repairs and treatments prior to the Closing Date, Purchaser may do so and receive reimbursement from Seller at closing. The Closing Date will be extended up to 15 days, if necessary, to complete repairs and treatments. (d) Environmental Matters: Purchaser is advised that the presence of wetlands, toxic substances, including asbestos and wastes or other environmental hazards, or the presence of a threatened or endangered species or its habitat may affect Purchaser's intended use of the Property. If Purchaser is concerned about these matters, an addendum required by the parties should be used.

10. SELLER'S WARRANTIES: Seller warrants that Seller has not received notification from any lawful authority regarding any assessments, pending public improvements, repairs, replacements or alterations to said premises that have not been satisfactorily made. These warranties shall survive the delivery of the above deed.

11. EARNEST MONEY: The Earnest Money as paid by Purchaser as set forth in Paragraph 3 hereof shall be deposited by Seller only upon the execution of this contract. The Earnest Money shall be nonrefundable to Purchaser except for the occurrences of Paragraphs 5, 6, or 14.

12. DEFAULT: If Purchaser fails to comply with this contract, Purchaser will be in default, and Seller may (a) enforce specific performance, seek such other relief as may be provided by law, or both, or (b) terminate this contract and receive the earnest money as liquidated damages, thereby releasing both parties from this contract. If, due to factors beyond Seller's control, Seller fails within the time allowed to make any non-casualty repairs, Purchaser may (a) extend the time for performance up to 15 days and the Closing Date will be extended as necessary or (b) terminate this contract as the sole remedy and receive the earnest money. If Seller fails to comply with this contract for any other reason, Seller will be in default and Purchaser may (a) enforce specific performance, seek such other relief as may be provided by law, or both, or (b) terminate this contract and receive the earnest money, thereby releasing both parties from this contract.

13. MEDIATION: Any dispute between Purchaser and Seller related to this contract that is not resolved through informal discussion [choose one:] _____ will _____ will not be submitted to a mutually acceptable mediation service or provider. The parties to the mediation shall bear the mediation costs equally. This paragraph does not preclude a party from seeking equitable relief from a court of competent jurisdiction.

14. SURVIVAL OF CONTRACT: All terms, conditions and warranties not performed at the time of delivery of the deed shall survive such delivery.

15. COMMISSION FEES: Purchaser and Seller agree that said contract was negotiated at arms length without assistance of any real estate agents or brokers and that no such fees shall be paid by either party in connection with this contract or sale.

16. ADDITIONAL PROVISIONS: Any additional Provisions set forth on the reverse side, initialed by all parties, are hereby made a part of this contract and this contract states the entire agreement between the parties and merges in this agreement all statements, representations, and covenants heretofore made, and any agreements not incorporated herein are void and of no force and effect.

17. SUCCESSORS AND ASSIGNS: This contract shall be binding upon any heirs, successors and assigns of Seller or Purchaser.

18. REVOCATION OF OFFER BY PURCHASER: This contract has been first executed by Purchaser and if not accepted by all parties by noon on _____, 20____, this offer shall be void.

19. DISCLOSURES:

_____

_____

_____

_____

_____

[The Seller should note any disclosures about the property that may be required under Federal or state law. Consult an attorney if uncertainty exists as to which disclosures may be required.]

PURCHASER:

_____   _____
Date   [purchaser's signature above/printed name below]

                         _____
                         [purchaser's signature above/printed name below]

SELLER:

_____   _____
Date   [seller's signature above/printed name below]

                         _____
                         [seller's signature above/printed name below]

Appendix B   Addendums to Real Estate Purchase Agreement

THIRD PARTY FINANCING CONDITION ADDENDUM
CONCERNING THE PROPERTY AT:

___

(Address of Property)

Purchaser shall apply promptly for all financing described below and make every reasonable effort to obtain financing approval. Financing approval will be deemed to have been obtained when the lender determines that Purchaser has satisfied all of lender's financial requirements (those items relating to Purchaser's assets, income and credit history). If financing (including any financed PMI premium) approval is not obtained within _____ days after the effective date, this contract will terminate and the earnest money will be refunded to Purchaser. Each note must be secured by an appropriate instrument authorized within the state, typically either (1) a mortgage or (2) vendor's and deed of trust liens. (Consult an attorney if you are unsure as to which instrument is appropriate for this transaction.)

CHECK APPLICABLE BOXES:

_____ A. CONVENTIONAL FINANCING:

_____ (1) A first mortgage loan in the principal amount of $_____ (excluding any financed PMI premium), due in full in _____ year(s), with interest not to exceed _____% per annum for the first _____year(s) of the loan with Loan Fees not to exceed _____% of the loan. The loan will be [choose one:] _____ with _____ without PMI.

_____ (2) A second mortgage loan in the principal amount of $ (excluding any financed PMI premium), due in full in year(s), with interest not to exceed % per annum for the first year(s) of the loan with Loan Fees not to exceed % of the loan. The loan will be with without PMI.

_____   B. FHA INSURED FINANCING: A Section _____ FHA insured loan of not less than $_____ (excluding any financed MIP), amortizable monthly for not less than _____ years, with interest not to exceed _____% per annum for the first _____ year(s) of the loan with Loan Fees not to exceed _____% of the loan. As required by HUD-FHA, if FHA valuation is unknown, "It is expressly agreed that, notwithstanding any other provisions of this contract, the purchaser (Purchaser) shall not be obligated to complete the purchase of the Property described herein or to incur any penalty by forfeiture of earnest money deposits or otherwise unless the purchaser (Purchaser) has been given in accordance with HUD/FHA or VA requirements a written statement issue by the Federal Housing Commissioner, Department of Veterans Affairs, or a Direct Endorsement Lender setting forth the appraised value of the Property of not less than $_____. The purchaser (Purchaser) shall have the privilege and option of proceeding with consummation of the contract without regard to the amount of the appraised valuation. The appraised valuation is arrived at to determine the maximum mortgage the Department of Housing and Urban Development will insure. HUD does not warrant the value or the condition of the Property. The purchaser (Purchaser) should satisfy himself/herself that the price and the condition of the Property are acceptable."

If the FHA appraised value of the Property (excluding closing costs and MIP) is less than the Sales Price, Seller may reduce the Sales Price to an amount equal to the

FHA appraised value (excluding closing costs and MIP) and the sale will be closed at the lower Sales Price with proportionate adjustments to the down payment and loan amount.

_____ C. VA GUARANTEED FINANCING: A VA guaranteed loan of not less than $_____ (excluding any financed Funding Fee), amortizable monthly for not less than _____ years, with interest not to exceed _____% per annum for the first _____ year(s) of the loan with Loan Fees not to exceed _____% of the loan.

VA NOTICE TO PURCHASER: "It is expressly agreed that, notwithstanding any other provisions of this contract, the Purchaser shall not incur any penalty by forfeiture of earnest money or otherwise or be obligated to complete the purchase of the Property described herein, if the contract purchase price or cost exceeds the reasonable value of the Property established by the Department of Veterans Affairs. The Purchaser shall, however, have the privilege and option of proceeding with the consummation of this contract without regard to the amount of the reasonable value established by the Department of Veterans Affairs."

If Purchaser elects to complete the purchase at an amount in excess of the reasonable value established by VA, Purchaser shall pay such excess amount in cash from a source which Purchaser agrees to disclose to the VA and which Purchaser represents will not be from borrowed funds except as approved by VA. If VA reasonable value of the Property is less than the Sales Price, Seller may reduce the Sales Price to an amount equal to the VA reasonable value and the sale will be closed at the lower Sales Price with proportionate adjustments to the down payment and the loan amount.

PURCHASER:

_____   _____
Date   [purchaser's signature above/printed name below]

                          _____
                          [purchaser's signature above/printed name below]

SELLER:

_____   _____
Date   [seller's signature above/printed name below]

                          _____
                          [seller's signature above/printed name below]

Note: This addendum is only necessary if the parties have checked the option in Paragraph 4(b) above.

LOAN ASSUMPTION ADDENDUM
TO CONTRACT CONCERNING THE PROPERTY AT:

_____

___

(Address of Property)

A. CREDIT DOCUMENTATION: Within _____ days after the effective date of this contract, Purchaser shall deliver to Seller the following: [check all applicable items:]
_____credit report _____verification of employment, including salary
_____verification of funds on deposit in financial institutions _____current financial statement to establish Purchaser's creditworthiness. Purchaser hereby authorizes any credit reporting agency to furnish to Seller at Purchaser's sole expense copies of Purchaser's credit reports.

B. CREDIT APPROVAL: If Purchaser's documentation is not delivered within the specified time, Seller may terminate this contract by notice to Purchaser within 7 days after expiration of the time for delivery, and the earnest money will be paid to Seller. If the documentation is timely delivered, and Seller determines in Seller's sole discretion that Purchaser's credit is unacceptable, Seller may terminate this contract by notice to Purchaser within 7 days after expiration of the time for delivery and the earnest money will be refunded to Purchaser. If Seller does not terminate this contract, Seller will be deemed to have accepted Purchaser's credit.

C. ASSUMPTION:

_____ (1) The unpaid principal balance of a first lien promissory note payable to which unpaid balance at closing will be $_____. The total current monthly payment including principal, interest and any reserve deposits is $_____. Purchaser's initial payment will be the first payment due after closing.

_____ (2) The unpaid principal balance of a second lien promissory note payable to which unpaid balance at closing will be $_____. The total current monthly payment including principal, interest and any reserve deposits is $_____. Purchaser's initial payment will be the first payment due after closing.

Purchaser's assumption of an existing note includes all obligations imposed by the deed of trust securing the note. If the unpaid principal balance(s) of any assumed loan(s) as of the Closing Date varies from the loan balance(s) stated above, the [check only one:]
_____cash payable at closing _____Sales Price will be adjusted by the amount of any variance; provided, if the total principal balance of all assumed loans varies in an amount greater than $350.00 at closing, either party may terminate this contract and the earnest money will be refunded to Purchaser unless the other party elects to eliminate the excess in the variance by an appropriate adjustment at closing. Purchaser may terminate this contract and the earnest money will be refunded to Purchaser if the noteholder requires (a) payment of an assumption fee in excess of $_____ in (1) above or $_____ in (2) above and Seller declines to pay such excess, (b) an increase in the interest rate to more than _____% in (1) above, or _____% in (2) above, (c) any other modification of the loan documents, or (d) consent to the assumption of the loan and fails to consent. An appropriate instrument authorized within the state, typically

either (1) a mortgage or (2) vendor's and deed of trust liens, to secure the assumption will be required, and it will automatically be released on execution and delivery of a release by noteholder. If Seller is released from liability on any assumed note, the instrument securing the assumption will not be required. If noteholder maintains an escrow account, the escrow account must be transferred to Purchaser without any deficiency. Purchaser shall reimburse Seller for the amount in the transferred accounts.

NOTICE TO PURCHASER: The monthly payments, interest rates or other terms of some loans may be adjusted by the noteholder at or after closing. If you are concerned about the possibility of future adjustments, do not sign the contract without examining the notes and the instrument securing the note.

NOTICE TO SELLER: Your liability to pay the note assumed by Purchaser will continue unless you obtain a release of liability from the noteholder. If you are concerned about future liability, you should use the a Release of Liability Addendum.

PURCHASER:

_____   _____
Date   [purchaser's signature above/printed name below]

                                 _____
                                 [purchaser's signature above/printed name below]

SELLER:

_____   _____
Date   [seller's signature above/printed name below]

                                 _____
                                 [seller's signature above/printed name below]

Note: This addendum is only necessary if the parties have checked the option in Paragraph 4(c) above.

SELLER FINANCING ADDENDUM
TO CONTRACT CONCERNING THE PROPERTY AT:

_____

____

(Address of Property)

A. CREDIT DOCUMENTATION: Within _____ days after the effective date of this contract, Purchaser shall deliver to Seller: [check all applicable items:] _____credit report _____verification of employment, including salary _____verification of funds on deposit in financial institutions _____current financial statement to establish Purchaser's creditworthiness. Purchaser hereby authorizes any credit reporting agency to furnish to Seller at Purchaser's sole expense copies of Purchaser's credit reports.

B. CREDIT APPROVAL: If Purchaser's documentation is not delivered within the specified time, Seller may terminate this contract by notice to Purchaser within 7 days after expiration of the time for delivery, and the earnest money will be paid to Seller. If the documentation is timely delivered, and Seller determines in Seller's sole discretion that Purchaser's credit is unacceptable, Seller may terminate this contract by notice to Purchaser within 7 days after expiration of the time for delivery and the earnest money will be refunded to Purchaser. If Seller does not terminate this contract, Seller will be deemed to have accepted Purchaser's credit.

C. PROMISSORY NOTE: The promissory note (Note) described in Paragraph 4 of this contract payable by Purchaser to the order of Seller will be payable at the place designated by Seller. Purchaser may prepay the Note in whole or in part at any time without penalty. Any prepayments are to be applied to the payment of the installments of principal last maturing and interest will immediately cease on the prepaid principal. The Note will contain a provision for payment of a late fee of 5% of any installment not paid within 10 days of the due date. The Note will be payable as follows:

_____   (1) In one payment due _____ after the date of the Note with interest payable _____.

_____   (2) In _____ installments of $_____, [check all applicable items:] _____including interest _____plus interest beginning _____ after the date of the Note and continuing at _____ intervals thereafter for _____ when the balance of the Note will be due and payable.

_____   (3) Interest only in _____ installments for the first _____ month(s) and thereafter in installments of $_____, [check all applicable items:] _____including interest _____plus interest beginning _____ after the date of the Note and continuing at _____ intervals thereafter for when the balance of the Note will be due and payable.

D. SECURING INSTRUMENT: [Choose the appropriate instrument authorized within the state:] A _____ mortgage, or _____ deed of trust lien, will provide for the following:
(1) PROPERTY TRANSFERS: [check only one:]

_____ (a) Consent Not Required: The Property may be sold, conveyed or leased without the consent of Seller, provided any subsequent Purchaser assumes the Note.

_____ (b) Consent Required: If all or any part of the Property is sold, conveyed, leased for a period longer than 3 years, leased with an option to purchase, or otherwise sold, without the prior written consent of Seller, Seller may declare the balance of the Note, to be immediately due and payable. The creation of a subordinate lien, any conveyance under threat or order of condemnation, any deed solely between Purchasers, the passage of title by reason of the death of a Purchaser or by operation of law will not entitle Seller to exercise the remedies provided in this paragraph.

(2) TAX AND INSURANCE ESCROW: [check only one:]

_____ (a) Escrow Not Required: Purchaser shall furnish Seller annually, before the taxes become delinquent, evidence that all taxes on the Property have been paid. Purchaser shall furnish Seller annually evidence of paid-up casualty insurance naming Seller as an additional loss payee.

_____ (b) Escrow Required: With each installment Purchaser shall deposit with Seller in escrow a pro rata part of the estimated annual ad valorem taxes and casualty insurance premiums for the Property. Purchaser shall pay any deficiency within 30 days after notice from Seller. Purchaser's failure to pay the deficiency constitutes a default under the securing instrument. Purchaser is not required to deposit any escrow payments for taxes and insurance that are deposited with a superior lienholder. The casualty insurance must name Seller as an additional loss payee.

(3) PRIOR LIENS: Any default under any lien superior to the lien securing the Note constitutes default under the deed of trust securing the Note.

PURCHASER:

_____   _____
Date   [purchaser's signature above/printed name below]

                            _____
                            [purchaser's signature above/printed name below]
SELLER:

_____   _____
Date   [seller's signature above/printed name below]

                            _____
                            [seller's signature above/printed name below]

COUNTEROFFER

Offer made by_____

To purchase the real property commonly known as_____

_____is not accepted in its present

form, but the following counteroffer is hereby submitted:_____

_____

_____

_____

_____

_____

_____

_____

_____

OTHER ITEMS: All terms to remain the same as the original Offer and Acceptance.
RIGHT TO ACCEPT OTHER OFFERS: Seller reserves the right to accept any other
offer prior to purchaser's acceptance of this counteroffer and seller's agent being so
advised in writing.

EXPIRATION: This offer shall expire unless a copy of hereof with purchaser's written
acceptance is delivered to seller or his/her agent within _____ days from date.

Date_____ Seller_____

Time_____ Seller_____

The above undersigned purchaser accepts the above counteroffer

Date_____ Purchaser_____

Time_____ Purchaser_____

Appendix D Property Inspection Form

PROPERTY INSPECTION FORM

AREA OR ITEM	OK	WORK TO BE DONE	COMMENTS
Floors (Check each room for the following)			
Carpets clean and in good repair			
No spots or discoloration			
Wood floors in good repair			
Baseboards clean and in good repair			
Floor electrical sockets clean and working			
Tile or linoleum no cracks or breaks			
No bubbles or sloping			
No discoloration			
Does furniture need to be moved for inspection?			
Walls (Check each room for the following)			
Do wall hangings need to be removed for inspection?			
Walls clean with no cracks			
Wallpaper seams (top and bottom) secure			
Holes patched and painted			
No discoloration			
Light fixtures in good repair			
Switch plates in good repair			
Socket plates in good repair			
Mirrors and glass unbroken and not stained			
Doors (Check each room for the following)			
Paint or finish in good repair			
No discoloration			
No chipping or loose panels			
Move smoothly and no dragging			
Handles, hinges, and locks work well			
No squeaks			
Windows and Window Coverings			
No broken glass			
No cracks in frames			
Open and close easily			
Hinges in good shape			
Latches, handles, and cranks in good shape			
Slide smoothly and tracks clean			
All locks working well			
Drapes and curtains clean and in good repair			
Blinds in good shape and working well			
Pull cords in good shape			
Drapes operating smoothly			

Area or Item	OK	Work to be done	Comments
Curtain rods straight and attached well			
No discoloration on walls or coverings			
Ceilings (Check each room for the following)			
No stains or discoloration			
No damage			
Paint or finish in good repair			
Acoustic in good repair			
Light fixtures in good repair			
Track lighting working properly			
Kitchen			
Refrigerator clean and in good repair (if it stays)			
Dishwasher clean and in good repair			
Stoves and ovens clean and in good repair			
Switches and buttons in good shape			
All drip pans in place and in good shape			
Sink in good shape (no chips or stains)			
Cupboards, shelves, etc. in good order			
Faucets not discolored or stained			
Faucets, sinks, and pipes no leaks or drips			
Window coverings in good shape			
Garbage disposal working properly			
All other appliances working properly			
Living Room			
Does it have a good feel?			
Good traffic flow			
Enough room for furniture			
Good lighting			
Fireplace, hearth, and mantel is what you want			
Convenient to other rooms			
Drapes and curtains clean and in good shape			
Blinds in good repair			
Shelves secure			
Is noise a problem?			
Wet bar in good order			
Bathrooms			
Bathtub clean (no stains or chips)			
Soap holders in place			
Tile walls (no chipping or peeling)			
Grout in good shape			
No mildew stains			
Shower curtains/doors clean and in good shape			
No water stains			
Faucets and handles in good order			
Cabinets and cupboards adequate			

Area or Item	OK	Work to be done	Comments
Any evidence of leaks or seepage?			
Toilet and toilet seat in good repair			
Towel holders affixed properly and secure			
All drains working well			
Any other devices working right			
Mirrors in good shape			

Bedrooms

Enough room for furniture			
Good lighting			
Sun faces room at the right time of the day			
Windowsills in good repair			
Curtains/drapes/blinds clean and in good shape			
Accessible to bathrooms			
Lots of privacy			
Closets large enough			
View is okay			
Good ventilation (heating and cooling)			

Closets

Enough closets			
Enough hanging space			
Well lit			
Hanging bars secure and straight			
Walls in good shape			
No odor			
All shelves in place and secure			

Laundry Area

No odor			
Well lit			
Exhaust connected properly			
No gas odor			
Cabinet and shelves in good order			
Proper connections for your appliances			
Sink in good repair (if there is one)			
No swelling in floors from leaks			

Staircases

Handrails, top and bottom posts secure			
Stairs tight and no squeaks			
Does sound carry through the house?			
Tile, carpet or other covering secure			
No rails protruding			
Side slats and vertical rail secure			
Decorative knobs and pieces secure			
Good lighting on entire staircase			
Plenty of head room			
Pull-down staircase working smoothly			

Area or Item	OK	Work to be done	Comments
Shelves, Bookcases, and Drawers			
Shelves level and secure			
Finish or covering in good shape			
Adequate lighting			
Drawers move easily			
Handles and knobs are tight			
Fireplaces and Wood Stoves			
Chimney clean with no excessive burn marks			
Grate in place and in good shape			
Fireplace tools in good repair (if staying)			
All fans and heating units in good repair			
Any signs of leaks—no gas odor			
Mantel and hearth in good shape			
Screens or doors working well			
Gas lighters and fans working properly			
Electrical			
Adequate number of outlets in every room			
All switches and plugs operative			
Specialty lighting working properly			
Any burned areas around switches or plugs?			
No open wiring or plugs			
Dimmers working properly			
Wall plates in good repair			
Pull cords in good shape			
Heating and Cooling			
Units and thermostats working properly and recently serviced			
If propane, is tank accessible year round?			
Vent covers in place and working properly			
Window units secure and sealed			
Exposed ducting clean			
Pilot lights stay lit			
Basement			
Well lit			
No odor			
Dry			
Is area usable?			
Safe stairways			
Easy entry and exit			
Shelves and cabinets in good repair			
Anything scary about the area?			
Any live bugs or other critters?			
Well ventilated			
Sound Inspection			
Showers and tubs running—how much noise?			

Area or Item	OK	Work to be done	Comments
Staircases—does sound carry?			
Conversations in rooms—does it carry?			
Does noise from appliances carry?			
Noise from outside			

Security System

Operates properly			
Instructions available			

Attic

No odor and well ventilated			
Shelves and cabinets in good repair			
No leaks			
Anything scary about the area?			
Easy entry and exit			
Well lit			

Porches, Patios, and Entryways

Convenient access to other rooms			
Is there a coat hanging area?			
No uncomfortable steps			
Well lit			
No odor			
Any rotting or damage?			
Locks and doors in good repair			
Stairs and guardrails in good shape			
Deck or flooring in good repair			
Floors and decks level			
Glass and screens in good shape			

Garage

Well lit with doors open or closed			
Neatly arranged with no excessive storage			
Rafter area in good repair			
Stains and spots removed from garage floor			
All cabinets and shelves in good repair			
Workbenches in good repair			
Washer and dryer accessible with cars inside			
Fans and ventilation in good order			
Doors and windows secure			
Doggy door in good repair			
Good storage for tools, equipment, etc.			
Electric outlets working			
Garage door opener in good repair			
Appliances out of the way (hot water heater, water softener, etc.)			

Pools, Spas, and Saunas

Decks in good repair			
Proper chemical balance in the water			
All pumps, heating, and drains in good repair			

Area or Item	OK	Work to be done	Comments
Skimmers, hoses, cleaners operative			
Ladders, slides, diving boards in good order			
Pool furniture well maintained			
Safety equipment and signs in place			
Gates lock properly and doors close tightly			
Lighting works properly			
Heating units and timers work properly			
Door closes and seals well			
Good storage for equipment			
No mildew or odor			

Home Exterior

Area or Item	OK	Work to be done	Comments
Foundation in good shape and no cracks			
Exterior finishes in good shape with no chipping, peeling, cracks, or holes			
No discoloration from water splashes, drains, or the sun			
Eaves not peeling, chipping, or molding			
Window frames caulked well and in good shape			
Crawl spaces covered and accessible			
Vents and eave vents opened and screened			
Any wooden structures against house? Termites?			
Bushes and trees trimmed away from the house			
Exterior doors (including garage door) clean, properly finished, and working well			

Roof

Area or Item	OK	Work to be done	Comments
No low spots or sagging			
No missing tiles or shakes			
No leaks			
No antennas or satellites causing damage			
No stain or discoloration			
No wires connected which cause damage			
Gutters secure and clean			
Caulking in good shape			
No trees or bushes scraping the roof			

Yard

Area or Item	OK	Work to be done	Comments
Do you like the yard?			
Grass, bushes, and trees in good shape			
Sprinkler system working properly			
Driveways, sidewalks, and walkways free of stains			
Fences in good repair			
Parking areas in good shape			
Animal areas in good shape			

Appendix E   Seller Disclosure Statement

Seller   Disclosure Statement

Property address: ....

....

Seller: ....

A seller must disclose to a buyer all known material defects about property being sold that are not readily observable. This disclosure statement is designed to assist the seller in complying with disclosure requirements and to assist the buyer in evaluating the property being considered.

This statement discloses the seller's knowledge of the condition of the property as of the date signed by the seller and is not a substitute for any inspections or warranties that the buyer may wish to obtain. This statement is not a warranty of any kind by the seller or a warranty or representation by any listing real estate broker, any selling real estate broker or their agents. The buyer is encouraged to address concerns about the conditions of the property that may not be included in this statement. This statement does not relieve the seller of the obligation to disclose a material defect that may not be addressed on this form.

A material defect is a problem with the property or any portion of it that would have a significant adverse impact on the value of the residential real involves an unreasonable risk to people on the land.

(1) Seller's expertise. The seller does not possess expertise in contracting, engineering, architecture or other areas related to the construction and conditions of the property and its improvements, except as follows: ....

(2) Occupancy. Do you, the seller, currently occupy this property? ..... yes ..... no

If "no," when did you last occupy the property?....

(3) Roof.

(i) Date roof was installed: ....

Documented? ..... yes ..... no ..... unknown

(ii) Has the roof been replaced or repaired during your ownership? ..... yes ..... no

If "yes," were the existing shingles removed? ..... yes ..... no ..... unknown

(iii) Has the roof ever leaked during your ownership? ..... yes ..... no

(iv) Do you know of any problems with the roof, gutters or downspouts? ..... yes ..... no

Explain any "yes" answers that you give in this section:

....

....

(4) Basements and crawl spaces (Complete only if applicable).

(i) Does the property have a sump pump?

..... yes ..... no ..... unknown

(ii) Are you aware of any water leakage, accumulation or dampness within the basement or crawl space? ..... yes ..... no

If "yes," describe in detail: ....

....

(iii) Do you know of any repairs or other attempts to control any water or dampness problem in the basement or crawl space? ..... yes ..... no

If "yes," describe the location, extent, date and name of the person who did the repair or control effort: ....

....

(5) Termites/wood destroying insects, dry rot, pests.

(i) Are you aware of any termites/wood destroying insects, dry rot or pests affecting the property? ..... yes ..... no

(ii) Are you aware of any damage to the property caused by termites/wood destroying insects, dry rot or pests? ..... yes ..... no

(iii) Is your property currently under contract by a licensed pest control company?

..... yes ..... no

(iv) Are you aware of any termite/pest control reports or treatments for the property in the last five years? ..... yes ..... no

Explain any "yes" answers that you give in this section:

....

....

(6) Structural items.

(i) Are you aware of any past or present water leakage in the house or other structures?

..... yes ..... no

(ii) Are you aware of any past or present movement, shifting, deterioration or other problems with walls, foundations or other structural components? ..... yes ..... no

(iii) Are you aware of any past or present problems with driveways, walkways, patios or retaining walls on the property? ..... yes ..... no

Explain any "yes" answers that you give in this section.

When explaining efforts to control or repair, please describe the location and extent of the problem and the date and person by whom the work was done, if known:

....

....

(7) Additions/remodeling. Have you made any additions, structural changes or other alterations to the property? ..... yes ..... no

If "yes," please describe: ....

....

(8) Water and sewage.

(i) What is the source of your drinking water?

..... public ..... community system

..... well on property ..... other

If "other," please explain: ....

....

(ii) If your drinking water source is not public:

when was your water last tested? ....

what was the result of the test? ....

Is the pumping system in working order?

..... yes ..... no

If "no," please explain: ....

....

(iii) Do you have a softener, filter or other purification system? ..... yes ..... no

If "yes," is the system: ..... leased ..... owned

(iv) What is the type of sewage system?

..... public sewer ..... private sewer

..... septic tank ..... cesspool ..... other

If "other," please explain: ....

....

(v) Is there a sewage pump? ..... yes ..... no

If "yes," is it in working order?

..... yes ..... no

(vi) When was the septic system or cesspool last

serviced? ....

(vii) Is either the water or sewage system shared?

..... yes ..... no

If "yes," please explain: ....

....

(viii) Are you aware of any leaks, backups or other problems relating to any of the plumbing, water and sewage related items? ..... yes ..... no

If "yes," please explain: ....

....

(9) Plumbing system.

(i) Type of plumbing: ..... copper ..... galvanized

..... lead ..... PVC ..... unknown ..... other

If "other," please explain: ....

....

(ii) Are you aware of any problems with any of your plumbing fixtures (including, but not limited to: kitchen, laundry or bathroom fixtures, wet bars, hot water heater, etc.)?

..... yes ..... no

If "yes," please explain: ....

....

(10) Heating and air conditioning.

(i) Type of air conditioning: ..... central electric ..... central gas ..... wall ..... none

Number of window units included in sale: ....

Location: ....

....

(ii) List any areas of the house that are not air

conditioned: ....

....

(iii) Type of heating: ..... electric ..... fuel oil ..... natural gas ..... other

If "other," please explain: ....

....

(iv) List any areas of the house that are not heated: ....

(v) Type of water heating: ..... electric ..... gas ..... solar ..... other

If "other," please explain: ....

....

(vi) Are you aware of any underground fuel tanks on the property? ..... yes ..... no

If "yes," please describe: ....

....

Are you aware of any problems with any item in this section? ..... yes ..... no

If "yes," please explain: ....

....

(11) Electrical system. Are you aware of any problems or repairs needed in the electrical system?

..... yes ..... no

If "yes," please explain: ....

....

(12) Other equipment and appliances included in sale (complete only if applicable).

(i) ..... Electric garage door opener

Number of transmitters .....

(ii) ..... Smoke detectors How many? .....

Location: ....

....

(iii) ..... Security alarm system ..... owned ..... leased

Lease information: ....

....

(iv) ..... Lawn sprinkler Number ..... Automatic timer .....

(v) ..... Swimming pool ..... Pool heater ..... Spa/hot tub

List all pool/spa equipment: ....

....

(vi) ..... Refrigerator ..... Range ..... Microwave oven ..... Dishwasher

..... Trash compactor ..... Garbage disposal

(vll) ..... Washer ..... Dryer

(viii) ..... Intercom

(ix) ..... Ceiling fans ..... Number Location: ....

(x) Other: ....

Are any items in this section in need of repair or replacement? ..... yes ..... no ..... unknown

If "yes," please explain: ....

....

(13) Land (soils, drainage and boundaries).

(i) Are you aware of any fill or expansive soil on the property? ..... yes ..... no

(ii) Are you aware of any sliding, settling, earth movement, upheaval, subsidence or earth stability problems that have occurred on or that affect the property? ..... yes ..... no

(iii) Are you aware of any existing or proposed excavations that might affect this property?

..... yes ..... no

(iv) To your knowledge, is this property, or part of it, located in a flood zone or wetlands area?

..... yes ..... no

(v) Do you know of any past or present drainage or flooding problems affecting the property?

..... yes ..... no

(vi) Do you know of any encroachments, boundary line disputes or easements? ..... yes ..... no

NOTE TO BUYER: Most properties have easements running across them for utility services and other reasons. In many cases, the easements do not restrict the ordinary use of the property, and the seller may not be readily aware of them. Buyers may wish to determine the existence of easements and restrictions by examining the property and ordering an abstract of title or searching the records in the Office of the Recorder of Deeds for the county before entering into an agreement of sale.

(vii) Are you aware of any shared or common areas (for example, driveways, bridges, docks, walls, etc.) or maintenance agreements?

..... yes ..... no

Explain any "yes" answers that you give in this section:

....

....

(14) Hazardous substances.

(i) Are you aware of any underground tanks or hazardous substances present on the property (structure or soil), including, but not limited to, asbestos, polychlorinated biphenyls (PCBs), radon, lead paint, urea formaldehyde foam insulation (UFFI), etc.? ..... yes ..... no

(ii) To your knowledge, has the property been tested for any hazardous substances? ..... yes .....no

(iii) Do you know of any other environmental concerns that might impact upon the property?

..... yes ..... no

Explain any "yes" answers that you give in this section:

....

....

(15) Condominiums and other homeowners associations (complete only if applicable).

Type: ..... condominium* ..... cooperative ..... homeowners association ..... other

If "other," please explain: ....

....

NOTICE REGARDING CONDOMINIUMS AND COOPERATIVES:

According to 68 Pa.C.S. ß 3407 (relating to resales of units) and 4409 (relating to resales of cooperative interests), a buyer of a resale unit in a condominium or cooperative must receive a certificate of resale issued by the association in the condominium or cooperative. The buyer will have the option of canceling the agreement with return of all deposit moneys until the certificate has been provided to the buyer and for five days thereafter or until conveyance, whichever occurs first.

(16) Miscellaneous.

(i) Are you aware of any existing or threatened legal action affecting the property?

..... yes ..... no

(ii) Do you know of any violations of Federal, State or local laws or regulations relating to this property? ..... yes ..... no

(iii) Are you aware of any public improvement, condominium or homeowner association assessments against the property that remain unpaid or of any violations of zoning, housing, building, safety or fire ordinances that remain uncorrected?

..... yes ..... no

(iv) Are you aware of any judgment, encumbrance, lien (for example, comaker or equity loan) or other debt against this property that cannot be satisfied by the proceeds of this sale?

..... yes ..... no

(v) Are you aware of any reason, including a defect in title, that would prevent you from giving a warranty deed or conveying title to the property?

..... yes ..... no

(vi) Are you aware of any material defects to the property, dwelling or fixtures which are not disclosed elsewhere on this form?

..... yes ..... no

A material defect is a problem with the property or any portion of it that would have a significant adverse impact on the value of the residential real property or that involves an unreasonable risk to people on the land.

Explain any "yes" answers that you give in this section:

....

....

The undersigned seller represents that the information set forth in this disclosure statement is accurate and complete to the best of the seller's knowledge. The seller hereby authorizes any agent for the seller to provide this information to prospective buyers of the property and to other real estate agents. The seller alone is responsible for the accuracy of the information contained in this statement. The seller shall cause the buyer to be notified in writing of any information supplied on this form which is rendered inaccurate by a change in the condition of the property following the completion of this form.

SELLER .... DATE ....

SELLER .... DATE ....

SELLER .... DATE ....

....

Executor, Administrator, Trustee

The undersigned has never occupied the property and lacks the personal knowledge necessary to complete this disclosure statement.

....

....

.... DATE ....

....

....

RECEIPT AND ACKNOWLEDGMENT BY BUYER

The undersigned buyer acknowledges receipt of this disclosure statement. The buyer acknowledges that this statement is not a warranty and that, unless stated otherwise in the sales contract, the buyer is purchasing this property in its present condition. It is the buyer's responsibility to satisfy himself or herself as to the condition of the property. The buyer may request that the property be inspected, at the buyer's expense and by qualified professionals, to determine the condition of the structure or its components.

BUYER .... DATE ....

BUYER .... DATE ....

BUYER .... DATE ....

Appendix F   Cost Analysis of Property Reconditioning

Property Address _____

Owner's Name _____

Telephone Number (Home) _____ (Work) _____

Age of Property _____

Listing Broker _____

Existing Loans And Status _____

Insured By _____ Amount _____

WORK NEEDED AND ESTIMATED COSTS

1. **Costs**

   Legal _____

   Accounting _____

   Advertising _____

   Insurance _____

   Loan Costs _____

   Interest _____

   Permits And Fees _____

   Taxes _____

   Other _____

   Contingency _____

                                   Costs Subtotal _____

2. **Interior**

   Kitchen Appliances

      Stove _____

      Refrigerator _____

      Dishwasher _____

      Washer/Dryer _____

      Cabinets _____

      Microwave _____

      Other _____

   Total Appliances: _____

   Master Bedroom _____

   Bedroom Two _____

   Bedroom Three _____

   Bedroom Four _____

   Bathroom One _____

   Bathroom Two _____

   Den _____

   Family Room _____

   Halls _____

   Floors _____

   Elevator _____

   Water Heater _____

   Water Softener _____

   Air Conditioning/Ventilation _____

   Heating System _____

Electrical _____
Plumbing _____
Fire Protection System _____
Furniture/Fixtures _____
Other _____
Contingency _____

Interior Subtotal _____

3. **Exterior**
Roof _____
Windows _____
Doors _____
Walls _____
Trim _____
Garage _____
Chimney _____
Yard _____
Landscaping _____
Well _____
Septic Tank _____
Sprinkler System _____
Driveway _____
Walkways _____
Porch _____
Fence _____
Steps _____
Pool/Pool Equipment _____
Light/Light Fixtures _____
Other _____
Contingency _____

Exterior Subtotal _____

4. **Amount Invested**
First Mortgage _____
Second Mortgage _____
Third Mortgage _____
Other Liens _____
Back Payments _____
Back Taxes _____
Closing Costs _____
Estimated Costs to Sell _____
Other _____

Amount Invested Subtotal _____

TOTAL COSTS (EXCLUDING SELLER'S EQUITY) (1+2+3+4) _____

Estimated Selling Price _____
Less Investment (Total Costs Excluding Sellers Equity) _____
Profit Before Cash Or Notes to Seller For Equity _____
Less Cash Or Notes To Seller _____
Estimated Gross Profit _____

Index